UPDATED EDITION

Enriching Content Classes for Secondary ESOL Students

Judith H. Jameson

Study Guide

Center for Applied Linguistics, Sunbelt Office, and Delta Publishing Company, A Division of Delta Systems Co., Inc. National Edition (2003)

Delta Publishing Company, A Division of Delta Systems Co., Inc., publishes and distributes these materials. Orders may be placed at www.delta-systems.com, 800-323-8270, or 1400 Miller Parkway, McHenry, IL 60050-7030.

This printing contains corrections and revisions made after the initial print run. The content and pagination remain the same.

Printed in the United States of America

Enriching Content Classes for Secondary ESOL Students: Trainer's Manual and Study Guide

ISBN # 1-887744-14-2 Package (Manual and Guide)
           1-887744-15-0 Package (Manual, Guide, and Video)
           1-887744-16-9 Additional Study Guides

Preface and Acknowledgments

These teacher training materials, *Enriching Content Classes for Secondary ESOL Students* (National Edition), have been a long time in the making. Since 1990, I have been extensively involved in working with teachers and schools in Florida and other states, and in developing teacher education materials to help teachers meet the challenge of their linguistically and culturally diverse classrooms. *Enriching* consolidates and refines this experience in a practical, easy-to-use teacher education curriculum. While *Enriching* is founded on the totality of my experience, this National Edition has been substantially modified from previous work.

Sincere thanks are due to all the authors and publishers whose work adds immeasurably to these materials. Special thanks are extended to the following:

Kris Anstrom for "Academic Achievement for Secondary Language Minority Students: Standards, Measures and Promising Practices," The National Clearinghouse for Bilingual Education

TESOL Journal for permission to reprint the article by Gloria Tang, "Teaching Content Knowledge and ESOL in Multicultural Classrooms."

Deborah J. Short for "Integrating Language and Content Instruction: Strategies and Techniques," The National Clearinghouse for Bilingual Education

Deborah Menkart for "Multicultural Education: Strategies for Linguistically Diverse Schools and Classrooms," The National Clearinghouse for Bilingual Education

The Journal of Educational Issues of Language Minority Students (now *Cultural Circles*)for permission to reprint the article "Achieving Multicultural Goals Through Children's Nonfiction" by Marsha K. Savage and Tom V. Savage

The Center for Applied Linguistics and The Media Group for permission to use the video *Communicative Math and Science Teaching.*

The most special thanks of all go to Allene Grognet, Director of the Center for Applied Linguistics Sunbelt Office, colleague, mentor, friend, and to Charlotte Kelso, administrative assistant and desktop publishing specialist for hanging in there with me through revision after revision.

Judy Jameson
Gainesville, Florida

Enriching Content Classes for Secondary ESOL Students

Study Guide

Table of Contents

Note to Presenters:
This printing contains corrections and revisions made after the initial print run.
The content and pagination remain the same.

Enriching Content Classes for Secondary ESOL Students

Study Guide

Introduction

Introduction

Goal

To understand the purpose and requirements of this course and the need for training due to the increasing linguistic and cultural diversity of the students in US schools.

Performance Objectives

- Describe the changing demographics in the US in terms of immigrants and LEP students.

- Reflect on the role of secondary content teachers with regard to the academic success of LEP students.

- Reflect on the activities in this section and their usefulness for ESOL students.

Course Goals and Requirements

Course Goals

- To learn how to adapt content instruction to help ESOL students understand academic content, develop academic language, and participate in classroom activities.

- To learn how to facilitate ESOL student adjustment to a new culture and how to help all students develop an appreciation for diversity.

- To effectively apply these skills and strategies to content area materials when working individually or with colleagues.

Course Requirements

- Attendance and participation in 54 in-class hours
- Two outside assignments (3 hours each) to apply new learning
- Portfolio: completed Study Guide + outside assignments
- Completed Journal

Demographics Anticipation Guide

Directions: Complete the following items to the best of your ability, then listen to the presentation and make any necessary corrections.

1. The number of immigrants to the US was the highest ever in which of the following decades?
   1900s   1920s   1980s   1990s

2. In 2000, _____% of the US population was foreign-born, compared to 14.7 % in 1910.

3. Among adults who speak a language other than English at home, about _____% report that they speak English well or very well.

4. Immigrants comprised 15% of the workforce in 2000, and are projected to comprise _____% of the workforce by 2020.

5. There are over _____ million limited English proficient (LEP) students enrolled in US schools. Since 1990-91, the LEP population has grown 105%, while the general school age population has grown 12%.

6. The five states or jurisdictions with the highest LEP enrollment in 2000 were
   _____.

7. Of the four US regions (West, Northeast, South, and Midwest), which regions
   (_____) are projected to have states with minority student enrollment between 40% to more than 50% by 2015? Which regions (_____) are projected to have states with less than 20% minority student enrollment by 2015?

8. Most LEP students are in elementary school. About _____% of LEP students are enrolled in high school.

9. Most LEP students speak Spanish as a first language. The second largest language group speaks _____.

10. About _____% of secondary school immigrant students in grades 7-12 were retained at least one grade in 2000.

Summary Reading

Directions: Read the following passage and write an appropriate title for it in the allotted space.

Title: _____

As teachers look at the students in their classrooms today, they see a scenario much different from the classrooms of their own childhoods. Today 1 in 3 children nationwide is from an ethnic or racial minority group, 1 in 7[14%] speaks a language other than English at home, and 1 in 15 was born outside the United States. The linguistic and cultural diversity of America's school population has increased dramatically during the past decade, and it's expected to increase even more in the future. While three quarters of Americans now claim European descent, by 2050 only half will. The concept of "minority" group will become obsolete as no group will form a majority.

Educating children from immigrant and ethnic minority group families is a major concern of school systems across the country. For many of these children, U.S. education is not a successful experience. While one tenth of non-Hispanic White students leave school without a diploma, one fourth of African Americans, one third of Hispanics, one half of Native Americans, and two thirds of immigrant students drop out of school.

 Confronted with this dismal reality, administrators, teachers, parents, and policy makers urge each other to do something different–change teaching methods, adopt new curricula, allocate more funding. Such actions might be needed, but will be meaningless unless we begin to think differently about these students. In order to educate them, we must first educate ourselves about who they are and what they need in order to succeed. Thinking differently involves viewing these students in new ways that may contradict conventional notions, and coming to a new set of realizations.

Eugene E. Garcia, Ph.D.
University of California, Berkeley

Reprinted with permission from ERIC Clearinghouse on Rural Education and Small Schools @ AEL, Inc., from Flores, J.L., Ed. (1996). *Children of la frontera: Binational efforts to serve Mexican migrant and immigrant students.* Charleston, WV: ERIC/CRESS, p. ix.

Evaluating Techniques for ESOL Students

Directions: Think back over the three instructional techniques or activities used in the Introduction: the Demographics Anticipation Guide, Creating a Title for a Passage, and Think-Write-Pair-Share. Use the Think-Write-Pair-Share Technique a second time to identify why each of these techniques would be helpful to ESOL students learning academic content. Make your notes below.

1. Demographics Anticipation Guide

2. Creating a Passage Title

3. Think-Write-Pair-Share

Enriching Content Classes for Secondary ESOL Students

Study Guide

Section 1
Academic Competence, Part A

Academic Competence, Part A

Goal

To understand and apply basic principles of modifying lessons to help ESOL students learn academic language and content in the basic subject areas.

Performance Objectives

• Identify characteristics of the content areas and how to use them to enhance ESOL student learning.

• Understand and apply three principles of lesson modification for ESOL students.

• Develop two lessons with appropriate modifications for ESOL students.

• Create links with other secondary content areas to make connections across the curriculum.

• Reflect on one's own priorities for implementation to help ESOL students achieve academic success.

Enriching Content Classes for Secondary ESOL Students (National Edition)
Study Guide Section 1: Academic Competence, Part A

11

VIDEO OBSERVATION FORM

Directions: View the videotape, *Communicative Math and Science Teaching,* and identify strategies that illustrate each of the Three Principles. Take notes on this chart.

	Clip 1	Clip 2	Clip 3	Clip 4
Increase Comprehensibility				
Increase Interaction				
Increase Thinking/Study Skills				

Enriching Content Classes for Secondary ESOL Students (National Edition)
Study Guide Section 1: Academic Competence, Part A

Easy as Pie Lesson Modification

Name:_____

Grade/Subject: _____

Topic: _____

Directions: Choose a chapter or topic in your text and plan to modify its presentation using the strategies/principles below. Describe briefly how you will modify your instruction for each item listed. Be prepared to explain your modifications to a partner.

1. Increase Comprehensibility using Teach the Text Backwards

     a. Do Application(s): relevance, prior knowledge

     c. Discuss Main Points: use oral language, visuals, hands on

     b. Examine Study Questions: overview, identify key concepts

     d. Read Text: make manageable for ESOL students

2. Increase Interaction

3. Increase Thinking Skills

Enriching Content Classes for Secondary ESOL Students (National Edition)
Study Guide Section 1: Academic Competence, Part A

13

Easy as Pie Lesson Modification
Partner Checklist

Your Name: _____

Partner's Name:_____

Partner's Grade/Subject: _____

Partner's Topic: _____

Directions: Ask your partner to explain his/her lesson modifications. Circle the appropriate number indicating your understanding of how your partner's modifications fulfill the three principles and help ESOL students learn academic content and language. Then answer the open-ended question.

Key:
1= I understand well.
2= I think I understand.
3= I'm not sure I understand.
4= I don't understand.

1. Increase Comprehensibility using Teach the Text Backwards

    a. Do <u>Application(s)</u>: relevance, prior knowledge   1 2 3 4

    b. <u>Discuss</u> Main Points: use oral language, visuals, hands on   1 2 3 4

    c. Examine <u>Study Questions</u>: overview, identify key concepts   1 2 3 4

    d. Read <u>Text</u>: make manageable for ESOL students   1 2 3 4

2. Increase Interaction   1 2 3 4

3. Increase Thinking Skills   1 2 3 4

Something I liked about my partner's modified lesson is:

SCANS Skills:
Skills Employers Want

Basic Skills: reading, writing, computation, oral communication

Thinking Skills: decision-making, problem-solving

Personal Qualities: responsibility, self-management

Organizing, planning, allocating resources

Working on teams, working in culturally diverse settings

Gathering, organizing, and interpreting information

Understanding and improving systems, monitoring and correcting performance

Selecting and using technology

Source: Secretary's Commission on Achieving Necessary Skills (1991). *What work requires of schools: A SCANS report for America 2000.* Washington D.C.: Department of Labor.

Enriching Content Classes for Secondary ESOL Students (National Edition)
Study Guide Section 1: Academic Competence, Part A

15

Six Types of Pair/Group Work
for Content Classrooms with ESOL Students

1. Think-(Write)-Pair-Share

- Teacher chooses a topic or question.
- Students individually think, then may write a few notes to record their thoughts.
- Pairs of students discuss their ideas and may agree on a response to share with the whole class.
- The whole class shares ideas.
- * Advantages for ESOL students: Gives students time to think in their new language and then to try out communicating their ideas with a partner before sharing with the whole class; "recycles" language and content at least three times.

2. Numbered Heads Together

- Teacher divides students into groups with equal numbers.
- Students in each group number off.
- Teacher asks a question.
- Students in each group "put their heads together" to decide on an answer. All students are responsible for knowing the answer.
- Teacher chooses a number at random. Students with that number raise their hands. Teacher calls on one or more to answer.
- * Especially good for reviewing material and checking comprehension.

3. Jigsaw

- Teacher selects a task that can be accomplished by dividing it into parts and then putting the parts together to accomplish the whole; e.g., reading a long chapter by dividing it into parts and then sharing the information.
- Teacher divides students into home groups and explains the overall task.
- Students number off. All students with the same number are assigned the same part of the task. These students may move into expert groups to complete their task and become "experts" on it.
- Students then return to their home groups to share their parts of the task and to accomplish the task as a whole.

4. Peer Tutoring

- Assign a more proficient English-speaker to help an ESOL student.
- Give the pair a task to accomplish so that there is a need to communicate.
- * For example: the more proficient student might read to a peer, highlight key passages in the text, and/or paraphrase difficult material; or the more proficient student might take dictation for a journal from a student who is unable to write independently.

16

Enriching Content Classes for Secondary ESOL Students (National Edition)
Study Guide Section 1: Academic Competence, Part A

5. Pair Assignments

- Assign two students to a common task. The students may confer with one another, contributing what they can.
- * For example: in a science lab project, the more proficient student reads the instructions and notes the observations while the ESOL student follows the directions and orally describes the observations.

6. Cooperative Projects

- Teacher divides students into groups of four to six to produce a product together; e.g., creating a skit, book, or mural. The project should include opportunities for cooperative planning, use of manipulative materials, synthesizing ideas, and reaching group consensus.
- * Students may need to be taught the necessary cooperative skills. Begin with a project that entails bringing individual pieces or work together (such as individual pictures and dictated or written poems edited and combined into a group-made book). Later on, assign group projects that require more sophisticated collaborative effort. Rotating leadership and roles can give students a chance to learn valuable skills.

Things To Remember When Using Pair/Group Work

1. Vary grouping strategies

2. Plan for positive interdependence and individual accountability

3. Teach and model activities before asking students to do them

4. Recognize and reward effective group work

Enriching Content Classes for Secondary ESOL Students (National Edition)
Study Guide Section 1: Academic Competence, Part A

17

Sequenced Topics

Directions: Choose two content areas and list five major topics for each. Then, working together, sequence the topics to facilitate making connections.

Content
Area # 1: _____   # 2: _____

Topics:
- _____   • _____
- _____   • _____
- _____   • _____
- _____   • _____
- _____   • _____

Sequence
_____

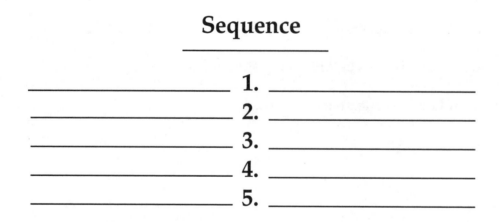

_____	1.	_____
_____	2.	_____
_____	3.	_____
_____	4.	_____
_____	5.	_____

18

Enriching Content Classes for Secondary ESOL Students (National Edition)
Study Guide Section 1: Academic Competence, Part A

SEQUENCED TOPICS: EXAMPLE

SECTION 1

Topics

Content
Area # 1: Literature   #2: American History

Topics: • Red Badge of Courage   • Discovery

        • Diary of Anne Frank   • Colonial Period

        • _____   • Civil War

        • _____   • WW I

        • _____   • WW II

Sequence

_____	1.	Discovery
_____	2.	Colonial Period
Red Badge of Courage	3.	Civil War
_____	4.	WW I
Diary of Anne Frank	5.	WW II

Shared Topics

Directions: Choose two content areas and brainstorm important concepts, attitudes and skills taught in each. Record these in the outer crescents. Then, working together, identify areas that overlap.

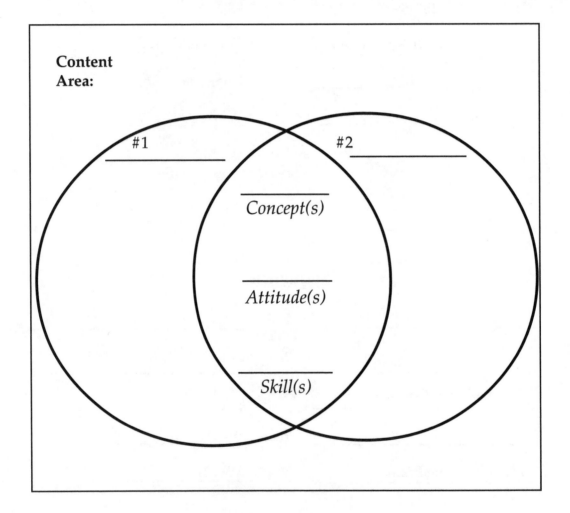

Content Area:

#1 _____

#2 _____

_____
Concept(s)

_____
Attitude(s)

_____
Skill(s)

Shared topics - Examples

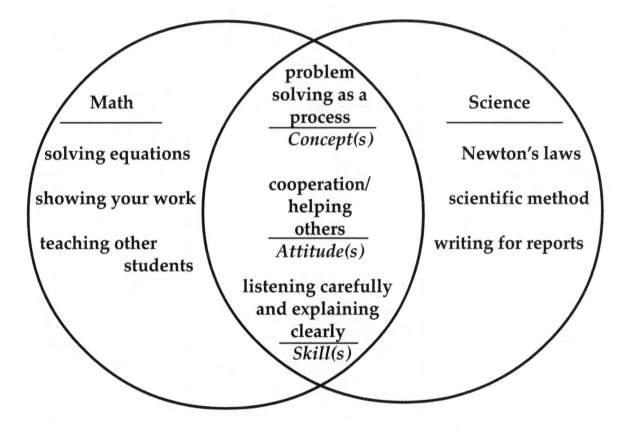

Math
solving equations

showing your work

teaching other students

problem solving as a process
Concept(s)

cooperation/ helping others
Attitude(s)

listening carefully and explaining clearly
Skill(s)

Science
Newton's laws

scientific method

writing for reports

Enriching Content Classes for Secondary ESOL Students (National Edition)
Study Guide Section 1: Academic Competence, Part A

21

Webbed Topics

Directions: Think back to topics that you have taught and, as an interdisciplinary team, (or a grade level team), see if you can find a theme that might have worked for all of you. It is often helpful to list major questions that study of the theme should answer.

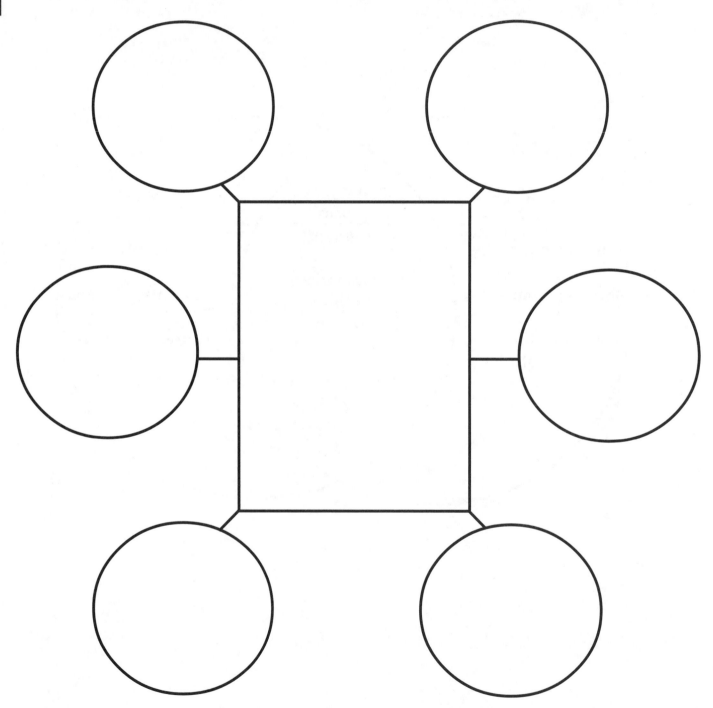

From *The Mindful School: How to Integrate the Curricula* by Robin Fogarty © 1991 IRI/Skylight Training and Publishing, Inc. Reprinted by permission of Skylight Professional Development, www.skylightedu.com or (800) 348-4474.

22

Enriching Content Classes for Secondary ESOL Students (National Edition)
Study Guide Section 1: Academic Competence, Part A

Webbed Topics - Example

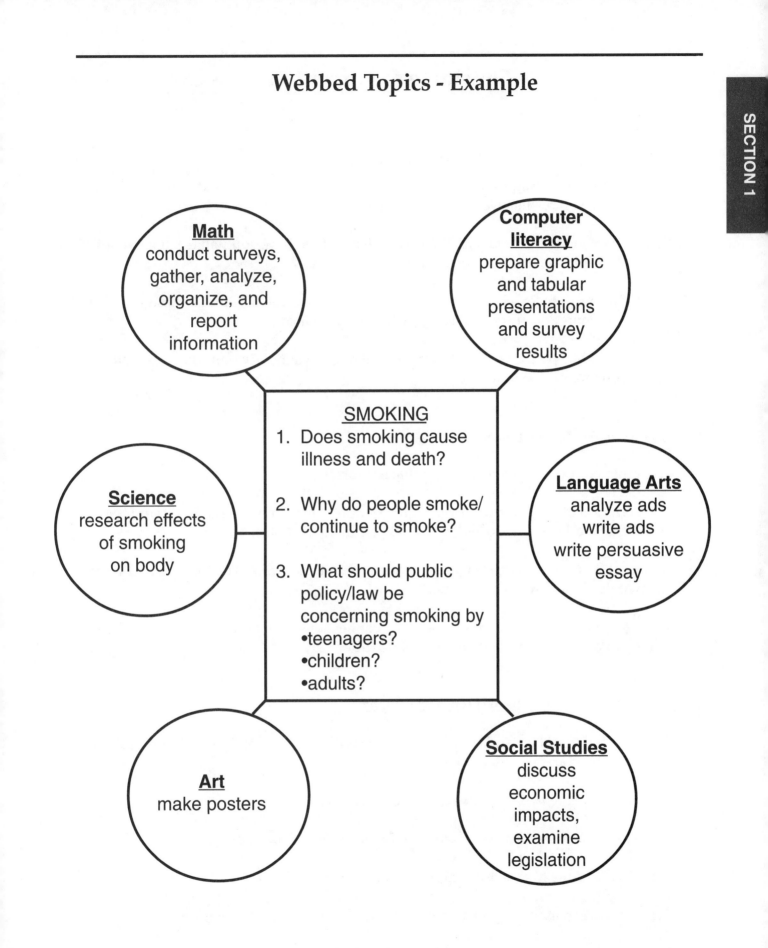

Math
conduct surveys, gather, analyze, organize, and report information

Computer literacy
prepare graphic and tabular presentations and survey results

SMOKING
1. Does smoking cause illness and death?

2. Why do people smoke/ continue to smoke?

3. What should public policy/law be concerning smoking by
•teenagers?
•children?
•adults?

Science
research effects of smoking on body

Language Arts
analyze ads
write ads
write persuasive essay

Art
make posters

Social Studies
discuss economic impacts, examine legislation

Enriching Content Classes for Secondary ESOL Students (National Edition)
Study Guide Section 1: Academic Competence, Part A

23

Outside Assignment #1

A. <u>Process</u>

1. Choose the Connecting Across the Content Areas model that you and your partner(s) want to develop further. Develop and enhance it.

2. Select a portion of the model in your content area. Plan how you will teach it using the Three Principles and connections to other content areas.

3. Teach this portion. Reflect on the experience and write it up as Outside Assignment #1. See the contents and criteria (below) for further guidance.

4. Work with your partner(s) to prepare a visual display and a five-minute presentation about your connected unit.

B. <u>Contents of Written Assignment</u>

1. A completed connections model (graphic organizer).

2. A description of how you will teach your portion of the connected unit. Be sure it is clear what students will do and how ESOL students will participate.

3. Reflect on your experience teaching the lesson/unit. Tell what worked well and what you would do differently next time.

4. Reflect on your experience developing the connections with other content areas. Tell what worked well and what you would do differently next time.

C. <u>Criteria for Evaluating the Written Assignment</u>

Note that the presenters and some participants will read your assignment and provide feedback. These are the criteria they will use.

1. Are there *meaningful* links between the content areas?

2. Is the lesson/unit sequenced to enhance ESOL student understanding?

3. What else is done to increase comprehensibility for ESOL students?

4. What is done to increase content-focused interaction among students?

5. What are the principal higher order thinking skills/tasks required of students?

24

Enriching Content Classes for Secondary ESOL Students (National Edition)
Study Guide Section 1: Academic Competence, Part A

6. Describe something that you liked or responded to in the lesson/unit you reviewed.

7. Describe something that you didn't understand or that might need further work.

8. Other comments:

D. <u>Presentation</u>

You and your partner(s) will prepare and display a visual presentation for your colleagues in this inservice. The visual should show the connections model that you used and the major elements of each partner's lesson/unit. You will have 3-5 minutes to explain your visual and answer questions about it.

Enriching Content Classes for Secondary ESOL Students (National Edition)
Study Guide Section 1: Academic Competence, Part A

25

Enriching Content Classes for Secondary ESOL Students

Study Guide

Section 2
Language Learning in School

Section 2
Language Learning in School

Goal

To understand the principles of language learning in order to facilitate the learning of English by ESOL students in content classrooms.

Performance Objectives

• Understand the principles, similarities, and differences of first and second language acquisition.

• Describe how the principles of second language acquisition can be used in the mainstream classroom to facilitate language development of ESOL students.

• Differentiate social and academic language and describe the implications for school programs.

• Develop activities appropriate to different stages of an ESOL student's language development.

• Describe program models for second language students and tell when each is appropriate.

• List ways that teachers, schools, and communities can support students' first language development in ESOL program models.

Enriching Content Classes for Secondary ESOL Students (National Edition)
Study Guide Section 2: Language Learning in School

29

Inferences About Language Acquisition

Directions: All of the following statements are true. In your small group, discuss each statement and make inferences about what the statement tells us in terms of how children acquire their first language in natural settings. Make notes on the accompanying chart.

1. Children seem born to want to communicate, first with their parents and later with playmates. Through language, humans communicate needs and ideas, interact with others, and develop themselves.

2. Parents and young children talk about toys they are playing with at the time or books with pictures that they are reading, playmates talk about games that they are playing.

3. A child understands a parent who asks "do you want a cookie with your juice?" even though the child may only be able to say "cookie."

4. Parents and older children naturally adjust their language when speaking to young children. They speak more simply and link the language to clues to its meaning such as objects, gestures, facial expressions, pictures, prior knowledge, etc.

5. Children acquire their first language in the home where they are loved by parents and encouraged to talk. Children feel free to use and experiment with language, and make mistakes without fear of ridicule or even overt correction.

6. In natural settings, children develop complex language rapidly and without formal instruction. A preschooler's tacit knowledge of grammar is more sophisticated than the thickest style manual or the most state-of-the-art computer language system. Further, virtually all children fully acquire one or more languages regardless of IQ.

7. We think children pick up their mother tongue by imitating their mothers, but when a child says "don't giggle me!" or "we holded the baby rabbits," it cannot be an act of imitation.

8. If a child says, "we holded the puppies" (meaning rabbits), the parent is likely to respond "yes, they're baby rabbits, aren't they?"

9. The child points to a picture and says "king," the mother says, "yes, that's a king, you can tell he's a king because he's wearing a crown."

10. A child is raised in a minority community in which children are expected to learn by watching adults; adult actions are seldom explained verbally to the child and children are not asked "known answer" questions.

30

Enriching Content Classes for Secondary ESOL Students (National Edition)
Study Guide Section 2: Language Learning in School

Statement Summaries	Inferences about L1 Acquisition
1. Children naturally want to communicate.	1. This innate need to communicate provides natural motivation to acquire a language.
2. Parents and young children talk about what they are doing at the time.	2.
3. A child understands a parent's language even though the child's language is more limited.	3.
4. People adjust their language when speaking to young children.	4.
5. Parents love and encourage children to talk.	5.
6. All children acquire incredibly complex language naturally.	6.
7. "We holded the baby rabbits," cannot be an act of imitation.	7.
8. Parents corrected "puppies" to "baby rabbits."	8.
9. The parent makes a sentence from the child's single word "king."	9.
10. A child is expected to watch adult actions to learn.	10.

Source: Navarette and Gutske (1996), Pinker (1994), and Short (1991).

Enriching Content Classes for Secondary ESOL Students (National Edition)
Study Guide Section 2: Language Learning in School

31

SECTION 2

Reading On Language Acquisition

Directions: Read the following passage which goes into more depth on some of the issues raised in the inference activity and adds new information. Then, be prepared to discuss it with the class.

Chomsky and Krashen

Since 1950, two linguists have exerted especially strong influences on the field. Chomsky asserts that a substantial part of language acquisition must be innate (inborn, like an instinct). Krashen places emphasis on the social and interpersonal aspects of language acquisition; his ideas have revolutionized language classrooms. Since it is unethical to experiment with brain surgery or social deprivation and then study the effects on language acquisition, theorists must rely on observations, naturally occurring experiments, and cross-cultural studies.

Language Acquisition is Innate

In the late 1950s and 1960s, Noam Chomsky, arguably the most influential theoretical linguist of the 20th century, reasoned that certain aspects of language were innate—that is, they were inborn in the human brain. This view contradicts both the behaviorism of the time and the current social science model. The former explained behavior as stimulus-response learning and the latter explains it as a product of the surrounding culture.

The innateness of language can be visualized as the general outline of a blueprint or electrical wiring diagram that is inborn as "channels" or "circuitry" in the brain. As the child develops, the blueprint is filled in and becomes more detailed, building on the basic structure. Clearly, the original innate blueprint must guide language development in any language to which the child is exposed—a Chinese child, raised in China will learn to speak Chinese; the same child raised by English-speaking parents will learn to speak English.

Chomsky called this concept Universal Grammar. The word grammar in this sense does not mean rules for correctness, but rather general characteristics that all languages possess. For example, all languages have categories of words that name objects and other categories that describe actions, and all languages can express ideas such as number, place, and time. The innate blueprint would help a child develop categories for words and unconscious rules for putting the words together in sentences and conversations. Incidentally, the argument that there are innate aspects of language is not an argument against individual differences. An analogy is lungs: all humans are born with lungs, and all lungs work according to the same basic blueprint, but some lungs are inherently more efficient than others (natural athletes) and other lungs can be trained to be more efficient.

The theoretical construct of Universal Grammar—the innate, generalized blueprint, common to all human brains—is supported by several types of observations:

32

Enriching Content Classes for Secondary ESOL Students (National Edition)
Study Guide Section 2: Language Learning in School

1. All human cultures, even primitive cultures, have complex, rule-governed language. This observation is consistent with the view that language is a biological adaptation, developed over hundreds of thousands of years, in order to communicate information. The forerunners of language can be seen in animal communication.

2. Children, in natural settings, learn language rapidly and without formal instruction. Their language utilizes thousands of rules that were acquired unconsciously and are transparent to them. Language is so complex that even state-of-the-art computers have difficulty producing it, yet, virtually all children learn language regardless of IQ, social class, formal education, and other social and cultural variables. Middle class Americans think that mothers teach their children language by speaking "Motherese," but other cultures do not speak directly to very young children, and the children still learn to speak on schedule.

3. If children are not exposed to rule-governed, complex language, they will create it. In Hawaii, about 1890, there was a sugar plantation where immigrant laborers came from many different countries and had no common language. The adults developed a makeshift pidgin with a limited vocabulary, few rules, and a limited ability to communicate complex ideas. But children born into this situation, created for themselves, a fully-developed, standardized, complex language in one generation. (Chomsky would say that they had no choice but to fill in their innate blueprint.) Language creation has also been observed in groups of deaf children with hearing parents.

4. There are several "naturally occurring experiments" such as traumatic injuries to the brain that destroy specific aspects of language such as the ability to put words together into sentences (grammar), but do not affect either knowledge of content words, cognition, or intelligence.

[For more information, see Steven Pinker (1994), *The language instinct*, NY: HarperCollins, especially chapter 2.]

Language Acquisition Requires Comprehensible Input

Perhaps the strongest influence on second language teaching and learning in the past 20 years is that of Stephen Krashen. Krashen's theory is based on the assumption that first and second language acquisition take place in very similar ways. This was a new idea as recently as 20 years ago. Prior to Krashen, people often learned second languages through grammar study so the similarity between natural, childhood, first language acquisition and later second language acquisition was not apparent.

The central role in Krashen's theory is played by "comprehensible input." Krashen believes that the language learner needs language "input" which consists of the new language along with clues as to what the language means; without these clues, the learner could hear a lot of language without ever learning to understand it. Without *comprehensible* input, hearing a new language would be like listening to Hungarian on the radio with no way to begin to understand individual words or even topics. Comprehensible input is the type of language that parents naturally supply to their children: it is slower and simpler, it focuses on the here and now, it focuses on meaning over form, and it extends and elaborates on the child's language.

Enriching Content Classes for Secondary ESOL Students (National Edition)
Study Guide Section 2: Language Learning in School

33

Krashen postulates that the comprehensible input that is most effective is just slightly beyond the learner's current level of competence. Sometimes this concept is written as "i + 1." If the input is either too easy or too difficult, it does not promote improvement as effectively—slightly "stretching" to understand is what promotes improvement. But, Krashen states, parents and teachers need not worry about pinpoint targeting of i + 1 for each language learner. Learners at different levels can each acquire benefit at his own level from a rich, interesting, and positive language acquisition environment.

Second, Krashen believes that there are two distinct ways of developing ability in a language: acquisition and learning. Acquisition is the natural, subconscious process of "soaking up" a language like that of children naturally developing their first language. Learning is a formal, conscious process often involving learning grammar, vocabulary, and rules. Krashen believes that acquisition is overwhelmingly the most important process in developing second language ability. Classrooms with second language learners should provide rich, natural, hands-on language acquisition experiences to facilitate this natural process.

A third key factor in Krashen's theory is that of the affective filter. "Affect" here is used as a noun. It is a psychological term meaning feeling or emotion. Krashen states that emotions and feelings determine how easily language is acquired. Emotional states such as anxiety, stress, or low self-confidence will "raise the filter" providing an emotional barrier to effective language acquisition. Optimal language acquisition occurs in states of low anxiety and stress and high motivation and self-confidence.

Fourth, language researchers have noted that children acquire (not learn) grammatical structures in a relatively predictable order, e.g., in English -ing forms and plural -s are acquired early, third person singular verb -s and possessive -s are acquired later. The order of acquisition for first and second language learners is similar, but not exactly the same. One of the implications of this observation is to discourage overt error correction because errors will tend to fall away when the learner reaches a certain stage of development, assuming that the learner is in a good environment for language acquisition. (Note that Krashen would NOT encourage teaching a second language based on this order because he believes that formal learning is not a good way to develop language ability. He would encourage placing the learner in a rich language <u>acquisition</u> environment which means the learner would hear and be exposed to lots of rich, natural, complex language from which the learner would begin to unconsciously internalize patterns. By controlling or adjusting the input to contain only certain grammatical structures, the learner's natural acquisition process is undermined.)

And finally, Krashen believes that conscious learning can, under limited circumstances, be used to edit or monitor language output, e.g., to make corrections as we speak or write or after we speak or write. In order to use conscious learning to make corrections, we must have time, be consciously thinking about correctness, be concerned with a limited number of rules, and know the rule. It is impossible to monitor hundreds of language rules when trying to speak or write fluently.

34

Enriching Content Classes for Secondary ESOL Students (National Edition)
Study Guide Section 2: Language Learning in School

At the risk of oversimplifying, the relationship of these factors could be illustrated as follows: Think of an ESOL student. He is presented with *comprehensible input* (comprehensible input and *i + 1*), and if the *affective filter* is low he can take in the input and use it to aid in *acquiring* new language. Some parts of the language will naturally be acquired before others (*natural order*). When the student produces language, it may contain errors because his language is in an intermediate state of development. In a few circumstances, when he is focusing on correctness, the student can use the *monitor* to make some self-corrections, but this focus will conflict with a focus on fluency and the content of the message.

[For more information, see Steven Krashen. (1981). Bilingual education and second language acquisition theory. In *Schooling and language minority students: A theoretical framework*. Los Angeles: Evaluation, Dissemination, and Assessment Center, California State University.]

Summary

Though Chomsky and Krashen assign central roles to different aspects of language acquisition, the theories are not necessarily in conflict: Comprehensible input could be an important, perhaps the most important, way the innate blueprint of Universal Grammar is filled in.

Enriching Content Classes for Secondary ESOL Students (National Edition)
Study Guide Section 2: Language Learning in School

35

Implications for the Classroom

Directions: The statements and statement summaries on this chart are the same as those on the earlier chart entitled Inferences About Language Acquisition (you may refer to it if needed). Complete the second column, making notes on the implications of language acquisition principles for the classroom; in other words, characteristics of classroom environments, instructional methods, curriculum, teacher behaviors, etc. that will facilitate learning English as a new language.

1. Children naturally want to communicate	1. Given an interesting, supportive, language-rich environment, students will be naturally motivated to learn English.
2. Parents and young children talk about what they are doing at the time.	2.
3. A child understands a parent's language even though the child's language is more limited.	3.
4. People adjust their language when speaking to young children.	4.
5. Parents love and encourage children to talk.	5.
6. All children acquire incredibly complex language naturally.	6.
7. "We holded the baby rabbits," cannot be an act of imitation.	7.
8. Parents corrected "puppies" to "baby rabbits."	8.
9. The parent makes a sentence from the child's single word "king."	9.
10. A child is expected to watch adult actions to learn.	10.

Facilitating Language Learning in the Classroom

(1.) <u>Create an environment that facilitates language learning</u>

- Actively engage students in challenging learning activities

- Use interactive activities so ESOL students talk with their peers and use academic English

- Use concrete, hands-on activities (and language) before more abstract (and language) activities

- Create an atmosphere in which ESOL students feel safe in taking risks with both English and content

(2.) <u>Adjust teacher talk to increase comprehensibility</u>

- Face the students

- Pause frequently

- Paraphrase often

- Clearly indicate the most important ideas and vocabulary through intonation or writing on the blackboard

- Avoid "asides"

- Avoid or clarify pronouns

- Use shorter sentences

- Use subject-verb-object word order

- Increase wait time for students to answer

- Focus on the student's meaning, not grammar

- Avoid interpreting on a regular basis

(3) <u>Support or scaffold ESOL student language development</u>

- Ask questions in simplified language

- Establish a pattern in the questions

- Ask for elaboration, "Tell me more about..."

- Be a good listener (eye contact, non-verbal support, plenty of time)

- Provide encouragement to continue, "Uh-huh. Really? What happened then?"

- Provide difficult words

- Ask for clarification, "I'm not sure I understand. Can you say it again?"

- Paraphrase what the student said

Enriching Content Classes for Secondary ESOL Students (National Edition)
Study Guide Section 2: Language Learning in School

37

Language Development Stages: Sample Behaviors in the Classroom

Stage	Sample Student Behaviors	Sample Teacher Behaviors	Questioning Techniques
Pre-production • Students are totally new to English • Generally lasts 1-3 months	• Points to or provides other non-verbal responses • Actively listens • Responds to commands • May be reluctant to speak • Understands more than can produce	• Gestures • Language focuses on conveying meanings and vocabulary development • Repetition • Does not force student to speak	• Point to... • Find the... • Put the ___ next to the ___. • Do you have the ___? • Is this a ___? • Who wants the ___? • Who has the ___?
Early Production • Students are "low beginners" • Generally lasts several weeks	• One or two word utterances • Short phrases	• Asks questions that can be answered by yes/no and either/or responses • Models correct responses • Ensures a supportive, low anxiety environment • Does not overtly call attention to grammar errors	• Yes/no (Is the trouble light on?) • Either/or (Is this a screwdriver or a hammer? • One word response (What utensil am I holding in my hand?) • General questions which encourage lists of words (What do you see on the tool board?) • Two-word response (Where did he go? To work.)
Speech Emergence • Students are "beginners"	• Participates in small group activities • Demonstrates comprehension in a variety of ways • Speaks in short phrases and sentences • Begins to use language more freely	• Focuses content on key concepts • Provides frequent comprehension checks • Uses performance-based assessment • Uses expanded vocabulary • Asks open-ended questions that stimulate language production	• Why? • How? • How is this like that? • Tell me about... Talk about... • Describe • How would you change this part?
Intermediate Fluency • Students are "high beginners, intermediate or advanced" May require several years to achieve native-like fluency in academic settings	• Participates in reading and writing activities to acquire new information • May experience difficulties in abstract, cognitively demanding subjects at school, especially when a high degree of literacy is required	• Fosters conceptual development and expanded literacy through content • Continues to make lessons comprehensible and interactive • Teaches thinking and study skills • Continues to be alert to incidual differences in language and culture	• What would you recommend/suggest? • How do you think this story will end? • What is the story mainly about? • What is your opinion on this matter? • Describe/compare... • How are these similar/different? • What would happen if...? • Which do you prefer? Why? • Create.

Source: Adapted from *Empowering ESOL teachers: An overview.* (No date). Tallahassee, FL: Florida Department of Education, pp. 93-95.

Enriching Content Classes for Secondary ESOL Students (National Edition)
Study Guide Section 2: Language Learning in School

Civics Classroom Vignette

Grade Level:	Eleventh grade in a mainstream civics class
Students:	22 native English speakers and 8 ESOL students at varying levels of proficiency
Language of Instruction:	English
Focus of Instruction:	Civics
Location:	Urban school district in the Northeast

Background

The following vignette describes an eleventh-grade, one semester civics course, which is composed of 22 native English speaking students and 8 ESOL students at varying levels of proficiency in a Northeast urban high school. Most ESOL students speak Spanish; other language groups include Haitian and Chinese. Four of the ESOL students are advanced-level in terms of English proficiency; two are intermediate-level and two are beginners. Mr. Phillipe, the teacher, is certified in civics and has attended workshops on English as a second language. It is near the end of the school year.

Instructional Sequence

Recognizing the importance of the development of academic skills, Mr. Phillipe has developed a series of lesson activities that will take approximately 1 full week to cover in a class that meets for 80 minutes every day. The lesson activities are centered around the theme of civic responsibility and include discussions of what it means to be an informed citizen and how one takes action regarding a community concern. The week-long project requires small student groups to research information from multiple sources and prepare for a debate to compare and contrast points of view on a topic generated by the class during the first day: a toxic waste dump planned for their neighborhood. Groups of four or five students are formed and they are given the task of comparing and contrasting articles from different newspapers, magazines, public interest groups' literature, and on-line sources. Whenever necessary, students of the same language discuss difficult ideas in their native language. Some teammates who are native speakers of English explain vocabulary and cultural dimensions to the assignment, such as the value of picketing. The students have had prior experiences comparing and contrasting reading selections and doing some library-based research.

As the research continues throughout the week, Mr. Phillipe occasionally calls the class together to share their findings. The ideas and issues that begin to crystallize are recorded on newsprint and mounted on the walls for further discussion. Positions and resolutions are compared and contrasted at times, using graphic organizers. Whenever necessary, the teacher asks open-ended questions based on the resources in order to guide students' reactions and understandings of the articles' ideas, photographs, graphics (e.g., charts), language, and tone. In some instances, they discuss bias-related elements in the research materials.

(cont. next page)

Enriching Content Classes for Secondary ESOL Students (National Edition)
Study Guide Section 2: Language Learning in School

39

On the fourth day students begin practicing for the debate. At this point, Mr. Phillipe assigns the positions. One half of the small groups join to represent the side in favor of the dump; the other half of the small groups join to oppose it. From the 15 students on each side, peers select 4 to present the case at Friday's debate. The others help plan the points to be offered and critique the practice performances.

After the debate is held, students are asked to write individual essays in which they describe which debate team was more convincing and why. They are then asked to take a position on the debate and support it in writing based upon their own informed perspectives.

Discussion

Students are encouraged to

- locate information appropriate to an assignment in text or reference materials

- research information on academic topics from multiple sources

- take a position and support it orally or in writing

- compare and classify information using technical vocabulary

- prepare for and participate in a debate

Mr. Phillipe recognizes the importance of a classroom environment that is conducive to language acquisition and learning. One way learning occurs is through meaningful activities, so he allows his students to select the topic they will explore for the civics assignment. He also provides his students with direction and material in order to build on their prior background and experiences. Through sharing and discussing, analyzing language and organizing information, responding to text and working in groups and as a whole class, the students participate in activities that develop their academic English, integrating all four language strands (listening, speaking, reading, and writing).

Students research information and generate opinions about a topic of interest to their lives within the context of the civics curriculum. They locate multiple sources of information and through class discussion come to understand the different genres in which information can be shared as well as the potential biases that writers can include in their material. This helps the students develop an awareness of the power and impact of language.

Students in Mr. Phillipe's class also acknowledge one another as resources and look to classmates for assistance. For example, native English speaking students and those who are not recent immigrants are able to act as cultural informants with respect to civic action. Mr. Phillipe, likewise, allows more proficient students to explain concepts in the native language of their peers.

SECTION 2

The students are also called upon to us their cognitive abilities as they prepare for a debate. They must clarify their own positions, argue persuasively, and anticipate the arguments of their opponents. In a supportive environment, students rehearse with their teammates' guidance. Help in this regard is further provided by the teacher's planned activities for comparing and contrasting viewpoints with the class as a whole. The recorded ideas, issues, and observations remain on the newsprint in sight of the students throughout the week.

After the group activity is completed, Mr. Phillipe gives a writing assignment that permits him to assess the knowledge individual students have acquired. The students argue a position in an essay drawing from the syntheses and analyses of information that they made in their groups and from their responses to the debate they observed.

Note: The background of the ESOL students in the vignette has been modified for the purposes of this activity.

Enriching Content Classes for Secondary ESOL Students (National Edition)
Study Guide Section 2: Language Learning in School

41

Civics Classroom Activity

Directions: Read the accompanying Civics Classroom Vignette, then, complete the following activity working in your small group.

1. List the academic tasks that the students are required to perform in this unit next to the appropriate language strand.

Listening:

Speaking:

Reading:

Writing:

2. How did Mr. Phillipe structure the students' activities to support the participation of the ESOL students?

3. What other modifications would you suggest to provide additional support to the beginning and intermediate-level ESOL students?

Beginning:

Intermediate:

42

Enriching Content Classes for Secondary ESOL Students (National Edition)
Study Guide Section 2: Language Learning in School

4. After the debate, Mr. Phillipe asks questions to check the students' comprehension. List two questions that he could ask of an ESOL student at each of the following stages:

Pre-production:

Early Production:

Speech Emergence:

Intermediate Fluency:

5. At the end of the unit, Mr. Phillipe wants each student to demonstrate his/her own learning (individual accountability) since most of the work for the unit was done in groups. Most of the students write an essay arguing a position, using the information they learned from the unit and the debate. Suggest an activity for the beginning and intermediate-level ESOL students to demonstrate their learning.

Beginning:

Intermediate:

Enriching Content Classes for Secondary ESOL Students (National Edition)
Study Guide Section 2: Language Learning in School

43

Program Models for Second Language Learners

Program Model	Short Description	Classroom Composition	Instructional Objectives
ESOL Models	The language of instruction is English		
1. Mainstream Classes (inclusion)	Mainstream classes with teacher using ESOL strategies	Native English-speakers with some ESOL students	Academic content, e.g., science
2. Self-contained Classes (elementary) and Sheltered Classes (high school)	ESOL students are grouped in special classes so that the teacher can modify instruction/curriculum to meet their needs, e.g., 2nd grade ESOL self-contained; Sheltered Science, ESOL English	100% ESOL students	Both academic content and development of English as a second language
3. ESOL Pullout	ESOL students leave their regular classes to receive ESOL instruction	All are ESOL students in the pull-out class	Development of English as a second language
Bilingual Models			
1. Two-way Bilingual Programs	English-speaking and LEP students are in the same class where some subjects are taught in English and other subjects are taught in the LEP students' L1	Half the students are English speakers and half are LEP students	Academic content and proficiency in two languages
2. Transitional Bilingual Programs	Some instruction is provided in L1 so that LEP students can progress academically while learning English; the goal is to support LEP students during their "transition" to an all-English program	All are LEP	Academic content and proficiency in English
3. Maintenance Programs	Some instruction is provided in L1 so that LEP students can "maintain" their L1 as well as learn English and academics	All are LEP	Academic content, proficiency in English, and maintenance of L1

Enriching Content Classes for Secondary ESOL Students (National Edition)
Study Guide Section 2: Language Learning in School

Case Studies

Directions: Identify the program model that each case study represents.

1. In this high school there is a separate science class for intermediate level LEP students. The teacher is a science teacher who has worked with an ESOL resource teacher to modify his curriculum so that he is sure to cover the most important basics of science, such as the scientific method, principles of experimentation, etc. He also spends more time on language-related skills such as how to state a hypothesis, how to state scientific principles in the student's own words, how to write a lab report, and common vocabulary words that have specific scientific meanings: force, power, pressure.

This Program Model is _____

2. This is a high school English class and students receive English credit. They are studying a novel by Pearl Buck entitled "The Good Deed" and are identifying the plot, setting, characters, etc. Each student reads part of the novel and then shares his/her learning with the other students. All the students are limited English proficient.

This Program Model is _____

3. This is a high school English class with 25 native English speakers and a few high-intermediate LEP students. The teacher is teaching the writing process. The LEP students work in small groups with the English speaking students who often help them by showing them what the teacher is looking for. The teacher also gives the LEP students extra help with their outside assignments.

This Program Model is _____

4. This is a third grade class composed of children with many different first languages, all of them learning English through the grade-level curriculum. The teacher uses many hands on activities, pays a lot of attention to developing students' language and literacy skills, often invites parents into the classroom, and encourages parents to read to their children in their native language.

This Program Model is _____

Enriching Content Classes for Secondary ESOL Students (National Edition)
Study Guide Section 2: Language Learning in School

45

5. In this class, half of the subjects (in the morning) are taught in Spanish and the other subjects (in the afternoon) are taught in English. Half of the students speak Spanish and are learning English as a second language and the other half speak English and are learning Spanish as a second language. Parents of both student groups regard this as a "gifted and talented" program which is preparing their children for a multicultural world.

This Program Model is _____

6. In this fourth grade class, most of the students stay with the teacher all day long, but a few students leave the class every day for a portion of language arts time for instruction in ESOL. The teacher realizes that this instruction is helping some of the students, but she worries that the students have an interruption in their learning environment and also are made to feel different.

This Program Model is _____

46

Enriching Content Classes for Secondary ESOL Students (National Edition)
Study Guide Section 2: Language Learning in School

Program Models for Second Language Learners

Directions: Take notes on this chart when this topic is discussed

Program Model	When Most Appropriate?	Pros	Cons
ESOL Models			
1. Mainstream Classes (Inclusion)			
2. Self-Contained Classes (elementary) and **Sheltered Classes** (high school)			
3. ESOL Pullout			
Bilingual Models			

Enriching Content Classes for Secondary ESOL Students (National Edition)
Study Guide Section 2: Language Learning in School

47

Language Minority Student Achievement
And Program Effectiveness

Teachers often have two basic questions about serving ESOL students in school:

1. How long does it take an ESOL student to learn English for school purposes and what factors affect this process?

2. What kinds of programs are effective in helping ESOL students succeed in school?

Needless to say, the answers to these questions are complex.

Virginia Collier (1995) reminds us that acquisition of either a first (native) or second language is a complex, long-term process. Think of a five-year-old, English-speaking child entering a U. S. kindergarten: his language is not fully developed by any means. As he grows older, he will develop language to express more complex and subtle meanings, he will learn to read and write, he will learn enormous amounts of vocabulary both in and out of school, he will learn how to use language differently in different situations and for varying purposes, and many other things. A student learning English as a new language must learn all these things as well, but he must learn under very different conditions: in an academic setting, often with peers who are native English speakers, and under severe time pressure. Students learning English in school also bring very different backgrounds to their task: age, prior education, socioeconomic levels, cultural differences, and others.

Virginia Collier and Wayne Thomas have studied the question of "how long does it take an ESOL student to learn English for school purposes" for many years. In brief, they found that in U.S. schools where all instruction is provided through English, the most significant student background variable is the amount of formal schooling students have received in their first language. Older students who have not had any schooling in their first language generally require *7-10 years to perform at the average level (50th percentile) of native English speakers on academic tests in English.* Students with 2-3 years of L1 schooling, generally require 5-7 years to perform at this level. This finding holds true regardless of other student background variables such as socioeconomic status or country of origin.

Note that these researchers have used a very demanding standard: the 50th percentile on academic tests in English—half the English speakers perform under this percentile. Further, this standard measures both content knowledge and use of English, and is higher every year as grade-level expectations increase. However, this is the standard at which ESOL students can be said to be performing (as a group) at a level equivalent to native English speakers. It is important to understand that Collier and Thomas are *not* implying that ESOL students cannot succeed in school for several years; they are documenting the sizable challenge that these students must meet, often in an environment that does not understand their needs well.

48

Enriching Content Classes for Secondary ESOL Students (National Edition)
Study Guide Section 2: Language Learning in School

The crucial role of schooling in the students' first language might be clearer if we think of two 16-year-old high school students. A native English speaker has been learning English for 16 years and U.S. school subjects for 10 years or more. An ESOL student must achieve comparable levels of language and content knowledge in much less time and the stronger his base of academic language and content is (even in L1), the more he will have to build on.

Collier summarizes the role of first language as follows: "The key to understanding the role of first language in the academic development of the second language is to understand the function of uninterrupted cognitive development. When students switch to second language use at school and teachers encourage parents to speak in the second language at home, both students and parents are functioning at a level far below their age" (pp. 6-7).

Teachers, however, have no control over the backgrounds their students bring and many schools cannot provide bilingual education to support their language minority students. What *can* teachers do?

First, teachers can recognize the important role that first language plays in student success in school and can look for ways to support ESOL students through L1 tutors (perhaps older students or members of community organizations), bilingual aides, books and websites in L1, and the appropriate use of L1 in the classroom (perhaps brainstorming, researching a new topic, or helping others). Second, classrooms can be highly interactive and emphasize student problem-solving and discovery learning. These classrooms offer opportunities to develop both cognitive and communication skills in English, not to mention a high degree of motivation to learn. Third, the school must offer an explicitly welcoming climate to its language minority students: perceptions of hostility, subordinate status, or remedial learning lead to isolation, self-doubt, and dropout.

In addition, academic achievement of ESOL students, especially at the secondary level, will be improved if the second language (English) is taught through academic content; teachers consciously focus on teaching learning strategies, thinking skills, and problem-solving; and teachers participate in ongoing staff development focusing on strategies appropriate for ESOL students as well as for other learners. These strategies include: "activation of students' prior knowledge, respect for students' home language and culture, cooperative learning, interactive and discovery learning, intense and meaningful cognitive/academic development, and ongoing assessment using multiple measures" (p. 9).

Source: Collier, V. P. (1995). *Acquiring a second language for school* (Directions in Language and Education, Vol. 1, No. 4). Washington DC: National Clearinghouse for Bilingual Education.

Enriching Content Classes for Secondary ESOL Students (National Edition)
Study Guide Section 2: Language Learning in School

49

Enriching Content Classes for Secondary ESOL Students

Study Guide

Section 3
Culture, Part A

Culture, Part A

Goal

To provide participants with a multicultural perspective, knowledge about cultural groups, and the opportunity to reflect on the role of students' home cultures.

Performance Objectives

- Discover US cultural values as a first step toward increasing cultural awareness.

- Interpret ESOL student behavior from a cultural perspective.

- Demonstrate in-depth knowledge of one culture represented in the ESOL student population.

- Practice interacting with an ESOL student concerning a personal cross-cultural conflict.

- Reflect on the role of students' home cultures in their adaptation to the U.S.

Cultural Diversity Profile

Directions: For each item, choose the value that comes closest to describing your own personal values. Record 'a' or 'b' in the box to the left of the item.

	1a. Hard work will accomplish any objective. 1b. Wisdom , luck, and fate are basic to success.
	2a. Communication should be frank and direct. 2b. Communication should be polite and indirect.
	3a. Commitments should be honored. 3b. Commitments signify intention, and may be superseded by a conflicting request or need.
	4a. Time should be effectively and efficiently used. 4b. Schedules should be viewed in relationship to other priorities.
	5a. An individual's work tells a lot about him/her. 5b. Individual identity isn't defined by work or accomplishments.
	6a. Success is earned by ability, experience, and hard work. 6b. Family ties and friendships determine mobility.
	7a. Teachers should consult with parents, who can contribute useful information. 7b. Decisions should be made by those in authority and others need not be consulted.
	8a. Competiton stimulates high performance. 8b. Competition leads to disharmony.
	9a. One should do whatever is necessary to get the job done. 9b. Some work may be below one's dignity or rank.
	10a. Change is healthy. 10b. Traditions should be preserved by observing rituals and customs from the past.
	11a. Both persons and systems should be evaluated. 11b. Personal evaluations should never be negative because they might cause a "loss of face."
	12a. Helping a fellow student on a test is cheating. 12b. One should help friends with schoolwork, even tests.
	13a. Present success and satisfaction are important. 13b. Materialism isn't important; spirituality is.
	14a. Students should be self-directed and take initiative in their studies. 14b. Students should wait for directions from the teacher.
	15a. An individual should do everything possible to achieve his/her goals and aspirations. 15b. The group is more important than the individual.

Total number of "a's" _____

Total number of "b's" _____

Source: Center for Applied Linguistics.

Valuing Cultural Diversity

Culture is the set of common beliefs and values that are shared by a group of people and that binds them together into a society. All people are members of at least one culture. The norms of a culture provide a framework that makes people's behavior understandable to one another. Culture allows the individual to predict how other people will behave. All cultures define certain roles, e.g., gender roles–men behave one way and women another– and age roles- children act in ways that adults do not. US culture also defines roles in relation to status and profession. A waitress, a flight attendant, a school principal, or a physician - all have a range of behavior that is appropriate to their positions.

Adults transmit their culture to their children in both conscious and unconscious ways. Parents consciously teach their children things like language, appropriate manners, religious beliefs, and family history. They emphasize positive behaviors such as valuing and behaving respectfully to older people or learning who is included in their kinship or family network. Children also gain unconscious knowledge of their culture-ideas of personal beauty and ways of communicating nonverbally are examples of things children assimilate without conscious awareness.

Through the transmission of culture, children define themselves and their identities. Their beliefs derive from their ethnic and family backgrounds, but they are also shaped by the experiences they have in school and in the larger society. For example, if a culture values the well-being of the group over that of the individual, children in that culture will usually be more comfortable in cooperative rather than in competitive settings. And if those children are placed in competitive situations, as they often are in US schools, they will likely not understand why they feel uneasy. The students will either adjust to and accommodate the competitive situations or fail to perform in a way satisfactory to the teacher.

Most people take culture for granted-it seems natural to them. They do not consciously analyze cultural roles until someone violates them. For example-most teachers in the US assume that a respectful and honest child will look them in the eye during any interaction. Indeed, failure to make eye contact is usually interpreted as a sign of dishonesty or shiftiness. But in many cultures, children are taught that they should look down when being spoken to by an adult. Looking away is a gesture of respect. These children must then master one system of showing respect to use at home and another one to use at school.

Language minority students are caught at the intersection of two cultures and they must find a personal accommodation. This process of accommodation is highly individual, and each person's adjustment will be unique. Students who do not find this comfortable accommodation may become alienated from both their native culture and US culture. These language minority children start school with positive attitudes about the culture represented at home. When the culture of school conflicts with what they learned at home they will sometimes reject their original culture in an effort to find comfort in school. On some level they feel that accepting the culture represented by the school will ensure that the school culture will accept them. However, they are usually still seen as different from the norm; they are still seen as "those ESL kids."

Often, then, these students reject the culture represented by the school. They join with other language minority students who are similarly alienated and have little satisfaction from either their original culture or the new culture. This is the typical picture of a student who does not finish high school and who gets involved in antisocial behavior both in and out of school.

Students who take pride in and feel satisfaction with their first culture are more likely to find a comfortable adjustment to a new culture. One of the tasks of teachers of ESOL students is to help students adjust to the new culture by reinforcing their pride in their original culture. Students must first learn to understand their own cultures and then they can begin to understand and to accept the cultures of others.

Some educators feel that promoting pride in students' home culture can foster a sense of alienation from mainstream culture. These educators believe that language minority students will be better adjusted to life in the US if they give up most of their cultural practices and become more like other members of the dominant culture. However, social scientists generally contend that the dominant culture itself is the result of the multiple acculturations of the groups who were here originally (Native Americans) and subsequent groups of immigrants. This national culture and identity is shared by all the groups here and minority group membership is an integral part of the larger culture. To say that there is a US culture does not mean that all Americans are alike but rather that there is a genuine sense of national community with its own principles of unity, history, and sense of belonging. The national culture consists of components which are shared by virtually all people in the US. Some of these values include:

- The importance of personal independence which includes the notion of individual rights. In fact, it is so fundamental to US culture that many people assume it to be a universal human value.

- Another basic and widely shared value in US culture is the sense of competition and fair play.

- Egalitarianism–that all humans are intrinsically equal in worth–is a widespread belief in the US.

- Action orientation characterizes the thinking of most people in this country. Doing something is more important than being something.

- There is a widespread belief in self help in the US. Many, if not all of our problems, can be solved by our own efforts if we just work hard enough to find the right solution.

Although many of the values listed above are also characteristic of other cultures, they are by no means universal. Language minority students may have learned conflicting values from various cultures. Educators face a complex challenge in working with students from various cultures. They want the students to maintain their sense of personal identity and self esteem that is derived from the home culture. But they also want students to function in US schools which require students to adjust to or even accept the strongest values of the dominant culture.

A good teacher demonstrates clearly that all students have the same self-worth and that no one student is the model for US culture. Good teachers encourage positive interaction and respect among students of different cultures and racial backgrounds. Good teachers not only tolerate cultural differences but also celebrate them.

Sylvia Boynton (1996). Used with permission.

Discussion Questions:

1. Give some examples from the reading or from experience of ESOL student behaviors that might be misinterpreted by US teachers or other students.

2. Give some examples of US behaviors that might puzzle or be misinterpreted by ESOL students.

3. Describe, in your own words, some of the feelings that ESOL students may go through in trying to find a personal accommodation to the differences between their home and school (US) cultures. How does a strong home culture help ESOL students?

4. List several things that teachers and schools might do to facilitate cross-cultural understanding by all students, teachers, parents, and the community.

Private Writing:
Awareness of Cultural Difference

1. How do you react when you hear someone speaking a foreign language?

2. How do you feel when a new student from a different cultural background is assigned to your classroom?

3. Are you aware of the presence of persons with a racial background different from yours? What do you think about when you recognize this awareness?

4. How do you feel when you are visiting someone with customs or traditions different from yours?

SOURCE: Strasheim, L. (1976). We're all ethnics. In: *The Culture Revolution,* edited by Robert C. Lafayette. Skokie: National Textbook Company.

Culture Study Group Tasks

Purpose: To study one culture, using multiple sources, and to identify information relevant to working with ESOL students.

Task 1: Study the culture using multiple sources, including first person interviews.

   a. Identify 3-5 key factors in the culture's history/immigration and mark the class Timeline.

   b. Identify features of the language on the class Language Matrix.

   c. Identify/infer positions on the value orientation continuums and mark these points on the class visual.

   d. Discuss cross-cultural teacher-student interactions and expectations. Add 2-3 items to the class chart.

   e. Discuss how parents of ESOL students might see American schools and teachers. Add 2-3 items to the class chart.

Task 2: Prepare a five-minute presentation for the class and a supporting poster or display.

   a. Choose <u>a part</u> of what you learned that really interested your small group.

   b. Design the presentation to present <u>a limited aspect</u> of the culture in <u>depth</u>.

   c. Prepare the short presentation and a poster or display. (Presentation may not be longer than 5 minutes.)

Cultural Vignettes Activity

Directions: You and your partner will simulate a teacher and student conducting and interactive journal writing activity. Each of you will be assigned one of the vignettes below. First, each participant will write a journal entry from the student's perspective. Second, you will exchange journals with your partner, then respond as a teacher to the "student" entry. Remember that each student is unique and that the purpose of the activity is not necessarily to solve a problem, but rather to help the student feels some degree of comfort with two cultures.

1. The student is a 12 year old girl from a Mexican family. The mother, who speaks no English, is extremely modest. The mother has to go to a physician for an embarrassing problem. The daughter has to accompany her mother into the examining room and translate the ensuing discussion with the physician. The experience is upsetting to the girl and she writes about it in her interactive journal.

2. The student is a fifteen-year-old Korean immigrant girl. At school she appears to have lots of friends especially among the girls. However she is not invited to any of the parties the students have. At school dances no boy ever asks her to dance. She feels physically unattractive and rejected and writes about this in her interactive journal.

3. A thirteen-year-old Native American boy has been invited to a special summer program for gifted students. However, if he goes he will miss the Green Corn Dance which is one of the most important events in his traditional religious calendar. His family does not want him to go but the school guidance counselor (Anglo American) sees this as a marvelous opportunity. The student has tremendous respect for his family and an excellent relationship with the guidance counselor. The student does not know what to do and writes about the problem in his interactive journal.

4. A 17-year-old Puerto Rican boy is confused about finding a social group in which he feels accepted. Physically, the boy has beige skin and dark brown, slightly curly hair. His mother has very dark skin and her hair is black and curly. His father has light brown, straight hair and fair skin. In Puerto Rico, his was not an unusual family. However, in the United States people seem to consider his mother black and his father white. People seem to be disapproving of what they consider an "interracial" marriage. This boy does not have a sense of himself as "black" or "white," nor does he feel as though he belongs to a different racial group from his dad. At school the white kids tell him he is black and the black kids say that he thinks he is white. The boy writes about this in his interactive journal.

5. Annette is a 14-year-old Haitian girl who has recently arrived in the United States. In Haiti, she attended school and was educated in French. However, upon coming to the United States, she was placed in a bilingual Haitian Creole class. She speaks Haitian Creole, but does not know how to read and write it. She speaks, reads, and writes French fluently, but neither speaks not understands English. The students in her school often tease the children who are Haitian, so Annette wants to be in an English class so that no one will know she is Haitian. She says it is a waste of time for her to be in the bilingual class since she cannot read or write Haitian Creole. She is very upset about the situation and writes about it in her interactive journal.

El Árbol

Directions: Read and reflect on the following, then write your thoughts in your journal. The author was raised in a family that worked in the fields. He later became director of a federal agency and a university professor.

One farm winter in the high plains of Colorado where I was born and raised, my father pointed to an árbol — a cottonwood tree as I recall — near our home. He asked simply "¿ Por qué puede vivir ese árbol en el frio del invierno y en el calor del verano?" (How can that tree survive the bitter cold of winter and the harsh heat of summer?). My father was not a man of many words — he was often characterized by relatives as quiet and shy — but a person who, when he spoke, all listened carefully. I remember struggling to find an answer. I was also characterized as quiet and shy. But I tried to respond to my father. I remember rambling on for some time about how big and strong the tree was and how its limbs and trunk were like the strong arms and bodies of my elder brothers...Then my father kindly provided a different perspective by referring to a common Spanish dicho (proverb): El árbol fuerte tiene raíces maduras (A strong tree has mature strong roots). In articulating this significant analysis that was absent from my youthful ramblings, he made very clear that without strong roots, strong trees are impossible, even though we don't see the roots. What became clear to me at that time was that if you have no roots, how can you withstand the tests of the environment that surely come. For me as an individual with a set of cultural and linguistic roots, if my roots were to die and I was to be stripped of the integrity that lies in those roots, then I would also disappear along with all that is important to me.

For many limited English proficient students in this nation, their roots have been either ignored or stripped away in the name of growing strong. Many have been directed to stop speaking the languages of their homes, to perceive their culture as one less than what it should be, and to assimilate as quickly as possible, so they can succeed in American society. And, unfortunately many have suffered the fate of the rootless tree — they have fallen socially, economically, academically, and culturally.

Eugene Garcia

Reprinted with permission from Eugene E. Garcia and Sandra H. Fradd from Fradd, S. H., and Lee, O. (1998). *Creating Florida's multilingual global workforce: Educational policies and practices for students learning English as a new language.* Tallahassee, FL: Florida Department of Education, p. VII-5.

Enriching Content Classes for Secondary ESOL Students

Study Guide

Section 4
Academic Competence, Part B

Academic Competence, Part B

Goal

To learn and apply additional strategies to modify lessons and adapt textbooks to help secondary ESOL students learn in content classrooms.

Performance Objectives

- Apply new strategies to modify a content lesson for ESOL students.

- Apply techniques and strategies to adapt content area textbooks for use with ESOL students.

- Teach a content chapter using the technique "From Text to Graphics and Back Again."

- Consolidate learning and set priorities for implementation in the classroom.

- Reflect on the meaning of this learning for one's own teaching.

SECTION 4

Enriching Content Classes for Secondary ESOL Students (National Edition)
Study Guide Section 4: Academic Competence, Part B

65

Academic Achievement for Secondary Language Minority Students: Standards, Measures and Promising Practices

Prepared by
Kris Anstrom, NCBE Information Analyst

Submitted to:
U.S. Department of Education
Office of Grants and Contracts Services

Table of Contents

Acknowledgments

The author is indebted to Dr. Kathleen Steeves, Dr. Sharon Lynch, and Dr. Linda Mauro of The George Washington University for their commentary and insight on secondary instruction within their respective content area fields. The author is also grateful for the assistance and direction given by Dr. Anna Chamot of The George Washington University and by Joel Gómez, Dr. Minerva Gorena, and Barbara Silcox of the National Clearinghouse for Bilingual Education at The George Washington University, Graduate School for Education and Human Development, Center for the Study of Language and Education.

SECTION 4

Overview

This document was prepared under contract by the National Clearinghouse for Bilingual Education in response to task order number D0003 for the U.S. Department of Education, Office of Bilingual Education and Minority Languages Affairs. In accordance with the task order requirements, this document summarizes, analyzes, and integrates findings from relevant research pertaining to the education of language minority students in the content areas. Specifically, the document focuses on several key questions outlined in the task order:

(1) What does the relevant literature pertaining to content area instruction of linguistically and culturally diverse learner (LCDLs) contribute to the theory and practice of standards for LCDLs?

(2) What does the relevant literature pertaining to content area instruction of LCDLs contribute to the theory and practice of measures of achievement, proficiency, and/or academic literacy for LCDLs?

(3) What does the relevant literature pertaining to content area instruction of LCDLs contribute to the field of promising practices in content area instruction for LCDLs?

In order to respond to the task order requirements and examine a specific facet of content area instruction particularly pertinent in this era of educational change, this study focused on the instruction of secondary-level language minority students in mainstream social studies, science, mathematics and language arts classes. Research included an extensive search of the National Clearinghouse for Bilingual Education (NCBE) bibliographic database as well as the ERIC Bibliographic database and various World Wide Web sites, such as the Eisenhower National Clearinghouse for Math and Science, for literature on the effective instruction of language minority students within secondary mainstream settings. Literature pertaining to curriculum and instruction, content standards, assessment, and teacher training and education was identified and analyzed for inclusion in the document.

This study also involved a series of interviews during the months of January to April 1997 with education faculty at The George Washington University in Washington, DC to determine current issues and effective practices within the various content area domains. These faculty members are responsible for preparing preservice teachers for mainstream classroom instruction at the secondary level within core content areas. The professors interviewed and their fields of specialization are as follows: Dr. Kathleen Steeves, social studies; Dr. Sharon Lynch, science; and Dr. Linda Mauro, English language arts. The results of these interviews, which were tape recorded and transcribed, helped inform the discussion of each of the content areas. In addition, these individuals are quoted throughout the document.

Site visits to a suburban high school that had implemented a team teaching approach for working with language minority students enrolled in mainstream classrooms were also

Enriching Content Classes for Secondary ESOL Students (National Edition)
Study Guide Section 4: Academic Competence, Part B

67

conducted in May 1997 in order to collect information in a "real-life" setting. Two team-teaching situations were observed. The first involved a Sophomore-level biology class in which an ESL teacher teamed with a mainstream biology teacher to provide an enriched environment for language and content instruction. In the second setting, a social studies teacher and an ESL teacher worked together, with the social studies teacher providing the content, and the ESL teacher focusing on making the content comprehensible to the language minority students. Both classrooms included native English speaking students and language minority students.

In addition to discussing instructional methodology and curriculum within the four core content areas, the study also examined national content standards documents written for these subject areas and related the ideas and recommendations contained therein to what is known about effective educational practice for language minority students. Specifically, the standards documents were analyzed to determine whether their theoretical bases were consistent with what educational research tells us is effective practice for language minority students. In addition, the documents were examined for commonalities between recommended instructional or curricular practice for mainstream students and recommended practice for language minority students. The following standards documents were included in this study: *National Standards for United States History: Exploring the American Experience, grades 5-12; Curriculum and Evaluation Standards for School Mathematics; National Science Education Standards*; and *Standards for the English Language Arts*.

The intent of this document is to provide teachers and teacher educators insight into how mainstream classroom instruction can be designed and implemented to enhance the academic achievement of language minority students. With this goal in mind the report was organized into four sections pertaining to the four main content areas. Within each of these sections, standards for the content area in question were examined and related to what research indicates is best practice for language minority students. Effective instructional and curricular models were described along with some of the background knowledge necessary for teachers to effectively implement these models. Throughout, vignettes of actual classroom experiences and comments by the various George Washington University professors add context and additional insight to the discussion. Sections on promising practices in the assessment of language minority students within the content areas and the preparation of mainstream teachers to work with these students were also included.

68

Enriching Content Classes for Secondary ESOL Students (National Edition)
Study Guide Section 4: Academic Competence, Part B

Introduction

Vignette 1: Biology Class Observation

As the bell signals the beginning of the second block period, biology students take their seats at seven tables spaced evenly around the classroom. Interspersed among the students are ten who have relocated to this large suburban high school from such places as Ghana, Liberia, Bangladesh, Vietnam, Korea, Pakistan and El Salvador. These students mix well with the diversity of "mainstream" students comprising this Sophomore-level class. At first glance, it is difficult to determine which students are the English as a second language (ESL) students and which are not. Two teachers conduct this class of more than 30 students, a biology teacher and an ESL teacher. As the instruction proceeds it becomes clear that the biology teacher introduces the content, in this case a lab experiment on measuring lung capacity, while the ESL teacher assists by clarifying certain points, writing key expressions on the board, or by circulating and quietly checking with individual students.

To augment the introduction of the lab, which consists of blowing up a balloon and measuring its width in order to determine differing lung capacities, the instructor explains key terms related to lung capacity by exaggerating her breathing motions, followed by having the students perform the same motions with her. She simultaneously relates her motions to the terms she has written on the board. She speaks somewhat more slowly than usual and enunciates her words carefully. To explain the lab assignment, she designates various students to read each step. After each step, she has a student sitting toward the front of the room demonstrate the corresponding step. When an ESL student is called upon to read, the ESL teacher assists by helping her with certain words she has difficulty pronouncing. At one point, the biology teacher demonstrates the amount of residual volume in the lungs by holding up a glass beaker so that students can visualize the approximate amounts for men and women. Part of the lab involves using mathematical formulas. These have been written on the board. The ESL teacher adds the formula for determining averages and gives an example to clarify.

After explanation of the lab, students work with partners at their tables. For the most part, ESL students are paired with native speakers. The room is noisy with the sounds of blowing up balloons and chatter back and forth among the students. Both teachers circulate throughout the room answering questions and checking student work. At one point the ESL teacher who is working intensively with two students near the front of the room pulls one student to the board to help him with the mathematical formula. She first questions him to find out what he knows, then elaborates to supply the needed information. Finally, she has him show her that he understands by applying his own measurements to the formula. At another point a native speaker, who has been doing the ESL student's work for her, is told in what ways she can help her partner— by explaining what she doesn't understand— but that she shouldn't do the calculations for her. Both teachers are active and involved with all students. The focus is on understanding the lab and completing it within the class period. Most students, including all the ESL students, complete the lab within the hour and a half time period. Some will meet later with the ESL teacher to complete questions relating to the lab. A block of time has been set aside toward the end of the day for such individualized instruction.

A Common Phenomenon...

The above scenario depicts what is becoming a common phenomenon in U.S. schools, the presence of significant numbers of language minority students in mainstream settings. During the past two decades, increases in the number of language minority students have had a major impact on our nation's classrooms. The degree to which mainstream classroom instruction meets these students' needs, however, varies dramatically from school to school and classroom to classroom. For the 1994-95 school year a total of 3,184,696 limited English proficient (LEP) students were enrolled in U.S. schools. This figure represents 6.7% of the total K-12 student population. In addition, this figure, while significant, most likely under represents the actual number of language minority students in need of services (Macías and Kelly, 1996).

Language minority students encounter a variety of difficulties in achieving academic success in U.S. schools. These difficulties may be related to language, educational background, socioeconomic status, psychological trauma, or any combination of these factors. Research indicates that the process of learning academic language requires much more time than that needed to learn language for interacting on a social level with English speakers. Ability with social language is usually developed within the first two years of arrival in an English-speaking setting; however, the language needed for learning academic content may require five to eight years, or longer, depending on the age and prior educational background of the student (Collier, 1995). This situation is exacerbated at the secondary level due to the higher cognitive demands of the curriculum and the fact that many secondary-age language-minority students may have significant gaps in their prior education (McKeon, 1994).

Who is Responsible?

> Because language minority students spend most of their time in mainstream classrooms, mainstream teachers must accept responsibility for educating these students.

Responsibility for instructing language minority students is increasingly falling on the shoulders of mainstream teachers. Reasons for this increased responsibility include the inadequacy of pull-out programs, still the most prevalent form of ESL instruction, which, at best, allow for one to two hours of instruction per day (Cornell, 1995). The downfall of pull-out programs is the tendency to assume that the short period of pull-out instruction is the learning for the day, while the time spent in mainstream classes is merely a waiting period until proficiency is acquired through the language program (Handscombe, 1989). Such an assumption is especially detrimental at the secondary level where students have "a window of a few years" to acquire the language ability necessary for successful academic course work (Whitten, 1995). Furthermore, pull-out time is often devoted to completing mainstream homework, which, though important, often forces the pull-out teacher to neglect language instruction. Self-contained ESL or bilingual classrooms, though capable of providing a richer environment for language and content learning, are considered unfeasible alternatives with many administrators due to the increased expenditures necessary to maintain them. For these and other reasons, language minority students spend most of their time in mainstream classrooms; thus, whether these students are given the opportunity to achieve academically depends to a great extent on the quality of mainstream instruction (Cornell, 1995).

Standards and the Language Minority Student

> A means to ensuring that language minority students have equal access to challenging academic content is the use of effective educational practices for these students in mainstream classrooms.

The last two decades have also witnessed the movement to establish rigorous academic standards in the various content areas. At the national level, most academic fields, such as English language arts, history, science, and mathematics, have issued content or curriculum standards for their respective areas. These core standards exist to guide state and local initiatives in setting standards and have influenced activity at these levels to a significant degree (Chris Green and Solis, 1997). Meeting these content standards will be disproportionately difficult for language-minority students since they will have to perform at much higher cognitive and linguistic levels than their native-speaking peers. In mainstream settings, native speakers, for whom English is nearly automatic, can focus primarily on the cognitive tasks of an academic assignment— learning new information, procedures, etc.— however, the student with limited ability in English must focus on both cognitive and linguistic tasks—learning new vocabulary, structures and academic discourse (McKeon, 1994). Thus, setting rigorous academic standards does not necessarily ensure that all students will have the opportunity to achieve them. An important issue concerns whether or not standards will be able to help educators meet the needs of language minority students without punishing them for previous educational neglect or for their linguistic and cultural diversity (Chris Green and Solis, 1997).

A means to ensuring that language minority students have equal access to challenging academic content is the use of effective educational practices for these students in mainstream classrooms. Many of the standards documents recommend instructional practices that will lead to achieving the standards. Thus, these documents have far-reaching implications for mainstream instructional practice— and, consequently, for the education of language minority students. In order to understand issues relating to effective practice and curriculum within the major content areas of social studies science, mathematics, and language arts, issues that will influence the instruction of language minority students within mainstream classrooms, the standards and recommended practices proposed for these areas must be examined in light of what is known about effective practice for language minority students.

Mainstream Teacher Preparation: Critical, Yet Often Neglected

> What do mainstream secondary teachers, as well as teacher educators, need to consider in order to plan and implement effective educational programs for language minority students?

The quality of mainstream instruction depends not only on the existence of effective instructional methodologies but also on whether teachers are well prepared to work with language minority students. Given that these students spend a much greater proportion of their time in mainstream classrooms, it is not enough to educate only ESL and bilingual

Enriching Content Classes for Secondary ESOL Students (National Edition)
Study Guide Section 4: Academic Competence, Part B

71

teachers to work with these students; mainstream teachers must also be prepared to meet the unique needs of this group. However, despite the fact that at least fifty percent of American teachers teach a language minority student at some point in their careers, many mainstream content area teachers receive little or no preparation in working with these students (McKeon, 1994). Underpreparation often leads to resentment and a willingness to pass off these students to the bilingual or ESL program. Secondary-level teachers are even more likely to react in such a way since they often perceive of themselves primarily as content specialists and not as language teachers (Constantino, 1994). Thus the need for preservice teacher education that includes issues related to the education of language minority students is critical to the implementing of effective mainstream programs for these students.

What do mainstream secondary teachers, as well as teacher educators, need to consider in order to plan and implement effective educational programs for language minority students? Areas important to consider include characteristics of secondary language minority learners and their relationship to the content being taught, standards and their implications for these students, classroom environments that encourage academic success, and teacher behaviors and instructional approaches that help make language and content accessible to language minority students. The following sections discuss these issues within the context of the content areas of social studies, science, mathematics, and English language arts. Concluding sections examine effective assessment practices for language minority students and the type of educational programming necessary to prepare mainstream teachers to work with students of culturally and linguistically diverse backgrounds.

Content Area Learning, Standards, and Instructional Approaches

Social Studies

Social studies content at the middle and secondary levels encompasses a range of knowledge bases including world and U.S. history, geography, political science, civics and economics. Curriculum and instruction in social studies are increasingly guided by standards at the national, state, and local levels. National standards have either been developed or are currently under development for U.S. and world history, civics, geography, economics, and social studies. National U.S. history standards bring together a number of these areas of knowledge under the umbrella of historical understanding and refer to them as spheres of human activity. These spheres include the social, political, scientific/technological, economic, and the cultural. Each of these spheres is then addressed within ten eras encompassing the whole of American history from its pre-European beginnings to contemporary times (National Center for History in the Schools, 1994).

U.S. History Standards and the Language Minority Student

> Content standards should reflect the best available knowledge about how LEP students learn and about how the content can best be taught to them (August, Hakuta, and Pompa, 1994).

The authors of the U.S. history standards emphasize that the study of history involves much more than the passive absorption of facts, dates, names and places. Students must be able to engage in historical thinking. Historical thinking demands that students "think through cause-and-effect relationships, reach sound historical interpretations, and conduct historical inquiries and research leading to the knowledge on which informed decisions in contemporary life can be based. These thinking skills are the process of active learning" (National Center for History in the Schools, 1994). The standards outline five historical thinking areas in which students should develop competence. These include:

- chronological thinking, which involves developing a clear sense of historical time;
- historical comprehension, including the ability to read historical narratives, identify basic elements of the narrative structure, and to describe the past through the perspectives of those who were there;
- historical analysis and interpretation;
- historical research, which involves formulating historical questions, determining historical time and context, judging credibility and authority of sources, and constructing historical narratives or arguments; and
- historical issues-analysis and decision-making, including the ability to identify problems, analyze points of view, and decide whether actions and decisions were good or bad.

Though no specific guidelines for providing equal opportunities for language minority students to learn such challenging content and abilities are given in this standards document, the authors declare that these standards should be expected of all students and that all students should be provided equal access to the educational opportunities necessary to achieve them (National Center for History in the Schools, 1994).

Standards Should Incorporate Best Practices for Language Minority Students

In outlining their recommendations to ensure that LEP children are considered and included in standards development, the Stanford Working Group on Federal Education Programs for LEP Students states that content standards should reflect the best available knowledge about how LEP students learn and about how the content can best be taught to them (August, Hakuta, and Pompa, 1994). In the *National Standards for U.S. History, Grades 5-12*, Standard 1A within the era "Three Worlds Meet" asks that students "demonstrate understanding of commonalities, diversity, and change in the societies of the Americas from their beginnings to 1620 by...(one among four objectives) comparing commonalities and differences between Native American and European outlooks, and values on the eve of 'the great convergence'" (National Center for History in the Schools, 1994). Such a standard, while outlining what a student should know and be able to do in history, fails to offer guidance on how teachers of language minority students can help these students learn this material.

A better example of how standards can reflect what is known about exemplary instruction for language minority students comes from *Standards for the English Language Arts*. For example, standard number three requires that "students apply a wide range of strategies to comprehend, interpret, evaluate, and appreciate texts...." The authors then elaborate on this standard, as they do with others, in the following manner: "Although students come to recognize many of these expectations and strategies as they read and discuss related

Enriching Content Classes for Secondary ESOL Students (National Edition)
Study Guide Section 4: Academic Competence, Part B

73

SECTION 4

groups of texts, teacher explanation and modeling of reading strategies and independent conscious study also contribute to students' proficiency. Students need encouragement to think and talk about how they are creating meaning as they read and to pay close attention to the strategies they are using to do so. Students should explore this meaning-making process explicitly, talking about how they move from predicting to confirming (or revising) their predictions, and back again" (International Reading Association and National Council of Teachers of English, 1996). In this expository fashion, the authors of the English language arts standards uphold and reinforce what educators of language minority students know about the development of reading strategies.

Standards Should Emphasize Diversity

> Using a multicultural social studies curriculum as a base, social studies teachers can emphasize and build on the cultural and world knowledge language minority students bring to class.

The Stanford Working Group also specifies that social studies content standards should reflect the diversity of this country (August, Hakuta, and Pompa, 1994). *The National Standards for U.S. History* meet this second recommendation concerning multicultural content. In reflecting upon the impact of these standards, Dr. Kathleen Steeves, a social studies education professor at The George Washington University, makes the point that the inclusion of multicultural content, what to include and what not to include, was perhaps the most troublesome issue for standards developers at both the national and local levels. "Do we look at history and talk about all of the warts? Do we include women and minorities? Do we make them part of the history or side bars?" These types of questions, and how they are answered, help define how students conceptualize diversity, a central concern of social studies education. "The general feeling is that we need to do a better job of inclusion— it's how you do it that's at issue."

Social Studies Curriculum: What Works for Language Minority Students

A multicultural history curriculum is an excellent content base for second language learners. According to Dr. Steeves, with such a curriculum, social studies teachers can emphasize and build on the cultural and world knowledge language minority students bring to class. For example, a unit on westward movement in the U.S. developed within the context of larger patterns of migration and immigration can lead language minority students to explore how they fit into these patterns of movement as newcomers to the U.S. (King, et.al., 1992). Thus, in conjunction with the students' own backgrounds and experiences, documents with a multicultural focus, such as the National Standards for U.S. History can serve as useful resources for curriculum development.

Use the Thematic Approach

> Thematically organized curricula have been found to work well with language minority students.

One method for organizing the curriculum to better meet the needs of language minority students is the thematic approach. A recent study noted that thematic units served as the predominant mode of organizing curriculum in schools where language minority students were particularly successful (Farr and Trumbull, 1997). Though useful in integrating material within one academic discipline, the thematic approach is particularly powerful in integrating instruction across disciplines. Lessons can be designed to help students make connections and achieve a deeper understanding of a concept by studying it from several disciplinary views. Themes derived from social studies can serve to unify several academic disciplines. In *School Reform and Student Diversity: Case Studies of Exemplary Practices for LEP Students*, the authors describe Hanshaw Middle School's use of thematic instruction to unify instruction across subject areas. A particular theme drawn from social studies was "I Have a Dream" from the Martin Luther King speech. The theme brought together social studies and language arts by focusing on the dreams held by people and the ways in which they realized their dreams. Students interviewed an immigrant using questions developed by the class, wrote essays about the immigrants' experiences, and investigated the immigrants' dreams concerning the U.S. (Berman, et.al., 1995).

Allow for In-depth Thinking

> Effective social studies curricula emphasize depth of coverage over breadth.

Curriculum designers in social studies, or other content areas, should note the following cautions. First of all, curriculum writers should not assume that comprehensive coverage of a subject must be the goal. Oftentimes comprehensive coverage results in superficial coverage of topics without giving students the opportunity to fully comprehend important concepts. Such an approach makes learning particularly difficult for language minority students who, as previously mentioned, must attend to both cognitive and linguistic tasks simultaneously. Curriculum planning must allow for more in-depth thinking about fewer topics. Additionally, curriculum developers should avoid trivializing instruction by merely adding insignificant details, such as foods and festivals, in order to "multiculturalize" the curriculum. A multicultural social studies curriculum does not simply add surface cultural details; rather, it involves students in thinking deeply about the meaning of cultural and linguistic differences (Farr and Trumbull, 1997).

Key Issues in Developing Social Studies Curricula for Language Minority Students

Certain issues pertaining to language minority students have important implications for social studies curriculum development. Curriculum in social studies, as in many other subject areas, depends on continuity, with content in any one course building upon content supposedly mastered in previous courses (Harklau, 1994). However, most secondary language minority students have not had eight or nine years of previous instruction in U.S. elementary and middle schools; thus their prior knowledge will be different than that of their native-English speaking peers who have benefited from such instruction. Furthermore, social studies materials are often too difficult for these students whose academic language abilities often lag well behind their grade-level peers. Unfamiliar vocabulary and linguistic constructions impede their ability to grasp new concepts (King, et.al., 1992).

Link Social Studies Concepts to Students' Prior Knowledge

As learning theorists and researchers have known for years, a learning situation can be meaningful only if the learner can relate the new learning task to prior knowledge. For the social studies teacher, this idea is critical. One of the more promising approaches to dealing with the issue of gaps in prior knowledge makes few assumptions about students' prior social studies learning. The curriculum should begin with the most basic concepts and gradually develop related ideas into broader units of study. In social studies, many of the primary historical events and developments can be related to basic concepts applicable to a variety of situations and settings. For example, prior to beginning study of the American Civil War, class discussion can center around the notion that differences may lead to conflict, a concept with which students are familiar from their own personal experiences and problems with being different. Extending this understanding into social, political, and economic differences among groups of people is a logical next step followed by focusing on differences between North and South prior to the Civil War. Finally the Civil War itself can be introduced within a context made rich by both personal experience and broad-based content knowledge. Thus, teachers can utilize students' experiential knowledge by relating it to an important social studies concept and the events leading to the Civil War (King, et.al, 1992).

Strive for Flexibility

> Flexibility is a key factor in successful curriculum development for and instruction of language minority students.

In her analysis of the ways in which mainstream classrooms and ESL classrooms differ, Harklau (1994) makes several observations which have implications for mainstream course curriculum and planning. Most importantly, she found that flexibility was a key factor in successful instruction of language minority students. The constantly shifting needs of the language minority population called for more flexible guidelines and much more autonomy in setting course curriculum. The ESL teachers Harklau studied responded by developing a spiral syllabus and unit-based approach to curriculum that could be easily adjusted up or down or supplemented, depending on the needs of the class (Harklau, 1994). Mainstream teachers working with language minority students may need to adopt a similar approach to curriculum, rather than the usual rigid grade-level guidelines.

Oral History Offers Language Minority Student Access to the Curriculum

An interesting and flexible approach to social studies curriculum and instruction involves using oral history as a medium to make history more accessible to language minority students. Oral history helps students understand that history is composed of stories in which they and their families have participated. Such an approach can support the learning of new concepts while making them more comprehensible. Concepts including religious persecution, tyranny of autocratic rulers and the rights and responsibilities of self governance are more accessible when developed from students' backgrounds and experiences. These backgrounds and experiences form the raw historical data from which a social studies curriculum can be built (Olmedo, 1993). In working with data obtained from interviews, students will be engaging in many of the historical thinking skills outlined in the U.S. history standards, skills such as chronological thinking, reading historical narratives, describing the past through the perspectives of those who were there, and historical analysis and interpretation.

In addition, oral history serves as an avenue through which students can strengthen their language skills. Oral language skills are involved when interviewing and presenting information to classmates. Literacy skills are developed through translating and transcribing oral interviews into English. Important offshoots of using oral history include the involvement of parents and families in the student's education, the use of the native language in meeting instructional goals, the validation of the student's culture and experience, and the enhancement of self esteem— all critical factors in the academic achievement of language minority students (Olmedo, 1993).

Steps in Implementing an Oral History Approach

(1) Identify which social studies concepts to teach. Olmedo (1993) lists some common concepts taken from the National Council for the Social Studies Task Force on Scope and Sequence (1989) including dependence and interdependence, interaction of human beings and their environment, resource development and use, scarcity, migration, acculturation, the impact of economic or technological changes on societies, issues of war causes and results, the meaning of culture rights and concepts such as the effect of climate and natural resources on economic structures and the way of life of the people.

(2) Develop questions or an interview guide jointly with students that can be used to interview family members, neighbors, or someone in the ethnic community.

(3) Translate or assist students in translating the questions into the students' native languages.

(4) Provide training and practice in using tape recorders and in conducting interviews.

(5) Invite a guest speaker from the community to be interviewed by the class as a practice activity.

(6) Have students select an interviewee.

(7) Assign students or small groups the tasks of interviewing, transcribing or summarizing the tape, and sharing knowledge gained with the class.

(8) Create a list of themes from the students' interviews and use them along with portions of the text or other classroom materials to reinforce social studies concepts.

(9) Finally, have students compare and contrast the experiences of their interviewees with information learned from reading historical biographies, excerpts from texts, and other source materials (Olmedo, 1993).

Social Studies Instruction: What Works for the Language Minority Student

According to Dr. Steeves, certain process-oriented approaches emphasized in social studies teaching are effective strategies for working with language minority students in mainstream settings. In addition to the previously mentioned thematic approach, these approaches include concept attainment and formation, cooperative learning, and inquiry learning. Concept attainment and formation is important in a field such as history which has a number of concepts, such as democracy and culture, that students must comprehend in order to make sense of the subject matter. In presenting new concepts, one approach is to give students characteristics that they can piece together to form the concept; conversely, the teacher can elicit pieces of the concept students already have and guide them toward a definition. The approach used depends on what the students already know about a particular topic; thus, an understanding of the students' prior knowledge is critical, particularly in the case of language minority students whose background knowledge in social studies may differ from that of other students. If the concept is one with which the students have some familiarity, instruction often begins by eliciting what students already know. If the concept is foreign, then the teacher can begin by sharing some of the defining characteristics and have students then determine what those characteristics mean and how they understand them.

Use Cooperative Learning

> Language minority students need frequent opportunities to interact with their native English speaking peers in academic situations.

In a recent study concerning attributes of effective instruction for English language learners, the authors highlight the importance of providing opportunities for and encouraging interaction between English language learners and native English speakers (August and Pease-Alvarez, 1996). Cooperative learning offers language minority students the opportunity to interact with their native-speaking peers in such a manner and to communicate their thoughts and ideas in a supportive and non-threatening environment. When students work cooperatively to complete a task, language minority students receive instruction from their peers that is individually tailored to their language ability and academic needs. Working in structured groups increases the variety of ways information can be presented and related to what is already known. Furthermore, active listening and speaking in cooperative settings, provides a rich language environment for both comprehensible input and practice in speaking that students cannot get in a more traditional classroom environment (Olsen, 1992). Care must be taken, though, to prevent cooperative learning projects from degenerating into group work where the best students do all the work. Language minority students do not benefit in this situation (McPartland and Braddock II, 1993).

An example of a social studies cooperative learning activity structured so that all students must participate involves creating a situation where different points of view are developed. By providing each group member with conflicting information, "creative controversy" develops.

Social Studies Cooperative Learning Activity: Creative Controversy

Students are given two maps and two readings that give different answers to the question "Who discovered America?" Depending on ability levels (language and knowledge), students might master their parts individually, in pairs, or in temporary expert groups— meetings of students from all the "home" teams who have the same map or reading. If expert teams are homogeneous for language, the native language can be used; if heterogeneous, more proficient English speakers can explain and clarify for the less fluent. Upon returning to home teams, each student must argue for his/her explanation of who discovered America. The cooperative learning structure "Roundtable" can be used to ensure that all team members offer their information. In Roundtable, there is one piece of paper and one pen for each group. Each student makes a contribution in writing then passes the paper and pen to the next student. This activity can also be done orally (Olsen, 1992).

Within a social studies classroom, communication in small groups can assume many forms,

Enriching Content Classes for Secondary ESOL Students (National Edition)
Study Guide Section 4: Academic Competence, Part B

one of which is role playing, a widely used strategy for fostering the development of communication skills with language minority students. As Dr. Steeves points out students might be asked to assume certain historical perspectives and to problem solve from those perspectives. For example, groups could function as American Indian tribal councils in order to examine a political issue facing that council during a particular historical period. Such problem solving and role playing provide opportunities for students to practice other communication skills, such as reporting out a group decision or presenting findings to the class.

Make Social Studies Content Accessible

> Using historical artifacts is particularly effective with students from other countries and cultures who may be able to share items that provide a different perspective on history.

Other important strategies for social studies teachers working with language minority students include the use of visuals and realia that transcend language barriers. Media materials for social studies are available in most school libraries. Prints and picture sets relating to specific themes are useful for conveying information and inducing thinking (King, et.al., 1992). Dr. Steeves advocates for the use of historical artifacts to initiate the inquiry process. The teacher may begin the lesson by handing an artifact, such as a tool, to students and having them guess what they think it might be, or what material it is made of, or how and when it was used, etc. Such an approach is particularly effective when students work in small groups where language minority students can feel less inhibited to venture guesses and share expertise. With this format, the teacher can also assess prior knowledge and encourage question asking, integral to the inquiry process.

Artifacts such as costumes, tools, photographs, record books, wills, written documents and other objects encourage students to begin thinking about their own family history and consider artifacts their own families may possess that can be brought in. This approach allows students to view history from a more personal perspective and as a subject relevant to their own lives. Students can begin to build concepts of what a particular era means by working with artifacts representative of that time. Classification of such artifacts motivates students to use higher order thinking skills to make sense of "data" and to generalize about a particular historical period.

The use of artifacts is particularly effective with students from other countries and cultures who may be able to share items that provide a different perspective on history or open up new avenues of discussion. Language minority students will benefit by having their contributions acknowledged and respected as integral parts of the curriculum.

Science

According to Dr. Sharon Lynch, science education professor at The George Washington University, science at the secondary level has traditionally been taught for the twenty percent of students who were college bound through textbook, test-driven methods. In contrast, effective science teaching encourages all students to become scientifically literate and to develop scientific habits of mind. The *National Science Education Standards* define scientific literacy in the following manner:

Enriching Content Classes for Secondary ESOL Students (National Edition)
Study Guide Section 4: Academic Competence, Part B

79

Scientific literacy means that a person can ask, find, or determine answers to questions derived from curiosity about everyday experiences. It means that a person has the ability to describe, explain, and predict natural phenomena. Scientific literacy entails being able to read with understanding articles about science in the popular press and to engage in social conversations about the validity of the conclusions. Scientific literacy implies that a person can identify scientific issues underlying national and local decisions and express positions that are scientifically and technologically informed. A literate citizen should be able to evaluate the quality of scientific information on the basis of its source and the methods used to generate it.... (National Research Council, 1996).

National Science Education Standards and the Language Minority Student

> National science education standards provide insight into more effective science learning for language minority students.

Such a goal requires a radical departure from traditional science teaching methods that emphasized the acquisition of specific facts and procedures and the idea that scientists work according to a narrowly conceived, logical method known as the scientific method. Rather, the national science standards advocate for the teaching of scientific inquiry as both "the diverse ways in which scientists study the natural world and propose explanations based on the evidence derived from their work" and the methods students use to develop an understanding of scientific ideas. Inquiry involves students in observing; asking questions and proposing solutions, explaining and predicting; planning experiments; referring to written and other source material to determine what is already known, using various implements to conduct investigations; and communicating outcomes. Authors of these standards view inquiry as the primary means of comprehending scientific concepts (National Research Council, 1996).

Involve Students in Scientific Inquiry

This restructuring of science education offers the potential for more effective science learning for language minority students and conforms with what is known about effective education for language minority students. Scientific inquiry involves language minority students in hands-on activities that provide opportunities for purposeful language use in meaningful academic experiences. For example, most scientific investigation requires data collection and reporting, which can be accomplished in various ways. Student work can include vocabulary charts, diagrams, graphs, timetables, schedules and pictures as well as the more traditional venues of written lab reports and science fair exhibits. These options help ensure that all students will have access to the content material in a variety of modes from highly contextualized cognitively undemanding experiences to more abstract, less contextualized tasks (Rupp, 1992).

> Effective science education for language minority students provides a variety of venues through which a student can learn a particular science concept.

However, as with any instructional adaptation, care needs to be taken that content is not "watered down." Dr. Lynch emphasizes that using a "menu approach" with students selecting different projects does not guarantee that the same concept will be learned. She describes a lesson in which students were allowed to select various projects, some of which were things they could build with their hands; others required drawing a diagram; and still others entailed writing an editorial. High verbal functioning students chose to write an editorial concerning scientists raiding an Egyptian tomb. Others made clay models of an Egyptian tomb. She doubts whether those making model tombs were learning the same concepts as those writing the editorial. She provides a more appropriate use of the menu approach in science in which the objective is to understand the basic properties of a cell— that it's a unit of life, has different parts, and divides to make more. Here, one student could construct a diagram or model of the cell; someone else could investigate cloning. In this instance the same concept is developed through cognitively and linguistically varied activities.

Advocate For a "Less is More" Curriculum

Another area emphasized in the national science standards involves students in conducting investigations over longer periods of time in conjunction with studying fewer fundamental science concepts. This notion of spending more time on learning fewer concepts is also one of the key points of the Third International Mathematics and Science Study (TIMSS). In comparing science and mathematics education in the U.S. with that in other peer countries, investigators criticized the lack of a cohesive vision for mathematics and science education in this country. They blamed what they termed "splintered visions" for emphasizing "familiarity with many topics rather than concentrated attention to a few..." which, the authors claim, most likely "lowers the academic performance of students who spend years in such a learning environment. Our curricula, textbooks, and teaching are all 'a mile wide and an inch deep.'" Authors of the study note that curricula in this country lack the strategic concept of focusing on a few key goals, linking content together, and setting higher demands on students. A result of this splintered approach to teaching and learning is that students may grasp pieces but not the whole (Schmidt, et.al., 1996).

> Science curriculum development involves the careful organization of concepts to form connections and patterns across the discipline.

Educators of language minority students also advocate for a "less is more" curriculum for their students. Such a "selective curriculum" should include major principles and unanswered questions rather than an accumulation of random bits of knowledge (Chamot, 1993). To develop this selective curriculum, Dr. Lynch suggests the use of a unit organizer, a conceptual map, which lays out a picture of the big ideas in a unit and how they're connected to one another. She cautions, "What can happen in science is, for example, if a teacher is doing a unit on sound, he may look through the text book and choose a series of experiments and other activities, and then perhaps he brings in his guitar and from all of this creates a set of experiences. I call this the 'beads on a string' technique of teaching— all the activities are sort of related to sound. If a student is from a typical middle class background, you can give them a string of experiences, and they'll come out the other end learning something. However, kids that come from other cultures need to have more explicit instruction. Consequently, a unit organizer can be helpful for teachers to understand how you structure activities and tie them together, making connections and patterns."

Teach the Language of Science

National science standards also emphasize the ability to reason and to communicate scien-

Enriching Content Classes for Secondary ESOL Students (National Edition)
Study Guide Section 4: Academic Competence, Part B

81

tific ideas and information (National Research Council, 1996). An important aspect of science instruction concerned with achieving such standards is the use of activities where students are actively engaged in discussion concerning the outcomes of predictions made and the meaning of data collected. Attempting to carry on a scientific discussion assists in developing the ability to ask questions, propose tentative answers, make predictions, and evaluate evidence. However, the acquisition of certain linguistic structures of argumentation is thought to be a prerequisite for the kind of advanced reasoning used in scientific communication. If language minority students do not have access to these linguistic skills, they will not be able to engage in the level of discussion essential to scientific inquiry, and will have difficulty with science reasoning. Certain linguistic structures, such as logical connectors, and specialized vocabulary, both science terminology and vocabulary that may have different meanings in a scientific context are problematic for language minority students. Moreover, discourse patterns common to science such as compare/contrast, cause/effect, and problem/solution require a high level of linguistic functioning. Thus, cognitive development in science is heavily dependent upon linguistic development (Kessler, et.al., 1992).

> Teaching the language of science and modifying speech and textual materials are ways in which mainstream teachers can provide greater access to science content for language minority students.

Mainstream science teachers must be aware of what students need to know linguistically in order to understand and express themselves in science activities and must be able to incorporate opportunities to learn the English language into their lessons. Examples of activities that may be used to supplement science lessons as a support for vocabulary learning include having students draw and label diagrams or pictures related to science concepts; classify words into specific categories; fill in charts; order sentences in correct sequences; and use key vocabulary to answer how/why/what questions, summarize information from readings or observations, draw conclusions, or state opinions (Kessler, et.al., 1992).

Teachers will also need to assist students in acquiring linguistic structures and discourse patterns used frequently in science. By identifying one or two such structures or patterns associated with a particular topic or activity and incorporating appropriate language learning activities, science teachers can encourage the linguistic development essential for language minority students' cognitive development. Kessler, et.al. (1992) provide a sample unit on electricity which focuses on the discourse function of agreeing and disagreeing. The teacher or other students can model frequently-used expressions for agreeing and disagreeing, as well as associated linguistic structures for language minority students. Oral language activities could involve sharing information about observations and agreeing or disagreeing with others about why balloons attract or repel one another. Written activities might involve recording results and agreeing or disagreeing with written statements given by the teacher or other students.

Provide Comprehensible Input in Science Classrooms

In addition to actively teaching language, science teachers can make their language more comprehensible to language minority students by modifying their speech. New terminology should be limited to a manageable number. These words should be accompanied by visual or real referents whenever possible and reintroduced in different contexts. Students can also be guided in using these words during scientific investigations. Since scientific language frequently contains complex sentences in the passive voice, these structures should be shortened and expressed in the active voice. For example the passive statement, "Nutrients are needed by living things," can be expressed as, "Living things need nutrients."

> Mainstream teachers can provide comprehensible input for their language minority students by modifying their speech and adapting written materials.

Important concepts should be presented in a number of ways and in a variety of situations. Repetition and paraphrase can be used to reinforce concepts and provide a rich environment for language acquisition. Teachers should also consciously intersperse more questions within their discourse, to help students understand, to encourage critical thinking, and to find out what students know. Questions should be varied for both linguistic and cognitive complexity. Teacher questioning in the science classroom improves interaction, acts as a model for student questioning and supports the development of inquiry skills. Finally, teachers should give oral feedback on language through restatement, not overt correction. Errors are natural when acquiring a second language and should be dealt with by modeling correct forms through restatement. For example, in response to the teacher's question, "What are some foods that contain protein?" a language minority student might answer, "Some food are eggs, milks, meats." The teacher can model correct language indirectly in the following manner: "Yes, some foods that contain protein are eggs, milk, and meat" (Fathman, et.al., 1992).

Adapt Written Materials for Language Minority Students

Making science information accessible to language minority students may also necessitate modifying written materials. Short (1992) provides suggestions for bringing written materials, whether in science or other content areas, within reach of language minority students for whom the vocabulary, linguistic structures and discourse patterns of many texts may be too difficult. She cautions that materials adaptation is more than simplifying vocabulary and shortening sentences, rather it implies adapting information to make it accessible to second language learners. Key to this adaptation is the presentation of visual information. Charts, graphs, and pictures make materials more accessible to students. For example, a flowchart with diagrams and pictures can convey a scientific process to students more rapidly than several paragraphs of text filled with complex structures and difficult vocabulary. Outlines can also serve to impart essential information more comprehensibly. Whereas timelines develop the higher-order thinking skill of sequencing, charts encourage comparison and contrast. Both formats emphasize essential points and reduce extraneous information.

Short (1992) recommends that teachers consider the students' proficiency level when reviewing possible formats for the material and question whether the material lends itself to an outline, chart, or simplified prose version. Students' prior knowledge about a topic should be considered when adapting materials. Background information may need to be added in order for the material to make sense. Limiting the amount of text and number of new vocabulary words, using simple verb tenses, and eliminating clauses helps make text more comprehensible as does simplifying grammatical structures. Teachers should also write in the active voice and reduce the number of pronouns. When used, paragraphs

Enriching Content Classes for Secondary ESOL Students (National Edition)
Study Guide Section 4: Academic Competence, Part B

83

should be structured carefully. Placing topic sentences first followed by supporting information helps students organize new information. Markers, such as first and next to indicate sequence and but to indicate contrast should be retained and taught to students as guides in managing the flow of information.

Teach Problem Solving and Learning Strategies

> Successful teachers are those who help language minority students acquire strategies that facilitate both second language acquisition and knowledge acquisition (August, and Pease-Alvarez, 1996).

Along with emphasizing conceptual and language development, educators of language minority students need to teach problem solving strategies. These strategies are actions or certain thought processes that students apply to help them accomplish challenging tasks. Authors of the study on attributes of effective instruction for language minority students emphasize that successful teachers are those who help students acquire strategies that facilitate both second language acquisition and knowledge acquisition (August, and Pease-Alvarez, 1996). Recent research has shown that these strategies can be taught and learned. Effective teaching of problem solving strategies involves explicitly showing students that various strategies exist and how to use them appropriately. Though knowledge of a variety of strategies is integral to effective strategy use, students also need to know how to regulate their strategy use. Such regulation, a metacognitive skill, requires explicit teaching about such contextual factors as when, where and how to use particular strategies. Different tasks require different strategies; thus, students need to learn to recognize when certain strategies will work and when they won't. Furthermore, teachers need to provide varied opportunities for students to practice using their strategies in pursuing academic learning (Padron and Waxman, 1993).

Spanos (1993) recommends the use of an integrated plan for learning which requires that teacher and students meet in a review session, in order to involve students effectively in the use of learning strategies. The following vignette provides an example of teacher follow-up after students had completed a series of science experiments in which they practiced specific learning strategies.

Vignette 2: Learning Strategies in Science

The instructor returned all of the student worksheets (he had been keeping the students' work in individual student portfolios) and asked them to complete checklists and evaluation forms that covered the four experiments. When they were finished, he conducted individual interviews with each student asking them to refer to their portfolios to clarify the checklists and evaluation forms. The interviews focused upon student perceptions of their learning both in terms of what they had learned and what they had learned how to do. The instructor was able to introduce learning strategy terminology...by simply asking questions such as: "What resources did you use?" "What can you infer from this experiment?" and "What words or information did you have to pay attention to do the experiment?" This provided a vehicle for the instructor to integrate learning strategy instruction with content and language learning rather than isolating the learning strategy instruction and making it an end in itself (Spanos, 1993).

Integrate Language and Content Learning with Learning Strategy Instruction

The Cognitive Academic Language Learning Approach (CALLA) is an instructional model that combines English language and academic development with learning strategy instruction. The CALLA model has been successfully used with science, as well as with other academic subjects. A strategy important in scientific learning is the ability to make use of one's own background knowledge (Chamot, 1994). Most students come to science classes with naive, informal theories of heat, energy, motion, etc. that are either inconsistent or incompatible with current scientific knowledge of these areas. However, despite the knowledge area, learners will attempt to interpret new information in light of what they already know. If lessons designed to teach new concepts do not account for existing knowledge, no matter how naive or incompatible, it is highly likely that students will ignore or misinterpret such lessons. This tendency is even more likely to occur when lessons are given in a language students are still learning (Gelman, 1995). Ability to employ prior knowledge as a tool in acquiring new knowledge is a skill teachers need to develop with their second language learners. Chamot (1994) recommends various brainstorming and discussion activities prior to introducing new scientific concepts. Dr. Lynch also suggests that teachers conduct introductory activities to determine the range of understandings concerning a concept. Such activities provide insight for teachers concerning common misperceptions about science and help students understand that intuitive knowledge may not always be relied upon in science.

An effective approach for teaching learning strategies is through modeling each strategy in an appropriate context. Teachers serve as intellectual role models for their students and, through "think aloud" techniques, coach their students in appropriate problem solving methods (Chamot, 1993). Dr. Lynch refers to this approach as "scaffolding the reasoning process." An example of scaffolding might occur in a lab situation after students have collected data with a lot of numbers. The teacher might take a sample of data and say, "Well, I can see that as this is decreasing, I see this is increasing. What might that mean?" She is using a think-aloud process to guide the students from data, to wondering, to hypothesizing.

Science Instruction: What Works for Language Minority Students

> By exploring a smaller number of science concepts in different ways, language minority students have the opportunity to learn important content in-depth and acquire necessary language skills.

Modeling is also involved in the following approach to teaching science to second language learners. Adhering to the call for depth over breadth in science curriculum, this approach explores each science concept in different ways. A particular concept is examined through three types of activities: a teacher demonstration, a group investigation, and an independent investigation. Through this three-tiered approach, students progress from a carefully guided presentation to an organized group inquiry to open-ended individual study. This sequencing allows students to progress naturally through stages of language learning: observing to solving, listening to speaking, and interacting to initiating (Fathman, et.al., 1992).

Enriching Content Classes for Secondary ESOL Students (National Edition)
Study Guide Section 4: Academic Competence, Part B

85

SECTION 4

Teacher Demonstration

Though initial activities are teacher directed, the focus in all three levels is on inquiry. During the demonstration phase the teacher guides students into questioning and discovering concepts. Teachers encourage critical thinking and problem solving strategies, and activities are open-ended to stimulate student initiative and different approaches to problem solving. The demonstration phase also involves determining students' prior knowledge on a given topic through methods such as those previously mentioned. Teacher demonstrations are used to introduce a concept, stimulate interest in a topic for individual investigation, show students how to do something, and raise questions or present problems to solve. Demonstrations, if used effectively, give language minority students the opportunity to listen and observe before having to produce any language. Thus, the teacher should take advantage of this opportunity ensuring that language is comprehensible through the use of visuals, gestures, models, drawings, graphs, and charts (Fathman, et.al., 1992).

Group Investigation

Following the teacher demonstration, the group investigation phase allows students to use new language through interaction with other students and offers the opportunity for further exploration of science concepts. Cooperative learning approaches work well at this stage (Fathman, et.al., 1992). Heterogeneous grouping of students provides opportunities for and encourages interaction between second language learners and native speakers. This opportunity for interaction was found to be one of the attributes of effective classrooms for language minority students. By interacting with native speakers in academic contexts, second language learners have access to language unavailable in traditional teacher-directed settings (August and Pease-Alvarez, 1996). Roles taken within these heterogeneous groups are varied according to each student's proficiency level. Fathman, et.al. (1992) provides the following example: "A student who is able to read and write English can record the results of an investigation while a student who writes little English might record numbers on a chart or draw pictures illustrating the group's findings."

Independent Investigation

After the group activity, independent investigation is used to allow each student to explore a science concept alone. At this point, inquiries can be extended outside the classroom. Teachers should remember that students at all levels of English proficiency can conduct individual investigations, but they will vary in their ability to communicate their findings in English (Fathman, et.al., 1992). Students can share their experiences through formats such as "science talk" used at Graham and Parks School, a predominantly Haitian-Creole middle school. In science talk, all students gather in a circle to discuss some area related to findings in their investigations. Students guide discussion, develop topics, argue evidence, explore their results and determine further questions. The teacher facilitates the discussion but relevant topics are introduced and pursued by students (Minicucci, 1996). Though at Graham and Parks, science talk is used in bilingual classrooms with most of the discussion in Haitian-Creole, this approach could be adapted to mainstream science settings as long as teachers ensure the participation of their language minority students.

86

Enriching Content Classes for Secondary ESOL Students (National Edition)
Study Guide Section 4: Academic Competence, Part B

Mathematics

Mathematics Standards and the Language Minority Student

These classroom vignettes demonstrate how problem solving in real life contexts is used to teach mathematics to language minority students. Current mathematics reform efforts emphasize that students learn best in settings that challenge and motivate them to fill in mathematical gaps in their knowledge. Thus, teachers are called upon to act as facilitators and provide intellectually challenging problems that encourage students to develop mathematically. Research supports the notion that students will develop their mathematical abilities to a higher degree when motivated by real-life problems (McLaughlin and McLeod, 1996).

> Teaching mathematics to language minority students requires instructional settings and situations where students are engaged in solving interesting real-life problems that encourage both critical thinking and basic skills development and practice.

Enriching Content Classes for Secondary ESOL Students (National Edition)
Study Guide Section 4: Academic Competence, Part B

87

In order for reform to occur, teachers need to accept that traditional text-book based instruction is no longer acceptable. At Andrew Jackson Middle School, reformers found that math teachers tended to lecture and then assign seat work for practice, which if not finished in class was taken home. The next day, homework was corrected, the next skill introduced and explained, then again student practice was followed by homework. Very little interaction among students occurred, and unless questions were asked, interaction between teacher and students was minimal (Smith, et.al., 1993). Reyhner and Davison (1993) point out that typical mathematics learning materials assume that all students learn mathematics in a verbal abstract manner. However, research on American Indian students indicates that many of these students prefer visual and tactile modes of learning. They suggest the use of a multisensory, activity-centered approach in mathematics. These findings indicate that both what is taught in mathematics and how it is taught need to change.

In 1989 the National Council of Teachers of Mathematics (NCTM) released *Curriculum and Evaluation Standards for School Mathematics*. This landmark document served as a catalyst for mathematics reform. This and other reform documents criticized both the mathematics curriculum as well as the way in which mathematics was taught. As with the previously discussed content areas of social studies and science, the traditional emphasis upon acquisition of facts and technical skills as opposed to the ability to pose and solve problems and engage in independent learning was found to be inadequate in preparing students to be mathematically literate in a rapidly changing, highly technological world. According to the report, problem solving should be central to mathematics curriculum and instruction:

Traditional teaching emphases on practice in manipulating expressions and practicing algorithms as a precursor to solving problems ignore the fact that knowledge often emerges from the problems. This suggests that instead of the expectation that skill in computation should precede word problems, experience with problems helps develop the ability to compute. Thus, present strategies for teaching may need to be reversed; knowledge often should emerge from experience with problems.... Furthermore, students need to experience genuine problems regularly. A genuine problem is a situation in which, for the individual or group concerned, one or more appropriate solutions have yet to be developed (National Council of Teachers of Mathematics, 1989).

Emphasize Problem Solving and Communication

> For language minority students, overemphasizing the learning of basic skills can inhibit students in developing problem solving, reasoning, and other higher-order thinking skills.

This shift in focus on the part of the mathematics community parallels thinking about how to best educate language minority students. Padron and Waxman (1993) note that the traditional notion of educating disadvantaged students in basic skills before exposing them to more challenging academic material has led to what he terms "learned helplessness." For language minority students, a basic skills mastery approach, such as occurs when students are required to learn basic language skills before being introduced to challenging content, can result in limited cognitive mastery, or the lack of ability in problem solving, reasoning, and other higher-order thinking skills. By teaching language minority students critical thinking and problem solving strategies in the context of real problems, the academic achievement of these students will most likely improve. Thus, teaching mathematics to language minority students requires instructional settings and situations, such as those described in the above vignettes, where students are engaged in solving interesting, real-life problems that encourage both critical thinking and basic skills development and practice.

Relate Mathematics to Students' Real-life Experiences

In working with language minority students, teachers must understand that though these students have had many experiences outside of school, the experiences do not necessarily prepare them for the academic work required of them in the classroom. Math teachers can best facilitate mathematical development in their language minority students by designing activities that relate to students' real life experiences. For example, math problems that evolve from after-school job situations allow students to connect what happens in the classroom with their outside world (Buchanan and Helman, 1993). McPartland and Braddock (1993) place relevance of school work high on their list of factors contributing to the school success of disadvantaged students, including those who speak minority languages. Disadvantaged students need to believe that school work makes sense for their current and long-term welfare. They recommend that classroom tasks be intrinsically interesting or directly relate to their current interests and identity

Encourage Mathematical Communication

The NCTM standards also emphasize communication and discourse within the context of mathematical problem solving. The standards explicitly recommend that teachers pose questions and design tasks that engage students' thinking and ask students to clarify and justify ideas orally and in writing (National Council of Teachers of Mathematics, 1989). By integrating math and language teaching, mathematics courses can provide the necessary experiences for language minority students to acquire higher order mathematical competencies and improve their communicative abilities in English. For such learning to occur, students need ample opportunities to hear math language and to speak and write mathematically (Buchanan and Helman, 1993).

Put Students' Needs and Interests First

> If rich real-world problem settings are to be the basis for the mathematics curriculum, then when designing curricula for language minority students, attention needs to be given to the social and cultural contexts underlying the problem settings (Secada, 1992).

Buchanan and Helman (1993) provide guidelines for teaching mathematics and language to language minority students based on NCTM guidelines for designing an environment in which all students will develop mathematical literacy. First of all, teachers must consider the interests and intellectual abilities of their students. Though students may need to work on primary level math concepts, the problems used should relate to their current interests. For example, secondary-level students learning to calculate percentages can use pay stubs from their after-school jobs to determine the percentages of their various withholding categories.

However, Secada (1992) cautions that if rich real-world problem settings are to be the basis for the mathematics curriculum, then attention needs to be given to the social and cultural

Enriching Content Classes for Secondary ESOL Students (National Edition)
Study Guide Section 4: Academic Competence, Part B

89

contexts underlying the problem settings. For example, an intermediate algebra class learning about percentages studied how decreasing rates for electricity are linked to increased consumption, and that increased consumption most often entailed using appliances only the wealthy could afford (air conditioners, pool filtration systems, etc.). Secada points out that this analysis of consumption implies a certain social class background. Such an analysis may, though rich in real-life problem solving potential, serve to alienate language minority students from the curriculum since the experiences may highlight class distinctions already very apparent to many of these students.

Orchestrate Classroom Discourse

> Command of mathematical language plays an important role in the development of mathematical ability.

A second NCTM guideline offered by Buchanan and Helman (1993) directs teachers to orchestrate classroom discourse in a manner that encourages mathematical learning. With language minority students, teachers must attend not only to their cognitive development but also to the linguistic demands of mathematical language. The importance of language in mathematics instruction is often overlooked in the mistaken belief that mathematics is somehow independent of language proficiency. However, particularly with the increased emphasis placed on problem solving, command of mathematical language plays an important role in the development of mathematical ability. Mathematics vocabulary, special syntactic structures, inferring mathematical meaning, and discourse patterns typical of written text all contribute to the difficulties many language minority students have when learning mathematics in English (Corasaniti Dale and Cuevas, 1992).

Teach the Language of Mathematics

Teachers must consider a number of factors concerning vocabulary when developing students' linguistic ability in mathematics. First of all, mathematics vocabulary includes both words specific to mathematics, such as equation, algebraic, etc., as well as everyday vocabulary that has different meanings when used in mathematical contexts. Examples include words such as positive, negative, table, and irrational. Mathematics also uses strings of words to create complex phrases with specific meanings, such as a measure of central tendency and square root. Furthermore, students must master the many ways in which one mathematics operation can be signaled. Addition is a prime example with at least six different words or phrases used to indicate it: add, plus, combine, sum, and increased by. However, simply memorizing these and other signal words will not suffice since the meaning of any given word is determined by the context. Students must also learn to associate mathematical symbols with concepts and the language used to express those concepts. Teachers must be aware that some symbols serve different functions in different cultures. The comma, for example, is used to separate hundreds from thousands in the United States, whereas, in other countries the decimal point is used (Corasaniti Dale and Cuevas, 1992).

Mathematical syntax involves many precise and difficult structures that are often used in a highly abstract context. Mathematical descriptions frequently use the passive voice, a complex and difficult structure for many non-English speakers. For example: *ten (is) divided by two* and *when 15 is added to a number, the result is 21; find the number*. One of the major

SECTION 4

difficulties of the syntax used in mathematics is the lack of one-to-one correspondence between mathematical symbols and the words they represent. For example, if translated word for word, the algebraic expression *the number a is five less than the number b* might be recorded as $a = 5 - b$ rather than the correct translation, $a = b - 5$. Researchers have found that non-native speakers tend to follow the surface syntax of problem statements; thus, teachers need to provide students instruction in how to correctly translate linguistic statements into mathematical statements (Corasaniti Dale and Cuevas, 1992).

> Those who teach mathematics to language minority students must have an understanding of the language students will need in order to comprehend and apply mathematical concepts and must be prepared to actively teach that language.

Inferring meaning from mathematical texts is frequently dependent upon knowledge of how key words relate to other words in a problem. Corasaniti Dale and Cuevas (1992) offer this example of a densely packed statement requiring facility with word reference: *Five times a number is two more than ten times the number.* Here students must understand that *a number* and *the number* refer to the same quantity. In addition to intricate semantic features such as word reference, written mathematics discourse has proved troublesome due to a number of features including lack of redundancy or paraphrase (a feature common in oral discourse and even in other types of written material), the use of symbolic devices, technical language with precise meanings, and the large quantity of concepts presented within a small amount of text (Corasaniti Dale and Cuevas, 1992).

Working with written text requires a number of abilities on the part of language minority students. Students must recognize familiar concepts and applications and determine when to apply them. They must also be able to determine when everyday background experience is helpful and when it may interfere with understanding new concepts. Moreover, the ability to think mathematically when reading mathematics text is critical. Mathematics teachers who work with language minority students should employ a dual approach, incorporating instruction on the mathematical language related to the particular concepts being taught along with the concepts themselves (Corasaniti and Dale, 1992).

Create Classroom Environments Rich in Language and Content

Orchestrating classroom discourse with language minority students requires more than a knowledge of the intricacies of mathematical language, it demands that teachers create classroom environments and instructional situations that support and promote the language and conceptual development of students. Teachers and/or students can create charts of commonly used mathematical terminology and display them around the room. In working from concrete problem solving situations to more abstract context-reduced ones, students can begin manipulating mathematical language by writing their own word problems drawn from their mathematical experiences and sharing them with other students.

Encourage Exploration and Reflection through Journal Writing

One useful tool encouraged by the NCTM *Curriculum and Evaluation Standards* is journal writing. Through journal writing teachers can encourage students to explore and write about various strategies for solving mathematical problems. Writing is more than a means

Enriching Content Classes for Secondary ESOL Students (National Edition)
Study Guide Section 4: Academic Competence, Part B

91

of expression; it is also a means of knowing what we think, a way of shaping and refining our ideas. Journal writing in mathematics classrooms allows students who may be too shy or intimidated to communicate their ideas and questions to write freely without concern for grammar or style. In their journal, students can summarize, organize and relate ideas, clarify concepts, and review topics. They can describe strategies, their reactions and accomplishments or frustrations and express positive or negative emotions (Bagley and Gallenberger, 1992).

Bagley and Gallenberger (1992) offer a number of suggestions for journal writing in mathematics classes. Though not specifically intended for language minority students, many of their suggestions would be productive with these students. In some instances, native language use could be encouraged; in others, students should be encouraged to write in English in order to practice working with mathematical vocabulary and linguistic structures, such as those specified above.

Examples of Prompts for Mathematical Journal Writing

(1) Display a picture. Construct a word problem about the picture that can be solved mathematically. Share your problem with a partner and solve it;

(2) What is the most important idea you've learned in algebra this week and why?

(3) Write a paragraph containing as many of these words as possible: ; and

(4) List some things you must remember when answering this type of question or doing this type of problem.

Integrate Reading into Mathematics Instruction

Siegel and Borasi (1992) encourage the integration of reading into mathematics education. Their perspective, though not explicitly stated as such, reflects the influence of the whole language philosophy. Again, though not specifically designed for language minority students, their recommendations for integrating reading and writing into mathematics instruction incorporate practices found to be effective with second language learners.

Integrating Reading into a Unit on Probability

1. Students are given a written survey in which they are asked to make guesses about the probability of certain events. Through discussion, the teacher elicits students' understandings of probability and encourages questions to guide them in further exploration of the topic.

2. Students then examine the historical events that led to the invention of probability by forming pairs to read selections on probability. In pairs, students take turns reading and then stopping to pose questions and discuss the ideas presented. This "say something"

---

strategy promotes social interaction between students which supports their efforts to work out a meaning for the text. It also encourages them to take ownership for their reading/ learning experiences and promotes an inquiry orientation to learning (Siegel and Borasi, 1992). Moreover, such a format works well materials on their own. By working with a partner, they are given extra support for developing both reading skills and their knowledge base on probability.

3. In follow-up exercises, the teacher asks students to put the historical information in their own words, make connections to the present, or discuss what piqued their interest while reading. By focusing on gaming in history, students can begin discussing various games in which probability plays an important role (Siegel and Borasi, 1992). Language minority students who may have experience with different games can share these with the class at this point.

4. As the teacher begins introducing the technical aspects of probability, students review newspapers and magazines for everyday uses of probability and record these instances on note cards which can then form the basis for a discussion on how probability is interpreted in everyday usage (Siegel and Borasi, 1992).

Through integrating reading, writing and discussion with mathematics content, teachers encourage both greater depth in students' understanding of topics such as probability and the development of academic language skills.

Make Connections to Students' Prior Knowledge and Experience

> Secondary language minority students may have difficulty learning mathematics through traditional text-book driven approaches. Thus, teachers will need to provide learning situations that relate mathematical concepts to students' cultures and life experiences.

A third NCTM guideline recommends that teachers seek and help students seek connections to previous and developing knowledge. This guideline involves both becoming aware of and utilizing students' cultural and educational background knowledge in helping them learn mathematics and connecting the math content to other fields, such as science, language arts and history excellent example of how various content areas can be interwoven around a central topic and how students' experiences with games from their own cultures can be integrated into instruction.

An effective approach for teaching mathematics to language minority students supports the above NCTM guideline by encouraging teachers to make instructional decisions based on students' developing knowledge and thinking about mathematics. Known as Cognitively Guided Instruction (CGI), this approach operates from the following premises:

(1) teachers must know how their students mentally organize mathematical content;

(2) instruction should focus on problem solving;

(3) teachers should determine what their students are thinking about the mathematical content studied;

Enriching Content Classes for Secondary ESOL Students (National Edition)
Study Guide Section 4: Academic Competence, Part B

93

(4) teachers should design instruction based on their students' thinking (Secada, 1992).

Vary Instructional Methods

A final caveat from NCTM advises that teachers provide opportunities for individual, small-group, and whole-class work (Buchanan and Helman, 1993). The study on attributes of effective instruction for language minority students emphasizes the importance of using a variety of instructional methods, such as direct instruction, guided discovery, cooperative learning, and computer-assisted instruction, tailored to students' needs. When choosing instructional methods, teachers must consider several factors including lesson goals and objectives, learner characteristics, and available resources. Furthermore, in mainstream English-medium classrooms, the level(s) of English language proficiency must also be considered when deciding upon an instructional approach. Through the use of multiple approaches, teachers can meet the needs of a wider variety of students (August and Pease-Alvarez, 1996).

Language Arts

English Language Arts Standards and the Language Minority Student

The recently released *Standards for the English Language Arts* are among the few national content standards documents that explicitly focus on the needs of language minority students. Two of the twelve standards directly relate to language minority student issues with one focusing on the importance of native language development, and the other promoting an understanding of and respect for diversity in language use. The authors also specifically address issues related to the educational needs of language minority students at various points throughout the document and use several vignettes involving language minority students in mainstream English language arts classrooms to illustrate effective instructional settings for these students (International Reading Association and National Council of Teachers of English, 1996).

> "If we deny second language learners the opportunity to read literature that is for them a mirror, we're doing them a disservice" (Dr. Linda Mauro).

In explaining the standard on developing an understanding of and respect for diversity in language use..., the authors make several important points concerning effective schooling for language minority students. They state that "the capacity to hear and respect different perspectives and to communicate with people whose lives and cultures are different from our own is a vital element of American society....Celebrating our shared beliefs and traditions is not enough; we also need to honor that which is distinctive in the many groups that make up our nation" (International Reading Association and National Council of Teachers of English, 1996).

Dr. Linda Mauro, English education professor at George Washington University, reinforces these statements in her discussion of the role minority literature can play in the lives of both native and non-native speakers. "I believe that adolescent literature needs to be a mirror of who they are and what they're struggling with as well as a window for understanding the world. So I think for a second language learner if we deny them the opportunity to ever read literature that is for them a mirror, we're doing them a disservice. And if we deny native speakers and native born students a chance to use literature as a window to understand other cultures and other students, we're denying them a chance to look beyond what they already know."

Select Appropriate Texts

> Literature containing themes relevant to the life experiences and cultures of language minority students are more appropriate initial choices than texts having little or no relation to these students' lives.

This standard and the comments by Dr. Mauro relate directly to one of the key issues in English language arts curriculum development, selection of appropriate texts. Teachers working in heterogeneous classrooms containing language minority students should carefully review the literature curriculum. Such a review involves analyzing literary texts for possible barriers to understanding for language minority students. These students may have difficulty with texts that are culturally unfamiliar to them, contain difficult vocabulary and complex themes, and academic or archaic syntax. Research into reading indicates that students use past experiences and background knowledge to make sense out of the unfamiliar texts; thus literature teachers need to understand their language minority students' experiences and background in relation to the texts they select for study. Literature containing themes relevant to the life experiences and cultures of these students are more appropriate initial choices than texts having little or no relation to these students' lives.

Literature teachers can facilitate the cognitive and language development of these students if instruction is planned so that more familiar works, such as folktales and myths from students' cultures, are introduced before less familiar texts. Also short stories written by minority authors, such as William Saroyan and Sandra Cisneros, and excerpts from authors such as Amy Tan and Maxine Hong Kingston tend to contain themes and characters with which students from the respective cultures of these authors will be familiar. These works also allow students from the majority culture the opportunity to learn from perspectives that may differ from their own (Sasser, 1992).

The following middle school vignette from the *Standards for the English Language Arts* demonstrates how language minority students and their families are integrated into the language arts classroom through the use of culturally familiar materials and through instructional methods that facilitate parental involvement and language and cognitive development.

Enriching Content Classes for Secondary ESOL Students (National Edition)
Study Guide Section 4: Academic Competence, Part B

95

Vignette 5: Using Folktales in Language Arts

Middle school students who are originally from a dozen different countries are studying folktales using resources in English and, when available, in their primary languages. Many sources come from their classroom, school, and public libraries, but some, especially those written in the students' primary languages, come from their homes. The students keep reflective reading journals and share responses to folktales they have read in small groups. As a class, the students read selected folktales together and watch videotaped dramatizations of several stories made by previous classes. Watching these tapes excites the students as they see stories from many different cultures being brought to life by their peers. Their teacher models different storytelling techniques, including puppetry, readers' theater, and role-playing.

After a week of reading a number of different stories, the students each select one special story to present to the class. Each student chooses the mode of storytelling that is best suited to his or her story, including staging a story as a mini-drama, drawing a picture, or creating puppets to represent key characters. Students then practice in small groups, and finally they present their folktales to the class. The teacher videotapes each presentation so that students can watch and critique their own presentations later. The videotape will also provide a model for students in next year's class.

As a further exploration of narrative, students ask their parents or caregivers to tell them stories from their own cultures. Working together, students and their parents write out these stories. In many cases, students write the stories both in their first language and in English.... The students work in groups to assemble all of these stories and create a book using the class computer. This book is duplicated so that each student has a copy. A copy is also donated to the school library so that other students may enjoy the stories and see different styles of writing from around the world (International Reading Association and National Council of Teachers of English, 1996).

Make Literature More Comprehensible

> To make literature more comprehensible use graphic organizers, have students keep journals, and provide opportunities for students to interact with their peers both orally and in writing.

The language arts standards also emphasize that students read a wide range of literature and apply a wide range of strategies to comprehend, interpret, evaluate and appreciate texts (International Reading Association and National Council of Teachers of English, 1996). In order to help language minority students meet such standards, teachers must adopt instructional approaches which help make literary material more comprehensible to these students and actively teach strategies that will aid them in their endeavors to unlock meaning in works of literature.

Sasser (1992) provides a number of tools teachers can use to engage students in these works. She recommends that graphic organizers, such as clusters, semantic maps, storyboards, matrices, semantic webs, and Venn diagrams, be used to help students visualize and organize thematic content and characters and to keep abreast of plot developments.

Through the process of locating and writing down information for various types of graphic organizers, students become involved in responding critically to the work. Students must sort, categorize, list, analyze, and evaluate both the content of the text and their own reactions to it. Moreover, graphic organizers force students to reformulate information from the text that may be highly abstract in a concrete from. Such activities aid students in comprehending and expressing difficult ideas. Students should also keep journal entries and interact with their peers both orally and in writing about literature. Together, all these activities give language minority students the extra support needed for successful academic experiences with literature.

Implement a Whole Language Approach

> Language arts teachers can work collaboratively with ESL/ bilingual teachers to design literature units and lessons that incorporate effective instructional strategies for language minority students.

The whole language philosophy, which views meaning and natural language as the foundations for literacy development, and the teaching/learning techniques associated with it have been found to conform with what is known about effective instruction for language minority students (Kauffman, et.al., 1995). Whole language approaches are particularly well-suited to language arts classrooms where students through reading, writing, speaking and listening are actively involved in constructing meaning from both their own experiences and through encounters with various texts. Kauffman, et.al. (1995) includes a description of a whole-language unit on *To Kill a Mockingbird* that was developed collaboratively by ESL and English literature teachers. The unit was designed for use in coordinated ESL and mainstream literature classes and asks students to consider the themes of love and conflict, the individual and society, blindness and sight, and passages and transformations. The unit is presented in three stages called INTO, THROUGH, and BEYOND.

Sasser (1992) describes the INTO stage as what occurs before reading begins. The purpose here, particularly for language minority students, is to interest the students in the text and elicit prior knowledge that may be useful in interpreting the work. Anticipation guides, often composed of simple true-false or agree-disagree statements, encourage students to identify and think through their positions on ideas prevalent in the literary work. The teacher can also introduce the reading by providing a summary of the plot in order to preview the plot and characters. During this stage, the teacher can also elicit predictions from the students about the content and outcome of the work. By having students write down their predictions prior to and through out the course of the reading, students can track their understanding and increased sophistication of their predictions and ideas.

During the THROUGH phase, students read the text. Silent reading can be enhanced by the teacher reading selected portions of the work aloud. In this manner, language minority students can get a better sense of inflection, pronunciation, rhythm and stress which can aid in understanding. To aid language minority students in developing the skills necessary for comprehension of a complex work of literature— skills such as following a sequence of events, identifying foreshadowing and flashback, visualizing setting, analyzing character and motive, comprehending mood and theme, and recognizing irony and symbols— teach-

Enriching Content Classes for Secondary ESOL Students (National Edition)
Study Guide Section 4: Academic Competence, Part B

97

ers might choose excerpts for discussion, helping students sort out what is significant from what is less so. Interchanges, either oral or written, allow students to share their ideas with one another and the teacher; in the process, students who may come from educational systems that stress only one right answer, begin to realize the possibility for multiple interpretations. In addition, during the THROUGH phase, the use of graphic organizers, as previously mentioned, becomes important as students grapple with the complexities of theme, character, and plot. Teachers can integrate writing by having students keep reading logs, assume the identities of characters to write letters, make up dialogue for characters, and rewrite scenes from different perspectives.

The BEYOND stage involves students in activities that extend beyond the text. At this point students write and discuss in order to refine their thoughts and deepen comprehension. Comparing a book with its film version or creating a drama from a scene in the work are appropriate at this point. Conducting further research on issues raised within a work or responding to a work through poetry writing are other examples of how teachers can further student involvement with a literary work. The description of the mainstream classroom's INTO, THROUGH, and BEYOND activities on the *To Kill A Mockingbird* unit follow:

Vignette 6: To Kill a Mockingbird

In the first stage, students read and discuss poems about truth and short stories such as "A Death in the House" by C. Simak. Following the discussion, students participate in a simulation exercise dealing with segregation. Students are divided into pairs with one member considered a first-class citizen (white) and the other a second-class citizen (Black). Pairs work together to find and write definitions for assigned words, identify suffixes, locate sentences in the text in which the words are used, and present the information to the class for discussion. Only the first-class citizen of the pair may present information, receive credit and be rewarded for their efforts. The second-class citizen, on the other hand, is expected to assist in completing the vocabulary activity and perform tasks involving physical labor (getting and returning the dictionary). At no point are any second-class citizens' efforts recognized or rewarded. At the conclusion, students discuss how they felt during the simulation and use the phrases, "I noticed," or "I learned. This activity is followed by viewing and discussing the film, "Amazing Grace."

In THROUGH, students complete daily writing activities, study questions and vocabulary development activities to better understand the novel. In one activity, students read a chapter or scene and choose a quote to represent it. Next, they illustrate the quote to depict its significance. Later students share their illustrations with the class and consider new perspectives for interpreting the chapters or scenes....

In BEYOND, students listen to and discuss the song "The Way It Is" by Bruce Hornsby. Next, they brainstorm criteria for a good novel and evaluate the book based on these criteria. At the end of the unit, they take an objective test (Kauffman, et.al., 1995).

Encourage Students to Maintain the Native Language

Authors of the English language arts standards stress the importance of native language development in learning English. This standard directly states that language minority students should make use of their first language both for learning English and content-area subject matter. A recent study found that among the major instructional features impacting the academic success of language minority students in predominantly English-medium settings was the opportunity for native language use. For monolingual English teachers or those teachers who do not speak all the languages of their students, the study outlines several ways in which teachers can facilitate native language use. These include structuring instructional activities that require students to use their native language; utilizing the services of aides or tutors fluent in the native languages of the students to assist in explaining content materials; and allowing students to respond in their native language to questions asked in English (Tikunoff, et.al., 1991). In addition, locating native language resources, such as books, magazines, films, etc. relating to the topic or theme supports native language development when other resources may not be available. Lucas and Katz (1994) describe how students not yet proficient enough in English can write in journals or keep reading logs in their native languages. Teachers can also utilize their students' linguistic resources by pairing students with the same native language but different levels of English proficiency so that more proficient students can tutor less proficient students. The following is an example of this type of peer tutoring arrangement used to facilitate student writing:

Vignette 7: Native Language Peer Tutoring

The teacher sets out the steps for the day's lesson on the process of writing a family history. The class, a heterogeneous grouping of middle school students whose native languages are Spanish, Vietnamese, and Korean, watch quietly and attentively as Norma (the teacher) brainstorms the topic, scribbling notes about her family history on the overhead projector as a model of how this prewriting technique can help them begin exploration of this topic. Next, Norma turns to the chalkboard, writing her first draft as she explains the students' task. When she is done, students turn to each other at their tables to exchange ideas for their own family histories. After about 5 minutes, Ana leans over Rosa's paper already three-quarters filled with writing in Spanish and English. Rosa has only been in the program for 1 month.... Norma describes her level of English as low intermediate. Ana, on the other hand, has high-intermediate English skills. Norma has carefully constructed students' groups to make sure each contains students with different skill levels so that students can help each other in either English or their native languages. Her brow furrowed, Rosa consults with Ana, discussing both what is on the sheet and what still needs to be added. She speaks quickly and quietly in Spanish, an occasional word from the sheet in English breaking the flow (Lucas and Katz, 1994).

Enriching Content Classes for Secondary ESOL Students (National Edition)
Study Guide Section 4: Academic Competence, Part B

99

Provide a Balanced Writing Program

Several of the language arts standards emphasize the importance of writing as a process and as a means of authentic communication with various audiences. Dr. Mauro also stresses the importance of a balanced writing program that promotes fluency, clarity and correctness. "If students can write correctly, but it's not clear and they aren't able to convey their meaning, that does students a disservice. There has been too much of a focus, in the previous generation, on correctness, and too much focus more recently on fluency by teachers who misunderstood the notion of the writing process." Dr. Mauro believes that teachers must actively teach correctness in the context of meaningful and authentic writing assignments. Clarity must also be taught using structured techniques that help students think about ways to organize their writing and that promote their working together to support one another's writing development. She provides the following classroom activity designed to teach persuasive writing that would work well with language minority students as well as native speakers:

Teaching Persuasive Writing

The class meets to select a topic that most everyone is interested in, a topic such as capital punishment. Students discuss the topic, sharing cultural and religious views, or views in other countries on the death penalty. Students also spend time reading various materials on capital punishment that are appropriate for their reading level. Native language materials could also be used if available. Students must then give two reasons why they might be in support of the death penalty and two reasons why they might be against it. Next they choose sides, identifying which side they have chosen with a name tag. Each student visits two other students who represent their own opinion, then two who are opposed to their opinion. They use a form to record their own responses, the responses of those who agree with them, and the responses of those who disagree. This process involves students in talking through other people's ideas in a respectful way. The next step involves teaching them how to explicitly and clearly structure a persuasive essay. Using their own ideas and those they gathered from others, they are taught how to raise the opponents beliefs through expressions such as, "Though some people may believe...," and expressions that counter the opponents' arguments. This activity teaches clarity in a setting where students are encouraged to talk and share with one another and requires that students build on the ideas of others (Dr. Linda Mauro).

Assessing Language Minority Students in the Content Areas

Fair and meaningful testing should be an integral component of the mainstream education of language minority students. All too often, though, these students are either asked to participate in tests that make unfair assumptions about their English language proficiency in order to assess their content knowledge or, conversely, are totally excluded from any testing until their English language proficiency has reached a certain level. Furthermore, often due to gaps in their educational experience, language minority students when measured against their native English speaking peers may fail to meet mainstream instructional goals; however, these students often achieve impressive academic gains when compared to where they began (Cornell, 1995).

Characteristics of Sound Assessment for Language Minority Students

> When assessing language minority students, teachers need to ask whether they are measuring language proficiency or content knowledge?

Authors of the study on attributes of effective instruction for language minority students list five attributes that should inform assessment for language minority students. A primary concern is that these students be assessed for both content knowledge and language proficiency. Secondly, whenever possible and appropriate, schools should make efforts to assess students' content knowledge and abilities in the native language as well as in English. Native language assessment is particularly important when students have learned certain content concepts and skills in their native language. Without such assessment, teachers are likely to underestimate students' academic achievement. A third characteristic of sound assessment practice entails ensuring that a diversity of measures (e.g., portfolios, observations, anecdotal records, interviews, checklists, criterion-referenced tests etc.) are used to measure content knowledge and skills. A varied approach to assessment allows the teacher to incorporate information about language minority students in "a variety of contexts obtained from a variety of sources through a variety of procedures." A fourth attribute concerns teacher awareness of the purpose of the assessment. Is the test intended to measure language proficiency or content knowledge? Finally, knowledge of a student's background, such as educational experiences and parents' literacy, should contribute to a more complete assessment picture (August and Pease-Alvarez, 1996).

Though recommendations list essential characteristics of good assessments, researchers do not know how to reliably measure how much children are learning except through standardized tests, which pose problems when administered to language minority students. Additionally, such tests are unable to measure the different kinds of learning discussed above and advocated for by education reformers. On the other hand, it is also unclear as to whether performance and portfolio assessment will meet the needs of language minority students (McLaughlin and McLeod, 1996). With this caveat in mind, however, these alternative forms of assessment offer the best opportunities for realistic assessment of the actual performance of language minority students on different types of learning tasks.

Alternative Methods of Assessing Language Minority Students

> Portfolios can be useful both for teacher appraisal of student work and for student self-appraisal.

Alternative assessment requires students to perform authentic academic tasks, similar to those originally used to teach the material, rather than merely regurgitate information. Such assessment is also continuous, allowing the teacher to track student growth throughout the school year. Options for alternative assessment include writing samples, group projects, oral history projects, historical and contemporary role playing, job interview role playing, games, science exhibitions, merit badges, student-run banks and stores, designing newspaper ads, and developing a class newspaper. Student responses on alternative assessments may include using checklists, learning logs, book reports, writing samples, explanations of problem situations,

Enriching Content Classes for Secondary ESOL Students (National Edition)
Study Guide Section 4: Academic Competence, Part B

101

science lab reports with diagrams, dialogue journals, self-evaluation of strategy use, and oral descriptions. Portfolios facilitate the organization of student responses to assessment tasks. Periodically, teachers and students discuss which samples of student work should be included in the portfolio, which should also contain teacher rating forms, checklists, observation notes and other information concerning student progress toward meeting instructional objectives (Chamot, 1993).

The Guide to Performance Assessment for Linguistically Diverse Students (Navarrete and Gustkee, 1996) describes a number of specific assessment techniques that can be used for improving performance assessments of language minority students in content area settings. These include:

- Allowing extra time to complete or respond to the assessment tasks;
- Designing administration procedures to match classroom instructional practices (e.g., cooperative small groups, individual conferencing, and assessing in the language of instruction);
- Simplifying directions in English and/or paraphrasing in the students' native language. Also providing additional clarifying information during and/or after administration of the assessment (e.g., synonyms for difficult words or phrases); and
- Permitting students to use dictionaries or word lists.

In addition to these recommendations, local schools and districts, in an attempt to be sensitive to their student's level(s) of language proficiency, have developed performance assessment tasks that consist of the following components:

- Supporting assessment tasks in a contextualized manner by:
  (a) incorporating familiar classroom material as a stimulus, such as brief quotations, charts, graphics, cartoons, and works of art;
  (b) including questions for small group discussion and individual writing; and
  (c) mirroring learning processes with which students are familiar such as the writing process and reading conferencing activities.
- Including teacher observations, student self-appraisals and parent judgments/observations of their child's progress.
- Designing assessment tasks that require different ways of demonstrating knowledge or skill (e.g., exhibits, dramatic renditions, interviews, observations, self reflections, and a variety of writing samples) (Navarrete and Gustkee, 1996).

The George Washington University education professors, Dr. Mauro, Dr. Lynch, and Dr. Steeves, all recommend alternative assessment practices for their respective content areas and express particular support for its use with language minority students. For social studies, Dr. Steeves encourages the use of oral tests with both native and non-native speakers. Such alternative test taking formats give native speakers the opportunity to experience a different style of test taking. At the same time, when given to all students, language minority students are not singled out. Oral storytelling and project-oriented assessment are other alternative methods of assessing second language learners. Projects could include journal writings, reactions to different time periods, etc. Though this type of assessment is worthwhile, it can be time consuming to evaluate. One solution is to have students present their projects through an exhibition format, such as "History Day." While students make public their best work through demonstration and explanation, teachers have the opportunity to evaluate it.

In the language arts, Dr. Mauro recommends the use of portfolios which can be used to look at student improvement over time as well as for grading individual pieces. She also advises that students select three ungraded pieces of their work that are best representative of their growth. Students then write about which pieces they like best and why, and how they think they have developed as a writer. Afterwards, teacher and students meet to discuss their progress.

Preparing Mainstream Teachers to Work With Language Minority Students

> Most mainstream preservice teachers lack the knowledge, skills and experience essential for working successfully with language minority students.

The above discussion on the education of language minority students within mainstream settings emphasizes the importance of effective instruction, curriculum and assessment for these students. However, such instructional and curricular decision making cannot occur unless mainstream teachers receive the type of preparation and training necessary to work effectively with these students. However as Chisholm (1994) reports, most preservice teachers lack the knowledge, skills, and experience essential for working with minority children, including language minority students. Many of these teachers also express a high degree of insecurity about working with these students. Such insecurity can lead to an aversion toward teaching in culturally and linguistically diverse schools. A recent survey found that only 9 percent of preservice teachers indicated that they would prefer to teach in urban or multicultural contexts, and fewer than 3 percent were capable of teaching in a language other than English (Chisholm, 1994).

> Teacher education is the key to improving mainstream instruction of language minority students.

Furthermore, most mainstream teachers received their teacher training under the assumption that their students would be native English speakers. This assumption often leads teachers to feel resentful and even fearful of language minority students. These assumptions and feelings are even more prevalent at the secondary level where teachers identify themselves as content specialists not responsible for the additional demands of language instruction (Constantino, 1994). However, research has shown that mainstream teachers who receive appropriate training in how to teach language minority students are able to create instructional environments supportive of second language and content learning (Castaneda, 1993). According to Castaneda (1993) training that promotes cooperative grouping strategies, sheltered ESL approaches, and collaboration between mainstream and bilingual staff were perceived to be most helpful by mainstream teachers involved in her study.

Teacher Education in Practice

Dr. Mauro involves her English language arts preservice teachers in an innovative activity designed to give them insight into the educational needs of many second language learners in mainstream classrooms. She first asks her students to write on an unfamiliar assigned topic. She tells them that she is tired of receiving sloppy, incoherent writing, and that they have 20 minutes to compose a well-written paragraph. Since, she continues, they have not been following the rules of the English language, simple rules they should know by now,

Enriching Content Classes for Secondary ESOL Students (National Edition)
Study Guide Section 4: Academic Competence, Part B

103

she will review them. On the board, she gives them a number of rules, such as making sure that adjectives follow nouns and various (non-English) methods of forming the past tense. She then reiterates that they have 20 minutes to write their paragraphs and that they can begin. As they're writing, she circulates, hovering over each of them.

What the students discover from this exercise is that they're almost incapable of writing with any meaning when (a) they don't understand what they're writing about, and (b) they're trying to write according to rules that are unfamiliar to them. From this exercise, students begin to understand the difficulties language minority students confront when teachers overemphasize correctness in a language students do not yet fully understand.

> The majority of new teachers will be teaching students who come from a variety of cultural and linguistic backgrounds.

Despite the recognition that most secondary teachers are unprepared to work with language minority students, secondary teacher education departments have generally not changed their programs partly due to the expectation that secondary education majors will take a great deal of their coursework outside the education department in their various content fields, where little effort is made to connect content with the teaching and learning of that content. Moreover, very little research has been done to assist teacher educators in preparing secondary teachers to work with language minority students in their classrooms. Finally, exacerbating the situation is the prevailing attitude that teaching language is the responsibility of the ESL or bilingual teacher and that these students should be ready when entering the mainstream classroom to learn academic content in English (Constantino, 1994).

Incorporate Language Minority Student Issues into Teacher Education Programs

An innovative program initiated in the Chicago Public Schools set out to train bilingual/ESL and mainstream teachers to work collaboratively with one another. Training topics the project emphasized for enhancing the instructional competencies of both mainstream and bilingual/ESL teachers might indicate some of the areas teacher education programs need to address.

Areas Mainstream Teacher Education Programs Need to Address

- Adapting mainstream lessons and learning materials to meet the needs of language minority students;
- Making oral presentations more comprehensible;
- Identifying suitable learning materials and matching them to the instructional needs of the students;
- Promoting the interaction of language minority and native English speaking students through cooperative learning activities;
- Promoting comprehension of academic English by teaching specific learning strategies;
- Incorporating ESL methods into the mainstream classroom;
- Managing multi-language level classrooms;
- Assessing and grading language minority students;
- Distinguishing between language difficulties and learning problems; and
- Working with teaching assistants (Sakash and Rodriguez-Brown, 1995).

104

Enriching Content Classes for Secondary ESOL Students (National Edition)
Study Guide Section 4: Academic Competence, Part B

Teachers as Cultural Translators and Cultural Brokers

Milk, et.al. (1992) refers to several major functions mainstream teachers need to perform in order to take a more active role in the education of language minority students. Mainstream teachers need to act as mediators and facilitators of both content learning and English language acquisition. They need to serve as language models and as mediators of mainstream culture. Chisholm (1994) aptly refers to teachers who perform these functions as cultural translators and cultural brokers. Mainstream teachers must also advocate for their language minority students and collaborate with both administrators and other teachers to provide information about these students and about the content of their classes. Overall, Milk calls for teacher education programs that, though they may differ in their specifics, focus on how language minority students learn, in light of their unique needs as second language learners from non-mainstream cultural backgrounds.

Make Coursework and Field Experiences More Relevant to Today's Diverse Classrooms

> Coursework at all levels should integrate methods for teaching language arts to language minority students and provide preservice teachers with a repertoire of methods and skills for adapting instruction

Teacher education programs must rethink who they are preparing teachers to teach. No longer will teachers face classrooms composed mainly of white, middle-class, English speaking students. Chisholm (1994) calls for a multiculturally infused teacher education curriculum which goes beyond the addition of one or two courses addressed to special needs issues, such as those of language minority students. Along with culturally relevant field experiences within diverse communities, she advocates for an infused curriculum in which all aspects of the education program, coursework and field experiences, involve preservice teachers in developing the skills and knowledge necessary for successful practice in diverse classrooms.

Coursework at all levels should integrate methods for teaching language arts to language minority students and provide preservice teachers with a repertoire of methods and skills for adapting instruction. Classes should familiarize education students with ESL teaching methods and strategies and alternative methods of assessing student progress. Knowledge of the contributions of linguistically and culturally diverse peoples to the content areas should be integrated throughout the liberal arts and teacher education components of the program. Coursework should help preservice teachers acquire a sound basis in assessment and incorporate test bias, alternative testing methods, interpretation of test results, and ethnographic and observational techniques. Education programs should prepare their students to recognize cultural bias in tests and to use valid and culturally sensitive assessment measures. Preservice teachers must be able to use technology in a culturally sensitive manner. They must be able to assess software for the accuracy of its cultural content as well as for its educational merit. Finally, coursework should teach education students how to incorporate differences in cognitive and learning style into classroom instruction and make them aware of the cultural underpinnings of many students' learning preferences (Chisholm, 1994).

Enriching Content Classes for Secondary ESOL Students (National Edition)
Study Guide Section 4: Academic Competence, Part B

105

An integral part of any teacher education program is the quality of its field experiences. Education programs serious about training teachers to work with language minority students must provide them with field experiences that allow them to both observe how effective teachers work with language minority students and to practice teaching in multilingual environments. Productive field experiences also give preservice teachers ample opportunities to reflect with their peers and collaborating teachers on their developing ability to work with these students. Finally, teacher education programs must assess the cultural competency of its prospective teachers. Sound evaluation of cultural competency should involve students in multiple opportunities and a variety of tasks to prove their ability. In addition, more than one culturally sensitive evaluator should be used. Such a multifaceted approach will more likely ensure reliability and fairness (Chisholm, 1994)

Educating our future teachers to work with language minority students is no longer a preference but a necessity. In examining whether preservice programs are up to the task of educating these teachers to work with a diverse population, teacher educators need to question the extent to which their program increases cultural self-awareness, an appreciation of diversity, and cultural competency; and prepares teachers to work effectively with a variety of students and parents.

Conclusion

Secondary-level language minority students placed in mainstream classrooms must no longer be treated as second class citizens whose learning is relegated to bilingual or ESL teachers. Just as new education standards call for the education of all students to high standards, all teachers must be responsible for and capable of educating their language minority students. In order for this to occur, tough new standards and knowledge of effective practices for these students must coincide with classrooms staffed by teachers trained to implement the kind of teaching necessary to assist language minority students attain these standards. Integral to this reform, is a shift not only in how all educators, both within middle and high schools and within college and university education departments, think about these students but in how they practice their profession. Contrary to popular opinion, Dr. Mauro argues that in order to change underlying philosophical beliefs, educators must first change their behaviors. In other words, practice influences belief. "Most teachers want to be good teachers. When someone is able to demonstrate an effective method for you that works with your students— they're excited about coming to class, their writing is good, and you see real development— you begin to do more of that method, and the more you do, the more you begin to advocate for it, and it becomes your philosophical base. Change in behavior can lead to philosophical change."

References

August, D., Hakuta, K. and Pompa, D. (1994). For all students: Limited English proficient students and Goals 2000. National Clearinghouse for Bilingual Education: Washington, DC.

August, D. and Pease-Alvarez, L. (1996). Attributes of effective programs and classrooms serving English language learners. National Center for Research on Cultural Diversity and Second Language Learning: Santa Cruz, CA.

SECTION 4

Bagley, T. and Gallenberger, C. (1992). Assessing students' dispositions: Using journals to improve students' performance. Mathematics Teacher, 85 (8).

Berman, et.al. (1995). School reform and student diversity: Case studies of exemplary practices for LEP students. National Center for Research on Cultural Diversity and Second Language Learning: Santa Cruz, CA.

Buchanan, K. and Helman, M. (1993). Reforming mathematics instruction for ESL literacy students. National Clearinghouse for Bilingual Education: Washington, DC.

Castenada, L.V. (1993). Alternative visions of practice: An exploratory study of peer coaching, sheltered content, cooperative instruction and mainstream subject matter teachers. Proceedings of the third national research symposium on LEP student issues: Focus on middle and high school issues. Volume I. U.S. Department of Education, Office of Bilingual Education and Minority Languages Affairs: Washington, DC.

Chamot, A.U. (1993). Changing instruction for language minority students to achieve national goals. Proceedings of the third national research symposium on LEP student issues: Focus on middle and high school issues. Volume I. U.S. Department of Education, Office of Bilingual Education and Minority Languages Affairs: Washington, DC.

Chamot, A.U. (1995, Summer/Fall). Implementing the cognitive academic language learning approach: CALLA in Arlington, Virginia. The Bilingual Research Journal, 19 (3&4).

Chamot, A.U. and O'Malley, J.M. (1994). The CALLA handbook: Implementing the cognitive academic language learning approach. Addison-Wesley: Reading, MA.

Chisholm, I.M. (1994, Winter). Preparing teachers for multicultural classrooms. The Journal of Educational Issues of Language Minority Students, 14.

Chris Green, L. and Solis, A. (1997). A measuring stick for standards and TEKS: Meeting the needs of second language learners. IDRA Newsletter, XXIV (2).

Collier, V.P. (1995). Acquiring a second language for school. National Clearinghouse for Bilingual Education: Washington, DC.

Constantino, R. (1994, Spring). A study concerning instruction of ESL students comparing all-English classroom teacher knowledge and English as a second language teacher knowledge. The Journal of Educational Issues of Language Minority Students, 13.

Corasaniti Dale, T. and Cuevas, G.J. (1992). Integrating mathematics and language learning. In P.A. Richard-Amato and M.A. Snow (Eds.), The multicultural classroom: Readings for content-area teachers. Longman: White Plains, NY.

Cornell, C. (1995, Winter). Reducing failure of LEP students in the mainstream classroom and why it is important. The Journal of Educational Issues of Language Minority Students, 15.

SECTION 4

Enriching Content Classes for Secondary ESOL Students (National Edition)
Study Guide Section 4: Academic Competence, Part B

107

Cuevas, G.J. (1991). Developing communication skills in mathematics for students with limited English proficiency. Mathematics Teacher, 84 (3).

Farr, B.P. and Trumbull, E. (1997). Assessment alternatives for diverse classrooms. Christopher-Gordon Publishers, Inc.: Norwood, MA.

Fathman, A. K., et.al. (1992). Teaching science to English learners. National Clearinghouse for Bilingual Education: Washington, DC.

Gelman, R., et.al. (1995). Integrating science concepts into intermediate English as a second language (ESL) instruction. In R.F. Macias and R.G. Gracia Ramos (Eds.), Changing schools for changing students: An anthology of research on language minorities, schools & society. UC Linguistic Minority Research Institute; Santa Barbara, CA.

Handscombe, J. (1989). A quality program for learners of English as a second language. In P. Rigg and V.G. Allen (Eds.), When they don't all speak English: Integrating the ESL student into the regular classroom. National Council of Teachers of English: Urbana, IL.

Harklau, L. (1994). ESL versus mainstream classes: Contrasting L2 learning environments. TESOL Quarterly, 28 (2).

International Reading Association and National Council of Teachers of English (1996). Standards for the English Language Arts. Authors: Newark, DE and Urbana, IL.

Kauffman, et.al. (1995). Content-ESL across the USA. Volume II: A practical guide. Center for Applied Linguistics: Washington, DC.

Kessler, C., et.al. (1992). Science and cooperative learning for LEP students. In C. Kessler (Ed.), Cooperative language learning: A teacher's resource book. Prentice Hall Regents: Englewood Cliffs, NJ.

King, M., et.al. (1992). Social studies instruction. In P.A. Richard-Amato and M.A. Snow (Eds.), The multicultural classroom: Readings for content-area teachers. Longman: White Plains, NY.

Lucas, T. and Katz, A. (1994). Reframing the debate: The roles of native languages in English-only programs for language minority students. TESOL Quarterly, 28 (3).

McLaughlin, B. and McLeod, B. (1996). The impact statement on practice and knowledge—educating all out students: Improving education for children from culturally and linguistically different backgrounds. National Center for Research on Cultural Diversity and Second Language Learning: Santa Cruz, CA.

McKeon, D. (1994). When meeting "common" standards is uncommonly difficult. Educational Leadership, 51 (8).

McPartland, J. and Braddock II, J.H. (1993). A conceptual framework on learning environments and student motivation for language minority and other underserved populations. Proceedings of the third national research symposium on LEP student issues: Focus on middle and high school issues. Volume I. U.S. Department of Education, Office of Bilingual Education and Minority Languages Affairs: Washington, DC.

Macías, R.F. and Kelly, C. (1996). Summary report of the survey of the states' limited English proficient students and available educational programs and services, 1994-1995. Author: Washington, DC.

Milk, R., et.al. (1992). Re-thinking the education of teachers of language minority children: Developing reflective teachers for changing schools. National Clearinghouse for Bilingual Education: Washington, DC.

Minicucci, C. (1996). Learning science and English: How school reform advances scientific learning for limited English proficient middle school students. National Center for Research on Cultural Diversity and Second Language Learning: Santa Cruz, CA.

National Center for History in the Schools (1994). National standards for United States history: Exploring the American experience, grades 5-12. Author: Los Angeles, CA.

National Council for the Social Studies Task Force on Scope and Sequence (1989, October). In search of a scope and sequence for social studies. Social Education, 53.

National Council of Teachers of Mathematics (1989). Curriculum and evaluation standards for school mathematics. Author: Reston, VA.

National Research Council (1996). National science education standards. National Academy Press: Washington, DC.

Navarrete, C. and Gustkee, C. (1996). A guide to performance assessment for linguistically diverse students. Evaluation Assistance Center-West: Albuquerque, NM.

Olmedo, I.M. Junior historians: Doing oral history with ESL and bilingual students. TESOL Journal, Summer 1993.

Olsen, R.E. W-B. (1992). Cooperative learning and social studies. In C. Kessler (Ed.), Cooperative language learning: A teacher's resource book. Prentice Hall Regents: Englewood Cliffs, NJ.

Padron, Y.N. (1993). Teaching and learning risks associated with limited cognitive mastery in science and mathematics for limited English proficient students. Proceedings of the third national research symposium on LEP student issues: Focus on middle and high school issues. Volume II. U.S. Department of Education, Office of Bilingual Education and Minority Languages Affairs: Washington, DC.

Reyhner, J. and Davison, D.M. (1993). Improving mathematics and science instruction for LEP middle and high school students through language activities. Proceedings of the third national research symposium on LEP student issues: Focus on middle and high school issues. Volume II. U.S. Department of Education, Office of Bilingual Education and Minority Languages Affairs: Washington, DC.

Rupp, J.H. (1992). Discovery science and language development. In P.A. Richard-Amato and M.A. Snow (Eds.), The multicultural classroom: Readings for content-area teachers. Longman: White Plains, NY.

Sakash, K. and Rodriguez-Brown, F.V. (1995). Teamworks: Mainstream and bilingual/ESL teacher collaboration. National Clearinghouse for Bilingual Education: Washington, DC.

Sasser, L. (1992). Teaching literature to language minority students. In P.A. Richard-Amato and M.A. Snow (Eds.), The multicultural classroom: Readings for content-area teachers. Longman: White Plains, NY.

Schmidt, W.H., et.al. (1996). Splintered vision: An investigation of U.S. science and mathematics education. Executive Summary. U.S. National Research Center for the Third International Mathematics and Science Study, Michigan State University: Lansing, MI.

Secada, W. (1992). Evaluating the mathematics education of LEP students in a time of educational change. Proceedings of the second national research symposium on LEP student issues: Focus on evaluation and measurement. Volume II. U.S. Department of Education, Office of Bilingual Education and Minority Languages Affairs: Washington, DC.

Short, D.J. (1992). Adapting materials and developing lesson plans. In P.A. Richard-Amato and M.A. Snow (Eds.), The multicultural classroom: Readings for content-area teachers. Longman: White Plains, NY.

Siegel, M. and Borasia, R. (1992). Toward a new integration of reading in mathematics instruction. Focus on Learning Problems in Mathematics, 14 (2).

Smith, S. Z., et.al. (1993). What the NCTM standards look like in one classroom. Educational Leadership, 50 (5).

Spanos, G. (1993). ESL math and science for high school students: Two case studies. Proceedings of the third national research symposium on LEP student issues: Focus on middle and high school issues. Volume I. U.S. Department of Education, Office of Bilingual Education and Minority Languages Affairs: Washington, DC.

Tikunoff, W.J., et.al. (1991). Final report: A descriptive study of significant features of exemplary special alternative instructional programs. Southwest Regional Educational Laboratory: Los Alamitos, CA.

Whitten, C.P., et.al. (1995). Review of the literature relevant to the education of secondary school students (grades 9-12) who are limited in English proficiency. DevTech Systems, Inc. and Juarez and Associates, Inc.: Washington, DC.

The National Clearinghouse for Bilingual Education (NCBE) is funded by the U.S. Department of Education's Office of Bilingual Education and Minority Languages Affairs (OBEMLA) and is operated under Contract No. T2950050001 by the George Washington University, Graduate School of Education and Human Development, Center for the Study of Language and Education. This report was prepared under Task Order D0003, Model 3. The opinions, conclusions, and recommendations expressed herein do not necessarily reflect the position or policy of the George Washington University or the U.S. Department of Education and no official endorsement should be inferred. The mention of trade names, commercial products or organizations does not imply endorsement by the U.S. government. Readers are free to duplicate and use these materials in keeping with accepted publication standards. NCBE requests that proper credit be given in the event of use.

NCBE Home Page
http://www.ncbe.gwu.edu

SECTION 4

Source: Anstrom, K. (1997). *Academic achievement for secondary language minority students: Standards, measures and promising practices.* Washington D.C.: National Clearinghouse for Bilingual Education.

Enriching Content Classes for Secondary ESOL Students (National Edition)
Study Guide Section 4: Academic Competence, Part B

111

Content Area Tasks

1. Read the Introduction section of the Anstrom article, the portion of the article dealing with your content area, and the remaining sections on Assessment and Teacher Preparation.

2. With your small group, identify three of the suggested strategies that are most feasible to incorporate into teaching, given the content taught, student characteristics, and teacher preferences. List these below and tell why you chose them and why they are especially helpful to ESOL students. Be prepared to share with the whole class if called upon.

   Strategy 1:

       Why chosen:

       Why helpful to ESOL students:

   Strategy 2:

       Why chosen:

       Why helpful to ESOL students:

   Strategy 3:

       Why chosen:

       Why helpful to ESOL students:

3. (a) Locate the assigned Promising Practice for your content area in the Anstrom document from the following list:

   Social Studies: Oral History Offers Language Minority Student Access to the Curriculum, Pages 76-77

   Science: Science Instruction: What Works for Language Minority Students (the three-tiered approach), Pages 85-86

   Mathematics: Integrate Reading into Mathematics Instruction, Pages 92-93

   Language Arts: Provide a Balanced Writing Program, Page 100

   (b) Using the assigned strategy and working in your small groups, outline a lesson that meets the five requirements of the *Easy as Pie PLUS Lesson Plan Checklist* (page 114). Record the sequence of activities that the lesson will follow on the next page.

   (c) Review the *Easy as Pie PLUS Lesson Plan Checklist* and make sure that each person in your small group can explain how the lesson meets each of the criteria.

4. Review the list of areas that mainstream teacher preparation programs (inservice and preservice) need to address. List one or two areas that you feel better prepared in as a result of this course and one or two areas that you still feel you need to work on.

Lesson Outline Using a Promising Practice

Enriching Content Classes for Secondary ESOL Students (National Edition)
Study Guide Section 4: Academic Competence, Part B

113

Easy as Pie PLUS Lesson Plan Checklist

1. Increase Comprehensibility

    a. Use a Lesson Sequence which proceeds
       (1) from prior knowledge to new knowledge
       (2) from the concrete to the abstract
       (3) from oral language to texts
       (4) from more contextual support to less contextual support
       (5) for example, Teach the Text Backwards
          (a) Do Application(s): relevance, prior knowledge (Engage)
          (b) Discuss Main Points: use oral language, visuals, hands on (Explore/Discuss)
          (c) Examine Study Questions: overview, identify key concepts
              (Overview Key Concepts)
          (d) Read Text: make manageable for ESOL students (Develop/Extend Learning)

    b. Use Contextual Support (visuals, hands on, non-verbal clues) to the communicate the overall message, then correlate the message with the language

2. Increase Interaction

3. Increase Thinking Skills/Study Skills

4. Make Connections

    a. To Other Content Areas

    b. To Students' Interests

    c. To Other Cultures

5. Modify Assessment

114

Enriching Content Classes for Secondary ESOL Students (National Edition)
Study Guide Section 4: Academic Competence, Part B

Selections from Textbooks

Directions: Read each selection and identify 2-3 difficulties that an ESOL student might have in reading this.

A. Tommy is growing up. Very soon he'll be shaving, he'll be driving, and he'll be going out on dates. Tommy can't believe how quickly time flies. He won't be a little boy much longer. Soon he'll be a teenager.

B. The members of the kingdom Monera, the prokaryotes, are identified on the basis of their unique cellular organization and biochemistry. Members of the kingdom Protista are single-celled eukaryotes, both autotrophs and heterotrophs.

C. It is usually a long process for a bill to become law. Sometimes a bill needs only one year to become law. But other bills need many years to become laws. For example, the 1986 immigration bill took six years to become a law.

D. "I found Rome a city of bricks and left it a city of marble." Augustus is supposed to have spoken these words as he lay dying. He was Rome's first emperor, and started the first of its great building programs. He claimed that he had had more than 80 temples rebuilt.

E. Sarah is playing a marble game. She shoots 4 marbles on the board. Each time a marble goes into a hole, she scores the number of points beside the hole. Sarah scores 25 pints for her 4 marbles. Which holes could the marbles have rolled into?

Enriching Content Classes for Secondary ESOL Students (National Edition)
Study Guide Section 4: Academic Competence, Part B

115

Selecting and Adapting a Content Area Text for Use with ESOL Students

Title of Text:	Content Area:

1. Strengths of the text for ESOL students:

2. Problems of the text for ESOL students:

3. Is this text appropriate for ESOL students in mainstream classrooms?

4. List three ways that you would adapt the text for ESOL students:

Strategies for Selecting, Adapting and Using Content Area Materials with ESOL Students

Criteria for Selecting Materials	• Materials are clearly and simply written. • Length is manageable. • There are many pictures that are closely related to the written text. • There are many charts and graphs. • There are many activities to use with text. • The text is clearly demarcated with headings, sub-divisions, and bold text for important points. • Materials take a multicultural point of view in illustrations, selections of materials, and background information expected. • The text includes a glossary with pronunciation information
Adapting less-than-ideal Materials	• Select excerpts including key points. • Find translations. • Supplement with or substitute more accessible materials. • Use concrete, specific examples of the concepts/points being explored. • Use many non-linguistic aids including pictures, graphs, charts, artifacts, tables, maps, and objects. • Focus students' attention on the essentials. • Allow students to explore the subject together and negotiate meaning through their native language.
Using Materials	• Use directed reading–preview, read, review. Ask many questions to guide and check comprehension strategy. • Teach students learning strategies for getting to the essence of the text. • Use text in combination with highly interactive activities, e.g., jigsaw, numbered heads. • Address and discuss cultural bias that is present; add other cultural points of view.

Source: *Empowering ESOL teachers: An overview.* (No date). Tallahassee, FL: Florida Department of Education, p. 159.

Enriching Content Classes for Secondary ESOL Students (National Edition)
Study Guide Section 4: Academic Competence, Part B

117

Summary of Graphics for
From Text to Graphics and Back Again *

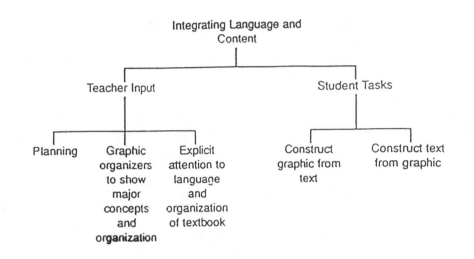

CLASSIFICATION/CONCEPTS	PRINCIPLES	EVALUATION
Homo Habilis—early tool-using ancestors of modern man **Homo Erectus**—first human to walk upright **Neanderthal**—more sophisticated tools and social structure **Cro-Magnon**—most technically advanced of early people	**Homo Erectus** • use of fire allowed migration to colder climates • development of stronger tools and weapons allowed Homo Erectus to kill larger animals **Cro-Magnon Man** • sophistication allowed them to survive the ice age • development of farming provided food for long periods of time	
	Homo Habilis • 1.75 million to 800,000 years ago **Homo Erectus** • 1.25 million to 250,000 years ago **Neanderthal Man** • 130,000 to 30,000 years ago **Cro-Magnon Man** • 30,000 to 10,000 years ago	
DESCRIPTION	**SEQUENCE**	**CHOICE**

* Excerpted from Tang, G. (Winter 1992/1993). Teaching content knowledge and ESOL in multicultural classrooms. *TESOL Journal* 2 (2), pp. 8-12. Used with permission.

Enriching Content Classes for Secondary ESOL Students (National Edition)
Study Guide Section 4: Academic Competence, Part B

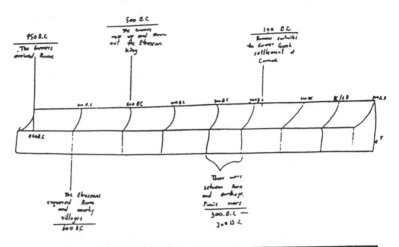

Cause	Effect
The Roman Empire expanded rapidly.	Romans had to spend a lot of time and energy defending their empire from invaders.
Angry Italians wanted the advantages of Roman citizenship. They threatened to rebel and attack Rome.	The Romans granted citizenship to the Italians.
Many internal problems existed • Poor people were starving • Government officials became corrupt • Consuls were assassinated • Slaves rebelled against rough treatment from masters.	The republican system was weakened.

There were 3 major events leading to the end of the Roman Republic. First, the rapid expansion of the Roman Empire caused the Romans to spend a lot of time and energy defending their Empire from invaders. The second reason was that angry Italians wanted the advantages of Roman citizenship. They threatened to rebel and attack Rome. The government survive without them so the Romans granted citizenship to the Italians. Last, the Republican system was weakened because poor people were starving, government officials became corrupt, consuls were assassinated and slaves rebelled against rough treatment from masters.

Written by
Jimmy

Enriching Content Classes for Secondary ESOL Students (National Edition)
Study Guide Section 4: Academic Competence, Part B

119

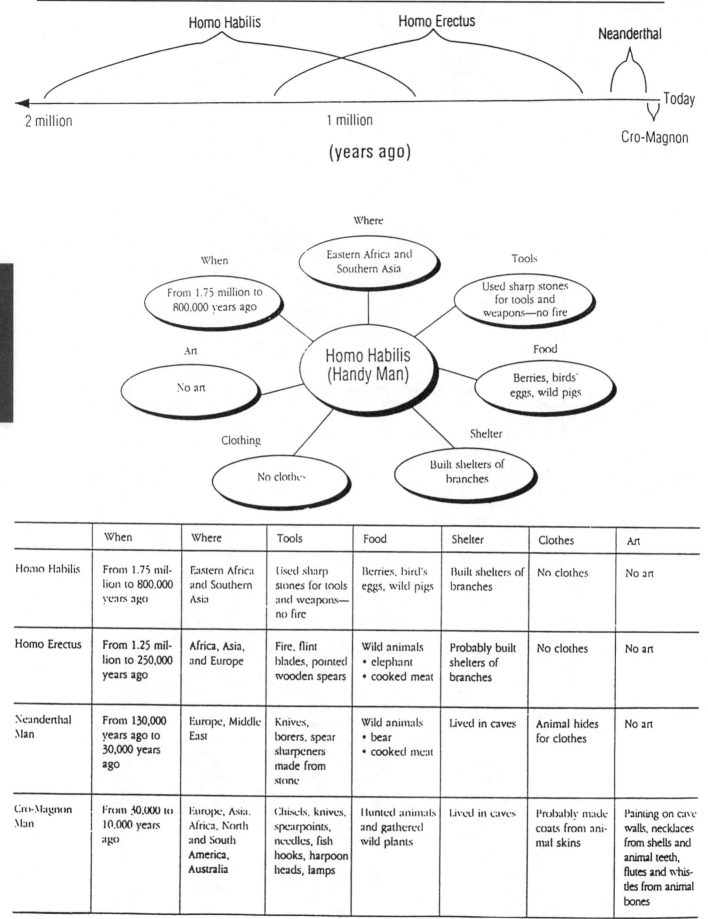

	When	Where	Tools	Food	Shelter	Clothes	Art
Homo Habilis	From 1.75 million to 800,000 years ago	Eastern Africa and Southern Asia	Used sharp stones for tools and weapons—no fire	Berries, bird's eggs, wild pigs	Built shelters of branches	No clothes	No art
Homo Erectus	From 1.25 million to 250,000 years ago	Africa, Asia, and Europe	Fire, flint blades, pointed wooden spears	Wild animals • elephant • cooked meat	Probably built shelters of branches	No clothes	No art
Neanderthal Man	From 130,000 years ago to 30,000 years ago	Europe, Middle East	Knives, borers, spear sharpeners made from stone	Wild animals • bear • cooked meat	Lived in caves	Animal hides for clothes	No art
Cro-Magnon Man	From 30,000 to 10,000 years ago	Europe, Asia, Africa, North and South America, Australia	Chisels, knives, spearpoints, needles, fish hooks, harpoon heads, lamps	Hunted animals and gathered wild plants	Lived in caves	Probably made coats from animal skins	Painting on cave walls, necklaces from shells and animal teeth, flutes and whistles from animal bones

Practice Activity Using "From Text to Graphics and Back Again"

Directions: Use this page as a worksheet for the practice activity. The steps in the activity are:

1. Preview a chapter and determine how it is organized and what its key concepts are.

2. Choose and draw a graphic organizer that will help students understand the organization of the text and/or important content and relationships in the chapter.

3. Write several, simple sentences that express the content and relationships illustrated in the organizer.

4. Describe a student writing task which would use the content, language, and relationships in the organizer.

Enriching Content Classes for Secondary ESOL Students (National Edition)
Study Guide Section 4: Academic Competence, Part B

121

Outside Assignment #2:

Using the "From Text to Graphics and Back Again" Technique in the Classroom

Directions:

1. Select a new chapter from your content text.

2. Develop a plan to teach this chapter using the "From Text to Graphics and Back Again" technique. Be sure to "close the loop" by including a student writing task.

3. Teach the chapter and reflect on your experience.

4. Write-up your unit and turn it in as Outside Assignment #2 using the following outline:

   a. Describe what you did
   b. Tell how it worked
   c. Describe what you would do differently next time
   d. Attach your assessment of your own unit using the instrument/ criteria developed by your small group

5. Be prepared to share your experience with others.

122

Enriching Content Classes for Secondary ESOL Students (National Edition)
Study Guide Section 4: Academic Competence, Part B

Worksheet for Draft Criteria
to Evaluate Outside Assignment #2

Directions: Work with your small group to draft a set of criteria to assess Outside Assignment #2.

Enriching Content Classes for Secondary ESOL Students (National Edition)
Study Guide Section 4: Academic Competence, Part B

123

Strategies and Techniques: Content Area Priorities

Directions: (a) Skim the article entitled *Integrating Language and Content Instruction*, then assign one or two of the categories below to each member of your small group, reread the article noting strategies that are good ideas for your content area in your assigned category. (b) Share the ideas generated in each category within your small group. (c) Review the list individually and circle one or two items in each category that you will implement in your classroom.

1. Increase Comprehensibility

-
-
-
-
-

2. Increase Interaction

-
-
-
-
-

3. Increase Thinking / Study Skills

-
-
-
-
-

4. Make Connections (to other content areas, to students' interests, and to other cultures)

-
-
-
-
-

5. Modify Assessment

-
-
-
-
-

Integrating Language and Content Instruction: Strategies and Techniques
by Deborah J. Short

Introduction

The number of limited English proficient (LEP) students in American schools for school year 1989-90 was estimated at approximately 1,927,828 which represented around 5.2 percent of all students in school (U.S. Department of Education, 1991). The previous school year (1988-89), the percentage of LEP students in U.S. schools was estimated at about 4.6 percent (U.S. Department of Education, 1991). The increase in LEP students has been dramatic in many areas of the country. This rapid growth implies that many teachers are finding an increasing number of students in their classrooms who have to master content matter in a language that is still in the process of being learned. Research indicates that the academic language utilized in content areas acts as a barrier to the success in school of many LEP students (Cummins, 1981). Postponing content instruction until these LEP students master English sufficiently to keep pace with their English-speaking peers often results in underachievement and eventual school leaving.

Current research in second language acquisition indicates that a critical element in effective English as a second language instruction is access to comprehensible input in English (Krashen & Biber, 1988). One way to provide comprehensible input directly to the LEP student is by teaching content in English using strategies and techniques that make the content comprehensible to the second language learner. Research confirms that students in classes where such strategies and techniques are employed acquire impressive amounts of English and learn content matter as well (Krashen & Biber, 1988). It has long been known that a second language can be effectively learned when it is the medium of instruction, not the object (Lambert & Tucker, 1972; Campbell, Gray, Rhodes & Snow, 1985)

The philosophical basis underlying language and content integration is that a child's whole education is a shared responsibility distributed among all teachers. The integration of language and content involves the incorporation of content material into language classes as well as the modification of language and materials in order to provide for comprehensible input to LEP students in content classes. The former is often referred to as content-based language instruction; the latter can be referred to as language-sensitive content instruction. An integrated approach bridges the gap that often separates the language and content classrooms. By utilizing an integrated approach, LEP students can begin academic studies earlier. Such an approach increases the understanding of subject matter by LEP students, which facilitates their academic success. At the same time, the LEP students are able to increase their proficiency levels in the English language.

An Integrated Language and Content Approach

The approach presented here focuses on three principal factors which apply equally to the language and the content teachers:
- the use of multiple media
- the enhancement of the students' thinking skills
- student-centered organization of instruction

Source: Short, D. J. (1991). *Integrating Language and Content Instruction: Strategies and Techniques* (Program Information Guide No. 7) Washington D.C.: National Clearinghouse for Bilingual Education.

Enriching Content Classes for Secondary ESOL Students (National Edition)
Study Guide Section 4: Academic Competence, Part B

125

In order to make English language input as comprehensible as possible, the teachers should present information through diverse media: realia, graphs, demonstrations, pre-reading, and pre-writing strategies. The focus of the instruction should be motivated by the content to be learned, which will help identify the language skills required to learn that content and the reasoning abilities needed to manipulate it (analyzing, synthesizing, and evaluating). Instruction should be student-centered where the teacher has the role of facilitator with the goal of increasing student-to-student interaction.

Content and language instruction can be integrated at any level. The focus here will be on middle and high schools (grades 6-12).

Strategies and Techniques

The following guidelines, strategies and techniques are for middle and high school teachers who wish to use an integrated approach in their classes. Many of these are things that good teachers do naturally; however, it is worth enumerating them here so that their relationship to integrated instruction is explicit. The list is not exhaustive; rather it reflects activities teachers can incorporate as they begin to integrate language and content instruction. Teachers may find that adaptations of techniques they currently use will be appropriate to an integrated approach as well.

Several of the strategies and techniques described below are used in the model lesson plans that follow. These lesson plans describe language and content objectives, the thinking/study skills that may be addressed, the general theme and vocabulary, the necessary materials, the basic procedure, and extension activities for enrichment and other uses.

Preparing for the Integrated Approach
The following sequential steps are recommended during the planning of integrated instruction.

Observe classrooms
The language teacher should see what academic language and instructional methods and materials the content teacher is using, while the content teacher can see which strategies the language teacher uses with LEP students.

Collaborate with colleagues
Working together, language and content teachers should identify the language and/or academic difficulties and demands that particular subjects or courses may present for LEP students. Some examples of those demands are
- reading textbooks
- completing worksheets
- writing reports
- doing library research
- solving mathematical and scientific word problems
- using rhetorical styles in essays (e.g., cause and effect, compare and contrast, argue and persuade)

126

Enriching Content Classes for Secondary ESOL Students (National Edition)
Study Guide Section 4: Academic Competence, Part B

Examine the content materials
The teachers should identify specific problems LEP students may have with material in advance. Such problems do not result solely from the complexity of the passages, but from factors like the skills needed to complete accompanying exercises.

Select a theme
The teachers can develop several lessons around a theme. The theme should be addressed in the language and content classes. For example, an environmental theme, such as deforestation, might be the focus of ESL and science lessons. (The model lessons that follow designed around themes.)

Identify objectives of the unit
While developing the curriculum and syllabus for a course, teachers should keep in mind the specific objectives and adjust the material accordingly in order to eliminate extraneous detail that may confuse a LEP student.

Identify key terms and words
Key terms can be pulled out and introduced in advance. The teachers should reinforce the new vocabulary throughout the lesson. Of particular interest are words that can clue students in to what is expected of them, such as the terms *altogether, more,* and *less* in math word problems, and *contrast* in expository writing.

Look for appropriate text materials
The language teacher can choose content passages that illustrate the language structures or functions being taught. The content teacher can look for alternate versions of general textbooks that present the subject matter more clearly for LEP students or can adapt materials to suit the language proficiency level of the students.

Adapt written materials
If a lesson objective is to present new content information to LEP students, it is important to make materials more comprehensible to the LEP students. (How to do this is discussed below.)

Helping the LEP Student Adjust to the Classroom
LEP students are still learning English and the style of the American education system, so teachers should take this into consideration when presenting information.

Announce the lesson's objectives and activities
It is important to write the objectives on the board and review them orally before class begins. It is also helpful to place the lesson in the context of its broader theme and preview upcoming lessons.

Write legibly
Teachers need to remember that some students have low levels of literacy or are unaccustomed to the Roman alphabet.

Develop and maintain routines
Routines will help LEP students anticipate what will happen (e.g., types of assignments,

Enriching Content Classes for Secondary ESOL Students (National Edition)
Study Guide Section 4: Academic Competence, Part B

127

ways of giving instructions) without relying solely on language clues.

List and review instructions step by step
Before students begin an activity, teachers should familiarize them with the entire list of instructions. Then, teachers should have students work on each step individually before moving on to the next step. This procedure is ideal for teaching students to solve math and science word problems.

Present information in varied ways
By using multiple media in the classroom, teachers reduce the reliance on language and place the information in a context that is more comprehensible to the students.

Provide frequent summations of the salient points of the lesson
- try to use visual reviews with lists and charts
- paraphrase the salient points where appropriate
- have students provide oral summaries themselves

Adjusting Teaching Style
It is important to provide LEP students with ample opportunities for interaction and participation in the classroom. Teachers should not rely on a lecture approach. They should be more conscious of their own speech patterns and tolerant of their students' mistakes.

Develop a student-centered approach to teaching and learning
Teachers need to become facilitators and let students assume more responsibility for their learning. When activities are planned that actively involve students in each lesson, the students can better process the material presented and acquire the language as well.

Reduce and adjust teacher talk
Increasing the amount of student communication about the subject matter is important.
- Allow students more time to speak.
- Concentrate on talking about the subject material rather than about classroom discipline.
- Be prepared to rephrase questions and information if the students do not understand the first time.

Increase the percentage of inferential and higher-order thinking questions asked
These questions encourage students' reasoning ability, such as hypothesizing, inferencing, analyzing, justifying, and predicting. The language used by the teacher or students need not be complex for thinking skills to be exercised. For example, to help students predict, a teacher might read the title of a story and ask, "What will this story tell us?" Teachers need to model critical thinking skills in a step-by-step approach to reasoning.

Recognize that students will make language mistakes
During the second language acquisition process, students make mistakes; this is natural in the process of learning a language. Make sure that the students have understood the information, but do not emphasize the grammatical aspect of their responses. When possible, though, model the correct grammar form.

Teaching Multilevel Classes
Frequently, teachers have classes with students of mixed abilities/proficiency levels. There

are several strategies that can help when these situations arise.

Use cooperative learning
This strategy provides for diversity and individuality in learning styles and aids students in the socialization process. Pair and group activities promote student interaction and decrease the anxiety many students feel when they must perform alone for the teacher in front of the class. It is important for each student in the group to have a task that he or she may accomplish and thus contribute to the activity (e.g., by being recorder, final copy scribe, illustrator, materials collector, reporter). The ideal size for these groups ranges from two to five students. (See Cochran, 1989, for additional suggestions.) Special considerations should be given to students whose home culture may make them feel uncomfortable participating in cooperative learning activities. While all students should be invited to participate, the teacher should respect the wishes of any student who prefers not to participate.

Incorporate peer tutoring
The students learn and share among themselves with the teacher as a facilitator who checks on the students' understanding and progress. The tutors learn to explain and clarify concepts while the tutored students have the benefit of one-on-one interaction in a non-threatening manner. Some supplemental textbooks, such as *English Skills for Algebra* (Crandall, et. al., 1989), are specifically designed as peer instruction materials.

Incorporate process writing
Process writing, though initially implemented in language arts classes, is easily extended into content-area classes. As with process writing exercises, students begin with pre-writing activities such as viewing a film or sharing the reading of an article that sets the stage for the content area topic. The class may also review key concepts and vocabulary to incorporate into the writing. During the process the students learn about language–specific to the content topic selected–in a meaningful and motivating manner. Word processing programs are particularly useful with process writing and should be used if available. They facilitate the draft and edit stages of the process and also allow students to concentrate on their writing style and organization, not on their handwriting.

Design lessons for discovery learning
These activities allow students to discover new information on their own with guidance from the teacher. Teachers help organize the data and sometimes set out the procedures for students to follow. Students, individually or in groups, discover the results. Problem-solving activities (math) and open-ended experiments (science) are examples of discovery learning.

Use inquiry learning
In these activities, students investigate a topic of their own choosing and teachers act as facilitators. They identify a problem, hypothesize causes, design procedures or experiments, and conduct research to try to solve the problem. These activities work well in science and social studies classes.

Include information gap activities
These activities, which include jigsaws, problem solving, and simulations, are set up so each student (in a class, or more generally, in a group) has one or two pieces of information needed to solve the puzzle but not all the necessary information. Students must work

Enriching Content Classes for Secondary ESOL Students (National Edition)
Study Guide Section 4: Academic Competence, Part B

129

together, sharing information while practicing their language, negotiating, and critical thinking skills.

Plan lessons around questionnaires/interviews
Designing questionnaires and interviewing respondents are excellent activities for heterogeneous groups. In the design phase, all students can contribute and evaluate questions for inclusion. In the interview phase, the number of people each student may be expected to interview can be adjusted to the student's ability. Also interviews may be conducted in students' first languages, though responses must be reported in English. A report and analysis of the interview responses may be conduct orally or in writing.

Motivating Students and Providing Background Knowledge
Many LEP students are at a disadvantage in content classes because they lack necessary background knowledge and/or experiential familiarity with the topic at hand. Teachers must plan activities in their instruction to provide some background schema for these students.

Motivate students with semantic webbing
Often used as a pre-writing activity, semantic webbing is also an excellent task for students before they read or discuss a new topic. This more sophisticated version of brainstorming allows students to organize their thoughts and categorize information. Students (with or without the teacher's assistance) may list items first and web later or they may web as they list, creating new strands as categories occur to them. The web is then used by the students as they write on the topic (in the example below, the War of 1812), using the categories to organize their thoughts into paragraph form.

In the following example, students start with the War of 1812 and add on more information about the historical event. (The numbers represent the order of students' ideas in building the web.)

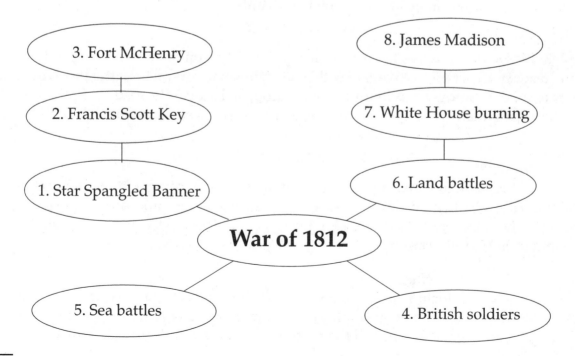

Use realia, illustrations, maps, photos
Although the use of realia and other visual materials is a common activity for language classes, it is less frequently found in content classes. These items provide a quick, often non-language-dependent means of introducing students to the lesson topic.

Organize students into small groups and then share with whole class
The teacher may announce the lesson topic for the day and ask small groups of students to list what they already know about it. After a few minutes, the teacher has the groups share their ideas with the class as a whole.

Include "theme" listening activities
Sometimes it is helpful to get students "in the mood" for a topic. The stage may be set by asking students just to listen to a song, a poem, or even a short story and having a brief discussion about it afterward.

Include discussion of student experience
While introducing new topics in class, encourage students to share knowledge they may already have about the topic, along with any relevant real-life experiences they may have had.

Begin units with the K-W-L technique
Using a standard from (see sample below), teachers distribute the "Know-Want-Learned" sheet to students individually at the start of each unit. Students complete the first two categories at this point. The "learned" category is completed at the close of the unit.

UNIT THEME: *Food Groups*

What I know about *Food Groups:*

What I want to learn about *Food Groups:*

What I learned about *Food Groups:*

Adapting Traditional ESL Techniques to the Content Classrooms
Language teachers providing content-based instruction and content teachers teaching LEP students can modify the following ESL techniques for their lessons.

Bring realia into the lessons
Teachers should use visual displays (e.g., graphs, charts, photos), objects, and authentic materials, like newspaper and magazine clippings, in the lessons and assignments. These help provide nonverbal information and also help match various learning styles.

Do demonstrations
When teachers use actions, they can show the meaning of new words (especially verbs), explain a science experiment, model language functions in the context of a dialogue, etc.

Use filmstrips, videotapes, and audiocassettes with books
Borrowing films and other audiovisual materials from school/district media centers can help improve a content lesson. It is useful to preview the audiovisual materials before

Enriching Content Classes for Secondary ESOL Students (National Edition)
Study Guide Section 4: Academic Competence, Part B

131

showing them to the class, both for possible language difficulties and misleading cultural information.

Have the students do hands-on activities
Content teachers should plan for students to manipulate new material through hands-on activities, such as role plays and simulations, TPR (total physical response), laboratory experiments, drawing pictures and story sequences, and writing their own math word problems.

Design lessons with music and jazz chant activities
Language teachers frequently use music and chants in their classes. These activities are motivating for students and also help teach English pronunciation and intonation patterns. Songs and chants on subject area topics would work well, too. Although some high school students may be reticent to sing aloud in class, all students should be able to do listening activities with music and chants.

Schedule sustained silent reading (SSR) sessions
As educators try to promote more student reading both in and out of school, many teachers (often reading, language arts, and ESL) have incorporated sustained silent reading in their classes. SSR adapts easily to content classes and is particularly effective in middle schools. Once a week, for example, students choose a book or magazine and read silently for 20-30 minutes. The teacher reads, too. Teachers with LEP students can stock their classrooms with magazines, picture books, reference books, and trade books on topics they are studying. There need not be any discussion about the reading selections, but some teachers may ask students to fill out reading logs (described below).

Meeting the Students' Cognitive Academic Needs
In many instances, LEP students need coaching and practice to improve their cognitive processing and production of content material. In order to do so, it is important for teachers to build upon the skills and knowledge students have already mastered. Each lesson should include critical thinking and/or study skills. Some of these skills may have been initially developed in the students' first language and will transfer to English.

Examine the topic through the students' listening and speaking skills first; then expand the topic through reading and writing activities.
Since the students' oral language skills usually develop more rapidly than their written skills, teachers can check the students' comprehension orally and clarify any trouble spots before introducing any reading or writing activities.

Be conscious of different learning styles
Teachers can help meet the different learning styles of their students by varying the presentation and reinforcement of information.
- Alternate activities to address the visual, aural, tactile, and kinesthetic modes of learning.
- Find out if your students prefer to learn from listening to theory or from applying information through hands-on activities.
- When reteaching information, choose a different mode of instruction. (For more information, see Hainer, et al., 1990.)

Incorporate thinking skill activities

When planning each lesson, teachers must create opportunities to focus on thinking skills. Thinking skills can be developed through teacher-student questioning or through scheduled activities like problem solving and decision making.

- Predicting, categorizing, and inferencing are easily addressed in the warm-up and motivation phases of a lesson.
- Observing, reporting, and classifying, which can be done orally, in writing, or pictorially, fit nicely into the presentation and application phases.
- Sequencing, summarizing, and justifying are skills that suit lesson reviews.

Teach study skills

LEP students frequently need assistance in learning how to study. This is especially true of students in middle schools. By teaching them study skills, teachers will give the students an important tool that they can use throughout their academic careers. Show students how to develop and use graphic organizers:

- **outlines** for summarizing, for making predictions
- **time lines** for organizing and sequencing events chronologically, for comparing events in different settings (e.g., states, countries)
- **flow charts** for showing progression and influences on an outcome, for showing cause and effect
- **mapping** for examining movement and spatial relations
- **graphs and charts** for organizing and comparing data
- **Venn diagrams** for comparing and contrasting

The following is a sample Venn diagram to use to examine Christopher Columbus and Neil Armstrong. Where the two circles intersect, students write some similarities. Where the circles do not intersect, students write some differences. (Some students may only write a few words,; others, several sentences.) This structure can become the draft for an essay comparing and contrasting the two explorers.

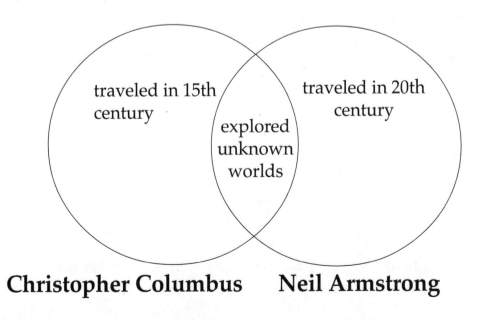

traveled in 15th century

explored unknown worlds

traveled in 20th century

Christopher Columbus   **Neil Armstrong**

Enriching Content Classes for Secondary ESOL Students (National Edition)
Study Guide Section 4: Academic Competence, Part B

133

Develop the students' ability to use texts and other written materials
Since the acquisition of details within a particular content topic is not the primary objective of the language course, teachers have more time to develop the students' skills in analyzing.

- **Text as a whole**-Teachers demonstrate how to use (a) the parts of a book (table of contents, index) to find information and (b) headings, subheadings, and illustrations in chapters to organize and enhance the information.
- **Passages**-Teachers help students learn to draw inferences, synthesize information, make judgements, and provide justifications.

However, because these skills are demanded of the students once they are mainstreamed, content teachers need to incorporate activities to review student knowledge in their areas, too.

Plan activities to train the students in attacking academic tasks, such as research projects, problem solving, and essay writing
Carefully planned academic activities help students make the transition from language class to mainstream content class. Teachers may plan a library project, for example, and walk the students through it step by step, preferably with peer tutors. They may also use process writing methods to help students write essays and research reports.

Present models for writing assignments
Assignments required by mainstream content classes, like research papers and laboratory reports, are of particular interest to LEP students and their teachers. It is beneficial to discuss the model clearly so that the students know how each section is structured and why each section is important. Students should then be given practice using the model before doing a required assignment with it.

Checking Student Comprehension of the Content

Use strip stories, sentence strips
Teachers write a summary of a lesson or reading passage or write out the steps for solving a math problem or for doing a science experiment on individual strips-either one sentence per strip or several sentences. These strips are distributed, out of sequence, to the students, in groups or as a whole class. The students then organize the strips into the proper sequence.
Sample strips for math:

$$2 \tfrac{1}{2} + 3 \tfrac{1}{4} =$$
$$5/2 + 13/4 =$$
$$10/4 + 13/4 =$$
$$23/4 =$$
$$5 \tfrac{3}{4} =$$

Set up dialogue journals
Many school systems are adopting "writing across the curriculum" approaches to encourage and improve student writing. Often teachers will use journal writing in their classes.

Dialogue journals go one step further by having teachers respond to student writing in positive and supportive ways. Dialogue journals are not vehicles for editing student work; they are opportunities for students to express themselves. (For further discussion, see Peyton & Reed, 1990)

Teachers decide how often they want students to write (e.g., daily, twice a week) and how often they will read and comment on the journals. Some teachers will respond to every piece of writing; others will respond once a week or less. The teacher comments may vary in length and depth also. Also, teachers may ask less proficient students to start with illustrations in their journals and slowly move into writing. In this way all students in a heterogeneous class can participate.

Some teachers choose to let writing be entirely student-derived; others provide the topics, at least some of the time. Some teachers use dialogue journals for lesson closure or motivation by having students summarize what they learned in the lesson (that day or the day before).

Although dialogue journals are not designed for correcting student work, they can guide teacher instruction. Teachers who see consistent problems in student writing or in student comprehension of the lesson topics can develop new lessons to address those issues.

Plan activities using drama and role play
Another language teaching technique that works well in the content classroom is using drama. Teachers can ask groups of students to act out an event or a topic studied, from the sprouting of a plant to a mock legislative debate in the state government. Teachers may assign roles impromptu or may have groups research and write dialogues before performing. Mime also works well with students from beginning to advanced levels of English proficiency.

Have students complete reading logs
These logs can be used in any content class to reflect reading done from a textbook, a supplemental reader, a trade book or magazine, and newspaper articles. Three categories may be set up on a standard from (see below):
What I understood, What I didn't understand, and what I learned.

Reading title: _____	
What I understood:	What I didn't understand:
What I learned:	

SECTION 4

Check comprehension with cloze exercises
Cloze exercises, popular for assessing reading comprehension, may also be applied to different subject areas. For many clozes, teachers write a summary or take an excerpt (of a reading passage or lesson or class activity) and then delete every *x*th word. Students then "fill in the blank" with teachers deciding if they will score by an exact word or an acceptable word method.

The following is an example of a cloze passage derived from a passage in a civics textbook:

> The First Amendment says we have_____of religion, speech, the press, and _____. We can follow any religion, say_____, write our thoughts, and meet in _____.

Have students do story summaries
As the graphic below shows, this activity has both a written and pictorial component. Students summarize a lesson, reading, or experience (individually or in groups) by drawing illustrations and describing them. A format may look like this:

Illustration	_____

_____	Illustration

Encourage students to write headlines
Students can practice their summarizing skills and, as they get more proficient, their descriptive language skills, by writing news headlines for lessons and topics discussed in class. For example, teachers may ask students to write a headline describing the results of a science experiment or to create a title of an imaginary book review of a book they had read.

Let students perform experiments
Teachers may plan performance-based activities to determine student comprehension of the subject matter. A traditional example is the lab practical for science classes. This idea can be easily adapted to math classes, especially those that use manipulatives.

Incorporate the LEA (Language Experience Approach) method
This method has grown out of the movement to teach adults literacy skills, namely to read and write. After students have an experience (e.g., going on a field trip), they dictate to the teacher a summary of what happened. (Teachers usually record on the board exactly what the students say.) Students then work together to organize the written ideas and if desired make corrections. Teachers may copy the dictation to use another day for review, motivation, or even a lesson on editing.

In a class with mixed proficiency levels of students, this activity can work well in small groups. The most proficient student in the group can be the scribe while the others contribute, organize, and edit their work.

Have students write character diaries
Frequently in social studies and from time to time in other subjects, the lives of important individuals in the field are studied. Students may read biographies and trade books or watch films and videos and then write a character diary, chronicling a week or two in the life of a particular individual. Students place special emphasis on the setting of the diary as well as the path toward accomplishment that the individual underwent during the week(s).

Developing Lesson Plans

In integrated lessons teachers and students work toward content and language objectives. When developing lesson plans for integrated instruction, it is important to identify both types of objectives and plan activities accordingly. It is often useful to specify critical thinking or study skills to target as well. A teacher's or school district's preferred lesson format can then be used to develop the lesson.

The lesson format presented below includes four phases: (1) warm up or motivation; (2) presentation of new material, in whole group or small group work; (3) practice and application of new material; and (4) review or informal assessment to check student understanding. Most lessons also contain extension activities to reinforce or extend the concepts covered. A series of lessons thematically linked into units provides for sustained student interest as well as the opportunity to build systematically on prior activities.

The model lesson plans in this section deliberately offer an extensive range of techniques and strategies. They demonstrate the possibilities available to teachers for making integrated language and content more comprehensible. It is important to note that teachers may not have time to incorporate all these suggestions into their lesson plans every day but should try to vary the activities they plan.

Certain procedures are more critical than others. These are

1. selecting principal vocabulary terms to teach as a pre-activity

2. providing the opportunity for students to discuss the information and material orally, preferably before any written work is assigned

3. designing class activities for student-to-student interaction

4. deciding to use real literature or adapted materials

The following model lesson outline may be used for integrated language and content lessons. While all lessons should include some language and some content objectives, an individual lesson need not address all the subcategories within. Some lessons may reach content objectives from different subject areas, such as math (use division) and science (calculate average rainfall). Some may have literature; some may not. Some may focus on reading skills without listening practice. Following the model are two sample lessons illustrating the use of this outline and some of the strategies discussed earlier. [Ed. note: Only one lesson has been excerpted here.]

Lesson Plan Format: Integrated Instruction
THEME
LESSON TOPIC
OBJECTIVES
    Language Skills
        Speaking/Listening
        Reading/Writing
        Structures
    Content Skills
    Thinking/Study skills
    Key Vocabulary
LITERATURE
MATERIALS
MOTIVATION
PRESENTATION
PRACTICE/APPLICATION
REVIEW/EVALUATION
EXTENSION

References

Campbell, R., Gray, T., Rhodes, N., and Snow, M. (1985). Foreign language learning in the elementary schools: A comparison of three language programs. *The Modern Language Journal.* Vol 69, Issue 1, pp. 44-54.

Cochran, C. (1989). *Strategies for Involving LEP Students in the All-English-Medium Classroom: A Cooperative Learning Approach.* Washington, DC.: National Clearinghouse for Bilingual Education.

Crandall, J. , Dale, T., Rhodes, N., and Spanow, G. (1989) *English Skills for Algebra.* Englewood Cliffs, NJ: Center for Applied Linguistics/Prentice Hall Regents.

Cummins, J. The role of primary language development in promoting success for language minority students. In California State Department of Education (Ed.), *Schooling and Language Minority Students: A Theoretical Framework.* Los Angeles, CA: California State University; Evaluation, Dissemination, and Assessment Center

Hainer, E., Fagan, B., Bratt, T., Baker, L., and Arnold, N. (1990). *Integrating Language Styles and Skills in the ESL Classroom: An Approach to Lesson Planning.* Washington DC: National Clearinghouse for Bilingual Education.

Krashen, S., and Biber, D. (1988). *On Course: Bilingual Education's Success in California.* Sacramento, CA: California Association for Bilingual Education.

Lambert, W. and Tucker, G.R. (1972). *Bilingual Education of Children.* Rowley, MA: Newbury House

United States Department of Education. (1991). *The Condition of Bilingual Education in the Nation: A Report to the Congress and the President.* Washington DC: Office of the Secretary, U.S. Department of Education.

Sample Lesson 2

This model lesson plan was created for ESOL students, but may be adapted for mainstream grades 6-12. If presented in full detail, the lesson may require one to two weeks.

KEY THEME: Environmental Pollution

TOPIC:	Littering (Solid Waste)
OBJECTIVES:	
Content:	Recognize environmental problems
	Identify litter and patterns of littering
	Identify human influences on the environment
Language:	
Listening/Speaking:	Recite/listen to a dialogue with meaningful content
	Discuss environmental issues as a whole class and in small groups
	Conduct interviews and report orally
Reading/Writing:	Design a questionnaire, writing questions
	Complete a list or chart
	Write in a journal
Structure:	Question Formation
Thinking Skills:	Analyze Problems Generate Solutions Infer reasons for human actions
Key Vocabulary:	Litter, garbage, dump, mess, environment, trash, cause, solution, solid waste, pollution, survey

Enriching Content Classes for Secondary ESOL Students (National Edition)
Study Guide Section 4: Academic Competence, Part B

139

Materials: Teacher-made dialogue, poster, items of trash (empty soda cans, paper wrappers, broken glass, etc.)

Motivation: *(Before lesson is presented)*

Two weeks before introducing this topic, hang a scenic poster on the wall. Some students may comment on the lovely view or ask vocabulary questions about objects in the scene. Every other day, attach an item that might be considered trash (candy wrappers, an empty box, an aluminum can) to the poster, thus creating a trash collage. The students may be curious, but do not reveal the purpose.

This activity whets the students' interest and visually represents some background information about the topic.

(To introduce the lesson)

Turn to the "Trash Collage" and ask students what they think it represents. Write student ideas on the board. Finally, through guided questioning, if necessary, lead the students to recognize that the lovely place is being ruined by litter.

Changing the focus, turn from the poster scene to the local environment, and add some additional vocabulary to the list. Then ask some of the more advanced students to explain why this happens and write comments on the board. Some students may venture consequences of the littering problem.

All students can participate. Teacher helps them make speech-print connections by writing their comments on the board.

Presentation: Ask two of the more advanced students to volunteer to come to the front of the class and role play the following dialogue:

LITTERING AT SCHOOL

Student 1: Don't throw that on the ground.

Student 2: Why not? What's the big deal?

Student 1: Our school looks like a garbage dump.

Student 2: So what? Tell one of the younger kids to clean it up.

Student 1: But you littered.

Student 2: Everyone does it. Teachers do it too.

Student 1: You're impossible. Do you know what our school will look like if everyone continues to litter?

This dialogue introduces, in an interactive way, some key vocabulary and causes associated with littering.

Enriching Content Classes for Secondary ESOL Students (National Edition)
Study Guide Section 4: Academic Competence, Part B

| *Having begun with concrete examples (poster, dialogue), students can now expand and organize their information.* | On the board, write the headings: PROBLEMS, CAUSES, SOLUTIONS, in chart form. Categorize and expand the vocabulary list with student input. Show students a written form of the dialogue. |

Having begun with concrete examples (poster, dialogue), students can now expand and organize their information.

On the board, write the headings: PROBLEMS, CAUSES, SOLUTIONS, in chart form. Categorize and expand the vocabulary list with student input. Show students a written form of the dialogue.

This activity incorporates some language practice for the students.

In order to check on comprehension and practice writing questions, have the students take dictation. Dictate the following questions:

Where are they?
Who is talking?
What happened?
Why is one student upset?
Does this happen at our school?

Have pairs compare their work and ask volunteers to write their dictations on the board. Encourage students to peer edit. Discuss relevant grammar points (e.g., question words, verb-noun positions).

Ask students to think of additional questions about the dialogue. Write the student-dictated questions on the board. Work as a class to edit errors.

If desired, add questions, such as "Why is there a problem?" (cause) or "What can you do?" (solution).

This paired activity allows for oral language practice in the context of the lesson topic.

Application 1: Have pairs role play the dialogue "Littering at School" and discuss the vocabulary and issues together. Then have pairs ask each other the class-generated questions (more advanced students should answer first).

Students work individually at first, then with peers.

Review: After this structured conversation, ask students to write ten questions and answers about the topic (littering). Before they hand it in, encourage students to peer edit.

This task applies the topic directly to their lives.

Home task: For homework, have students write in their journal about the trash they see as they go to and from school for several days. As this task continues expand the vocabulary list under PROBLEMS and put it on a poster or chart to hang in the room. Make two other posters, one with CAUSES, and the other with SOLUTIONS as well.

This group work offers all students a chance to participate.

Application 2: In small groups, have students discuss the causes of littering, then share ideas with the class. Write them on the CAUSES poster. Then ask groups to consider solutions. Share their suggestions and write on the SOLUTIONS poster.

This activity reinforces the language structure objective.

Next have small groups design a questionnaire to interview classmates, teachers, neighbors, family, and friends. The

Enriching Content Classes for Secondary ESOL Students (National Edition)
Study Guide Section 4: Academic Competence, Part B

141

SECTION 4

questionnaire should be limited to five questions. If needed, help groups plan their questions, but do not provide them with a full list. Possibilities include:

> Does litter bother you?
> Do you litter?
> What do people throw away as litter?
> Why do people litter?
> Who is responsible for solving this problem?
> What can be done about this problem?

Home task: Have students conduct a survey for three days, each interviewing 10 people. (If they interview non-English speakers, they may ask questions in the native language but should write responses in English.)

This task encourages interaction with non-classmates on the topic and may provide clarification practice, as students explain their task to others.

Follow-up and Extension: Have students share this information in their groups. Have recorders in the group organize the results of the survey and a representative of the group reports to the whole class. Help the whole class find ways of organizing and presenting the results of the survey. (Some students may list the results on posters, others may do a chart and quantify the responses. Some may prepare an oral report or a debate between individuals who litter and those who don't. Other students may create a role play or drama. Some may design a visual display or collage, highlighting *before* and *after* scenes.)

Each group contributes to the whole class. Optional presentations allow each group to choose the one best suited to their learning styles and academic skills.

Have students write a composition. Display the papers and, if appropriate, encourage some students to submit their work for publication in a school/class newspaper.

Long-term Projects: Expand this introduction to individual generation of and influence on solid waste pollution to heighten the awareness of students to other sources of solid waste (industrial, agricultural, municipal) and methods of disposal. Design additional lessons to help students research sources of solid waste in their communities and learn about local disposal methods, such as dumping, burying, burning, recycling, etc. Students may want to form action groups to decrease solid waste pollution in their towns.

These projects further students' problem-solving and study skill development.

142

Enriching Content Classes for Secondary ESOL Students (National Edition)
Study Guide Section 4: Academic Competence, Part B

Enriching Content Classes for Secondary ESOL Students

Study Guide

Section 5
Literacy Development and Study Skills

Literacy Development and Study SKills

Goal

To learn to assist ESOL students in developing academic competence through student-development of reading and study skills.

Performance Objectives

• Identify principles and guidelines which assist ESOL students in developing reading strategies in English.

• Apply reading, thinking, and other strategies to content materials.

• Identify ways content teachers can assist ESOL students with low-literacy skills and little formal schooling.

• Identify resources in the school and community to aid teachers and students in these situations.

SECTION 5

Enriching Content Classes for Secondary ESOL Students (National Edition)
Study Guide Section 5: Literacy Development and Study Skills

145

Passages Worksheet

Directions: Listen carefully to the presenter give specific directions for each passage. Then, write, in your own words, the reading principle that this passage illustrates and sample classroom strategies that would implement this principle in your content area. Do not share ideas with other participants until the presenter indicates that you may do so.

Passage #1

a. Topic: _____

b. Reading Principle: _____

_____

c. Classroom Strategies: _____

_____

Passage #2

a. Topic: _____

b. Reading Principle: _____

_____

c. Classroom Strategies: _____

_____

Passage #3

a. Topic: _____ Two Boys _____

b. Reading Principle: _____

_____

c. Classroom Strategies: _____

_____

SECTION 5

DRTA - Directed Reading/Thinking Activity

This strategy begins where Teach the Text Backward ends–i.e., with "read the text." Teachers should teach and model the strategy, but move students toward increasingly independent use.

1. PREVIEW the reading: Teach students to look at the title, headings, summary, and pictures; identify key vocabulary.

2. PREDICT the content: Teach students to make questions from the headings to help identify what they want to learn from reading each section; ask "What is this chapter about?, What seems important in this chapter?, What seems interesting?"

3. READ in sections: Teach students to read in sections, check their predictions, and summarize the main points before continuing. Usually students read silently or for homework; assign shorter sections to ESOL students or use a jigsaw.

4. CHECK the predictions: Teach students to check their predictions by focusing on answers and evidence they found related to their initial questions and predictions; ask students to show the part of the reading that answered a question; use higher order thinking questions and strategies.

5. SUMMARIZE the main points: Teach students to summarize and state the main points or what they learned in their own words either orally or in short written form.

Enriching Content Classes for Secondary ESOL Students (National Edition)
Study Guide Section 5: Literacy Development and Study Skills

147

DRTA Worksheet

Directed Reading/Thinking Activity

Directions: Work in pairs to "walk through" a chapter in a content text using DRTA as if you were teaching students to use this strategy. Record how you will do each of the five steps below. Give examples of questions that you will ask the students where appropriate.

1. PREVIEW the reading

2. PREDICT the content

3. READ in sections

4. CHECK the predictions

5. SUMMARIZE the main points

SECTION 5

Teaching Thinking Skills

QUESTIONING FOR QUALITY THINKING

Knowledge - Identification and recall of information
 Who, what, when, where, how_____?
 Describe_____.

Comprehension - Organization and selection of facts and ideas
 Retell_____in your own words.
 What is the main idea of_____?

Application - Use of facts, rules, principles.
 How is _____an example of _____?
 How is _____related to _____?
 Why is _____significant?

Analysis - Separation of a whole into component parts
 What are the parts or features of _____?
 Classify_____ according to_____.
 Outline/diagram/web_____.
 How does ____compare/contrast with____?
 What evidence can you list for_____?

Synthesis - Combination of ideas to form a new whole
 What would you predict/infer from_____?
 What ideas can you add to_____?
 How would you create/design a new_____?
 What might happen if you combined_____ with_____?
 What solutions would you suggest for____?

Evaluation - Development of opinions, judgement, or decisions
 Do you agree_____?
 What do you think about_____?
 What is the most important_____?
 Prioritize_____.
 How would you decide about_____?
 What criteria would you use to assess_____?

STRATEGIES TO EXTEND STUDENT THINKING

*Remember "wait time I and II"**
 Provide at least three seconds of thinking time after a question and after a response
*Utilize "think-pair-share"**
 Allow individual thinking time, discussion with a partner, then open up for discussion
*Ask "follow-ups"**
 Why? Do you agree? Can you elaborate? Tell me more. Can you give an example?
*Withhold judgment**.
 Respond to student answers in a non-evaluative fashion
*Survey the class**
 "Could you please summarize John's point?"
*Allow for student calling**
 "Richard, will you please call on someone else to respond?"
*Ask students to "unpack" their thinking**
 "Describe how you arrived at your answer." ("think aloud")
*Call on students randomly**
 Not just those with raised hands
*Student questioning**
 Let students develop their own questions
*Cue students' responses**
 "There is not a single correct answer for this question. I want you to consider alternatives."

Source: Language Development and Early Learning Branch, Division of Instruction, Maryland State Department of Education, no date. Used with permission.

Enriching Content Classes for Secondary ESOL Students (National Edition)
Study Guide Section 5: Literacy Development and Study Skills

149

Student Study Guides

A. Guidelines for Preparing Study Guides

    1. Read the passage.
    2. Find the main idea.
    3. Find several supporting details.
    4. Sequence the details logically.
    5. Write the main idea and supporting details in *complete* sentences.
    6. Simplify the sentence structure and vocabulary as much as possible.
    7. Incorporate key vocabulary in the sentences.
    8. Do not include definitions.
    9. Do not include names, dates, or places as a general rule.
    10. List the vocabulary and star items which will be new for the whole class.

B. Uses of Study Guides

    1. Teaching Guide: Teachers can use the guides to focus on the critical concepts and vocabulary that they want to get across to students.

    2. Reference Guide for Tutors: Tutors, paraprofessionals, or buddies can use the guides to focus on the most important points and vocabulary when helping ESOL students study.

    3. Reading Guide for Students: ESOL students can use the guides as outlines for their reading. They should use them to preview the reading, refer to them during reading, and study them after reading.

    4. Primary Reading for Students: Students who have great difficulty reading the textbook may be allowed to read and study the guides as a substitute.

    5. Study Guide for Students: Students can use the guides to review and study for tests.

    6. Developing Evaluation Tools: Teachers should use the guides to develop tests. Removing key words from the main idea and supporting concepts provides a ready-made fill-in-the-blank test.

(Source: Lopez-Valadez, J. and Reed, T. (1989). *Building competencies to serve LEP vocational students: An inservice manual.* Des Plaines, IL: Northwest Educational Cooperative.)

SECTION 5

STUDENT STUDY GUIDE

UNIT_____   TEXT _____

LESSON _____   PAGES _____

MAIN IDEA:

SUPPORTING CONCEPTS:

KEY VOCABULARY:

Enriching Content Classes for Secondary ESOL Students (National Edition)
Study Guide Section 5: Literacy Development and Study Skills

151

STUDENT STUDY GUIDE: EXAMPLE

UNIT _____   TEXT ____ Automotive Encyclopedia ____

LESSON _____   PAGES ____ 271-272 _____

MAIN IDEA:

Air cleaners clean the air that goes into the carburetor.

SUPPORTING CONCEPTS:

Air cleaners remove the dust from the air.

Air cleaners are installed at the air intake of the carburetor.

There are four types of air cleaners:

1) oil wetted mesh cleaners
2) oil bath cleaners
3) polyurethane cleaners
4) paper element cleaners

You clean oil and polyurethane cleaners with kerosene or solvent.
You either replace a paper cleaner or you clean it by tapping.

KEY VOCABULARY:

Remove	Polyurethane	Carburetor
Retain	Accumulated	Filter
Immerse	Wetted	Air Intake
Replace	Perforated	Solvent
Squeeze	Pleated	Particles
Trap		Housing
		Kerosene
		Mesh
		Surface
		Oil
		Cleaner

RAGS—READ AROUND GROUPS

This is an activity designed to help students recognize good written work (lab reports, math problems, explanations, summaries, essays, statements of hypothesis or conclusion, etc.) and the criteria that make it good.

Procedure:

1. Samples of student work for a written assignment is collected, e.g., lab reports, math problems, explanations, summaries, essays, statements of hypothesis or conclusion.

2. Students code their written work with numbers instead of using their own names.

3. Papers are collected by the teacher and students are divided into groups of four or five and given the same number of coded papers.

4. Everyone in each group reads all the papers assigned to their group. This is done by reading for a short timed interval, and then passing the papers around the circle and repeating the process until all papers are read.

5. Each group votes on the one or two papers that meet the criteria best and explains their choice.

6. The teacher tallies the results of the papers voted "best" on the chalkboard and students share their ideas about how and why these papers are most effective in achieving the given purpose, e.g., organization of information, use of descriptive terms, persuasiveness, effectiveness in making its point.

Enriching Content Classes for Secondary ESOL Students (National Edition)
Study Guide Section 5: Literacy Development and Study Skills

153

Suggestions for Working with Low-Literacy Students

1. Make classroom posters which list important things to remember: classroom rules, learning strategies, rules for group work. Label work materials on shelves and in closets.

2. Have students create their own books using pictures, translations, and simplified English summaries of important concepts. Buy or make audio or videotaped "read along" books and student study guides.

3. Use lower grade-level texts and native language materials when available. Explore other resources (see Study Guide Appendix, *Resources*).

4. Keep new vocabulary to a minimum. Have students make flash cards or a picture dictionary for content vocabulary.

5. Simplify language used in an explanation. Limit sentence length. Ask questions to see if s/he understands. Initially, have students point to items to identify or locate instead of requiring student production of language. Later, allow for short, controlled responses progressing from Yes/No to single word answers.

6. Use drama. Create, present, and write short role plays on content topics.

7. Pair a low-literacy student with an English-speaking partner. Vary partners from time to time.

8. In a group situation, such as cooperative learning or a science lab, give the student responsibility for a non-reading activity. Place the student in an average or above average group (NOT a low performing group) to provide good models.

9. Establish a routine. Start each lesson with a statement of what students will do that day and close with a simple summary of the most important points.

10. Share ideas and report progress and successful strategies with the student's other teachers. Take advantage of information and support available from the ESOL office.

11. Be optimistic and enjoy the student's presence.

12. Other:

First Days

- Sensitize the class, promote empathy.

- Pronounce the student's name correctly. Do not anglicize it unless the student asks you to.

- Introduce the student to the class. Make the student feel welcome.

- Learn a few phrases in the student's language and a little about the student's country.

- Be a model for all students by showing respect for the new student.

- Ask an experienced student to be a buddy for the first few days.

- Plan interactive activities that help the new student get to know his peers.

- Find out a little about the student's interests, make connections with other students, classroom lessons, and extracurricular activities.

- Develop long-term goals, minimum competencies for the course, and a grading structure. Communicate these to the student and his parents.

- Help the student learn school routines, rules, and expectations of behavior.

- Use school and community resources: other students, ESOL Resource Teachers, an adult volunteer or mentor.

Source: Adapted from Law, B. and Eckes, M. (2000). *The more-than-just-surviving handbook: ESL for every classroom teacher.* Second ed. Winnipeg, Canada: Portage and Main Press (Peguis Publishers), pages 7-29. Used with permission.

Enriching Content Classes for Secondary ESOL Students (National Edition)
Study Guide Section 5: Literacy Development and Study Skills

155

SECTION 5

Study Skills and Learning Strategies

A. General Study Skills/ Learning Strategies

Preview
Plan what to do
Selective attention: key words/ideas, main idea/specific information
Self-management: plan when, where, how to study; think positively
Monitor own comprehension
Self-assess and reflect

B. Specific Study Skills/ Learning Strategies

Use reference materials
Take notes
Construct graphic organizers
Summarize
Use the writing process
Ask questions
Cooperate with classmates

C. How to Teach Study Skills/ Learning Strategies

1. Increase student awareness

   - Ask students how they learn new vocabulary, read a chapter, approach a new project
   - Think aloud and ask students to think aloud

2. Teach study skills/ learning strategies

   - Model the use of skills and strategies
   - Name the technique and call it by name
   - Explain why the technique helps students learn
   - Describe when and for what kinds of tasks the technique is useful

3. Practice the technique in class and assign it with homework

4. Evaluate its use

   - Debrief students after using the technique
   - Ask for suggestions from successful users

5. Transfer strategies to new tasks

   - Remind students to use a strategy
   - Praise students for independent use

Source: Adapted from Chamot, AU and O'Malley, JM. CALLA handouts at a University of Florida workshop, 1994.

156

Enriching Content Classes for Secondary ESOL Students (National Edition)
Study Guide Section 5: Literacy Development and Study Skills

Enriching Content Classes for Secondary ESOL Students

Study Guide

Section 6
Assessment

Assessment

Goal

To learn to adapt traditional assessments and design alternative assessments to allow ESOL students opportunities to demonstrate their knowledge in the content areas.

Performance Objectives

• Compare and contrast classroom and standardized assessments.

• Identify and reduce language and cultural bias on teacher-made tests.

•Evaluate and improve teacher-made tests.

• Prepare materials to teach test-taking strategies to students.

• Develop personal guidelines for grading ESOL students in mainstream classrooms.

• Develop a practical alternative assessment for content material.

SECTION 6

Classroom vs. Standardized Assessments: Worksheet

	Classroom Assessments	Standardized Assessments
Examples:		
Purposes:		
Pros:		
Cons:		

Enriching Content Classes for Secondary ESOL Students (National Edition)
Study Guide Section 6: Assessment

Teacher -Made Test Checklist (2 pages)

Name _____ Content area _____ Grade Level ____

Directions: Look at the test "through the eyes of an ESOL student" and complete the checklist.

Checklist	Good	Could Be Improved	Don't Know	Comments/Examples
1. Items are clearly written.				
2. Directions are clearly written and easily understood.				
3. Examples of how to respond to items are provided.				
4. Readability level of items and directions is lower than actual grade / age level of students.				
5. Test moves from easy to more difficult items, with the majority of items being average in difficulty.				
6. Test has logical groupings, (e.g., in a history test, items related to colonial history are grouped separately from items related to the civil war).				
7. Test has 3-5 items for each curricular objective in order to yield a better picture of mastery.				
8. Items which require higher order thinking skills are included.				
9. There is a match between what is being tested and the method used for testing (e.g., a multiple choice test of spelling would be inappropriate).				

SECTION 6

Teacher Checklist cont.

Checklist	Good	Could Be Improved	Don't Know	Comments/Examples
10. Test stresses important concepts, not trivia.				
11. Items do not require cultural knowledge.				
12. Test results will help students learn and teachers plan instruction.				
13. Test is criterion-referenced.				
14. Teacher scores short answers and narrative responses based on student's meaning not grammatical errors.				
15. Test is not too long for the time allowed.				
16. Other:				

Source: Adapted from: *Empowering ESOL teachers: An overview.* (No date). Tallahassee, FL: Florida Department of Education, pp. 93-94.

Enriching Content Classes for Secondary ESOL Students (National Edition)
Study Guide Section 6: Assessment

SECTION 6

Test-Taking Strategies

In order to perform well on tests, it is important that students learn about and apply test-taking strategies. Both general test-taking strategies and strategies related to taking specific types of tests are included in this reading. They are intended to serve as the basis for study and class discussion both before and after students take classroom or standardized tests. (Source: Lopez-Valdez, J., and Reed, T. (June 1989). Building competencies to serve LEP vocational students: An inservice manual. Des Plaines, IL: Northwest Educational Cooperative.)

General Strategies

A. Preparing for Tests

1. Try to find out what kind of test will be given. If you know what kind of test to expect, you can practice by asking yourself similar types of questions.

2. Begin preparing for the test as soon as possible. Remember that studying often for short periods is more effective than studying for long hours at one time.

3. When you prepare for a test, think of the task positively! It is the best opportunity to really learn the material for future application.

4. Ask the instructor which concepts and topics are most important to study. Instructors will usually give you this information, although they will not tell you the exact questions on the test.

5. Look at all your notes and readings and organize the information into logical units, such as main topics.

6. Make a study plan by writing down the main topics and adding the most important points to concentrate on.

7. Read all lecture notes and notes from readings, and review important exercises you have done.

8. Make a new set of study notes which contains the most important information.

9. Practice writing difficult words and their definitions.

10. Review your notes on several different days.

11. Test your memory of important facts by looking away from your notes and asking yourself questions.

12. If it's difficult for you to study alone, form a study group. Discussing the subject

SECTION 6

matter with other students helps the memory. However, you should know the basic facts <u>before</u> you study with other people. This is important for two reasons: 1) so that you can contribute your knowledge to the study session, and 2) so that you can recognize incorrect statements when your study partners make them.

B. <u>Before the Test</u>

1. Get a good night's sleep before the test. Being well rested makes it easier to remember what you have learned and studied.

2. Relax. Being too nervous makes it difficult to recall information you know.

3. Don't study anything new the day of the test--this will only make you nervous.

4. Eat a light meal a few hours before the test. Do not take a test on either an empty stomach or a full stomach; this will negatively affect your ability to concentrate.

5. Arrive in the test room a little early so you can make yourself comfortable.

6. Keep an optimistic attitude; don't let negative comments from other students make you nervous.

C. <u>Taking the Test</u>

1. Listen carefully to the teacher's instructions before and after the test is passed out.

2. When you receive the test, look at all of the different parts and pages to see what types of questions and how many questions there are.

3. Budget your time. If it is a long test you may have to decide how long to spend on each part.

4. Read all directions carefully; they may be different from what you expected.

5. Study all examples carefully.

6. If you don't understand what you are supposed to do, ask the instructor.

7. When you begin to write, skip questions which are very difficult and return to them after you have finished the other questions. Often you will find clues to the answer in another part of the test.

8. If you don't know the answer to a question, make a guess (unless it is the type of test on which you lose points for incorrect answers). The concept of "educated guessing" is crucial to test-taking. "Guessing" is the underlying strategy to improving test scores beyond what knowledge of the content area alone would allow. Guessing involves applying knowledge of specific test format and identifying clues in the test items.

9. Your first response is usually correct. Don't change an answer unless you are sure you made a mistake or misunderstood the question.

10. When you have finished answering all the questions, spend as much time as you have left to go back and check your answers.

11. Make sure your name is on the test or answer sheet before you turn it in.

D. After the Test

1. When you get the test back, go over the results carefully.

2. Pay equal attention to the items you got right and those you missed.

3. Add any new information to the ones you got right and make corrections to the items you missed directly on the test form.

4. For the items you missed, try to determine the reason why. Was your study plan a good one?

5. Use the test results to help you improve your plan for studying for the next test.

Specific Strategies

Multiple Choice Test Strategies

1. Try to figure out the answer before you look at the choices.

2. Read all the choices before you pick one. If they do not seem 100% correct, take the closest one.

3. If you are recording your answers on a separate answer sheet (especially machine-graded answer sheets), make sure that you mark your answers accurately.

4. Choices with absolute expressions such as "always, all, never" and "none" are usually incorrect.

5. Choices with expressions which are more "flexible," such as "usually, often", and "generally" are often correct.

6. If two choices are similar, usually one of them is correct.

7. If two answers are direct opposites, usually one of them is correct.

8. Make sure the choice agrees grammatically with the stem.

9. If two quantities (numbers) are almost the same, one is usually correct.

10. If the quantities (numbers) cover a wide range, usually one in the middle is correct.

True-False Test Strategies

1. Read each word carefully, If one word is false, the whole statement is false.

2. Don't spend too much time analyzing the statements; true-false questions test your knowledge of facts and usually don't require interpretation.

3. Statements with absolute expressions such as "all, always, never," and "only" are usually false.

4. Statements with "flexible" expressions such as "usually" are usually true.

5. There are usually more "trues" on a test than "falses."

Fill-in-the-Blank Test Strategies

1. These questions usually test how well you have memorized certain words or facts. Your answers should be short and clear. Do not give interpretations.

2. Look ahead to the other questions to make sure you don't give the answer to a question which is coming up.

3. Often you must define a word. When giving a definition of a concept or an object, remember to consider:

> WHAT- What category it is in; what it looks like; what its characteristics are
>
> WHERE- Where it is found or used
>
> WHEN- When it is used or takes place
>
> HOW- How it works, how it is used
>
> Examples:
> Define solid
> Answer: A form of matter which has a definite shape.
>
> Define coping saw
> Answer: A wood saw that's used to saw curved lines in wood.
>
> Define piston
> Answer: A part in an internal combustion engine which moves up and down in a cylinder.

SECTION 6

Open-Book and Take-Home Test Strategies

1. Prepare well for the test. This is the most important strategy because these tests are often the most difficult kind.

2. Know where to find the information in your book(s). This type of exam doesn't test what you know as much as it tests your ability to find important information quickly.

3. Use the table of contents and the index to help you find the information you need.

4. When you find an answer to a test question, try to write the answer using your own words.

5. If you copy more than a few words directly from the book, put the words in quotation marks and give the name of the book and the page number.

"Pop-Quiz" Strategies

1. The only way to prepare for these is to do your homework! Complete all study and reading assignments on time and keep up with the course syllabus.

Top Ten Test-Taking Strategies

Directions: Read the section General Strategies in the reading entitled *Test-Taking Strategies*. Then, work with others in your small group to identify the top ten most important general strategies for ESOL students in your content area. Rewrite these strategies below using clear, short phrases or sentences. Later, use this list as a poster or handout to guide your teaching and reinforcement of test-taking strategies in your classes.

1. _____

2. _____

3. _____

4. _____

5. _____

6. _____

7. _____

8. _____

9. _____

10. _____

Specific Test-Taking Strategy

Directions: Read the section Specific Strategies in the reading *Test-Taking Strategies*. Then, determine which of these (or another) specific strategy would be most helpful to ESOL students in your classes. Work alone or with your group to plan how you will teach and reinforce this strategy to your students. Make notes for your own use below.

Specific Strategy: _____

How/when I will teach students to use this strategy:

How/when I will reinforce student use of this strategy:

A Teacher's Concern About Grading ESOL Students

Note: This reading is from a teacher interview conducted to evaluate ESOL inservice programs.

One secondary English teacher discussed his dilemma in evaluating the LEP students in his classes. He said that he felt his expectations for achievement and assessment often did not match the expectations of some of his ESOL students. He found it difficult to fairly evaluate LEP students, whose language skills (written and verbal expression skills) were not equivalent to those of the native speaking students in his class, despite the fact that the ESOL students might have made great progress over the course of the semester. He worried that grading LEP students relative to the native English speaking students was unfair, but that his grades had to reflect a student's true ability to express himself in English, and grades also had to be meaningful and credible to those considering grades for other purposes, such as college admissions.

"I ran into a situation this year with a student who was very successful in his other classes, and in my class he earned a 'B.' This was after I had the ESOL course. If I had not had the ESOL workshop, I probably would have evaluated this student's papers with a 'C' grade, thinking I was being generous. But since I had the ESOL training, I evaluated this student's papers and assigned a 'B' grade, thinking I was being generous but fair. But the student seemed disappointed that he wasn't getting 'A's!" Even though he didn't say it, I could see that. The fact that they are speaking English as a second language and that their English skills are limited makes it very hard for a person to evaluate them fairly and assign a grade in consideration with all the other students. Those are issues I did not feel were made clear to me in the workshop.

"We have to consider what the grade means when other people look at it. For example, if I had given that student an 'A' in English and he had gone to the University of Florida, how would those professors feel when they saw his real skill level? On the other hand, what I saw the student doing was so super compared to how short a time he had been speaking the language, I felt he deserved a 'B.'

"It's not an intellectual issue, it's a heart issue. But it becomes an intellectual issue when you start to apply it to what someone outside the school might be looking for, say Harvard University. What is the credibility or integrity of the grade itself when it stands alone as opposed to what the ESOL teacher knows or what I might know about this individual student?...So when you're putting ESOL students in with the regular population students and you're asking for a comprehensive grade..."

Source: Harper, C. (1995). An evaluation of ESOL inservice training in Florida (Technical Report). Gainesville, FL: University of Florida, p. 24. Used with permission.

Enriching Content Classes for Secondary ESOL Students (National Edition)
Study Guide Section 6: Assessment

SECTION 6

Grading Options and Guidelines

1. Focus on the ESOL student's *meaning* and *content knowledge,* not language errors such as grammar mistakes or awkward phrasing. Ask yourself: Did the student understand the question? Did he/she answer the question? and, if appropriate: How well did the student develop his thoughts?

2. Grade a combination of *process* and *product.* Using only *product* criteria can be unfair to any student. Thomas Guskey, a well-known educator, illustrates with a hypothetical gym-class situation. Imagine assessing two students: one is a brilliant athlete; the other has poor movement skills but always tries his hardest and is unfailingly sportsmanlike. Using only product criteria (such as how high the student can jump and how fast he can run) would not recognize the second student for the things he does well. (Process criteria in this example could include teamwork and sportmanship.)

3. Explain to students what and how you grade early in the class. Show examples of good work. Talk to students after grading if you think their expectations were different from the grade they received.

4. Have grades reflect a variety of measures (some less dependent on fluent language skills) such as participation, projects, portfolios, and oral explanations.

5. Adapt tests and test administration (allow more time for ESOL students, read the test to them, etc.). Teach test-taking skills and strategies. Use criterion-referenced tests.

6. Teach students how to learn. Arrange support such as a buddy or study group.

7. Teach students how to evaluate their own work. Conduct self-evaluations.

8. Grade ESOL beginners as satisfactory/unsatisfactory or at/above/below expectations until the end of the year, then assign a letter grade for the year.

9. Put a note on the report card and transcript to identify the student as an English-language learner. Write comments to clarify how you graded the student.

10. Recognize effort and improvement in ways other than grades.

Designing Alternative Assessments

1. What do you want the students to know and be able to do at the end of the unit?

2. Is there an alternative assessment that will demonstrate this?

3. What are the criteria for excellent performance? (List at least three.)

4. Do students have ongoing support and ongoing feedback during this work?

5. Does the activity require students to learn new knowledge and skills (not just do nifty things)?

6. How are students made aware of what they have learned and how they have learned it?

Practical Alternative Assessments for the Content Areas

1. <u>Learning Logs and Journals</u>

Each student keeps a journal which summarizes his learning in the class in his own words. A good way to start journals is for each student to write a one sentence summary of what he has learned at the end of each class period (or unit). The summaries in the journal create a personal record of learning over time. Teachers may need to teach students to write good summary statements and may wish to discuss sample summary statements occasionally to help students edit and improve their own.

Teachers can vary the contents of the students' learning journals by varying the prompts or sentence starters. Good sentence starters (for the students to complete) include:

> I learned ...
> I had reinforced ...
> I was reminded of ...
> I want to learn more about ...
> I think ...
> This topic made me wonder about ...
> What I really enjoyed was ...
> I didn't like ...

Journals can also be used for content-based dialogue between students and teachers. Themes or topics are selected from the curriculum and the student can ask questions, provide reflections on information learned, integrate concepts, synthesize material and more. The teacher responds to the student in writing and asks questions that will elicit more information. These journals provide an opportunity for students to combine their personal reflections with the information learned. The teacher can use these student contributions to assess the students overall comprehension of content.

In learning journals or logs, teachers should focus on the *meaning* of the student communication and its indication of content understanding, not the mechanics of writing.

2. <u>Role Play</u>

Students role play characters from literature, social studies, or other relevant content areas. This provides an opportunity for the teacher to assess students' mastery of specific content, and an opportunity for students to use different skills, talents, and varieties of language in an interactive and meaningful context. Role plays need not simply enact known events, but can create responses to hypothetical situations that are consistent with known facts, such as a conversation between King George and Thomas Jefferson.

3. Student Self-Ratings

Students rate their own performance using either a teacher-developed checklist or one they compose cooperatively based on curricular objectives. This provides an indication for the teacher of how the student assesses his own abilities. In addition to rating their performance or knowledge, student self-ratings can address learning styles and preferences. For example, ask students:

> Which activities helped you learn best? Why?
> Do you prefer to work in groups or alone? Why?
> How do you feel about your ability to learn in this class? Why?
> What can I, the teacher, do to help you learn better?
> What can you, the student, do to learn better?

4. Venn Diagrams and Other Graphic Organizers

Students compare two concepts—ideas, books, or other concepts in any content area—using a Venn diagram format (two overlapping circles). This type of assessment provides the student with an opportunity to utilize higher-order thinking skills individually or in pairs. The graphic organizer focuses student attention on ideas and reduces concern with language (e.g., putting the ideas into complete sentences). Matrices, webs, and timelines can be used for assessment as well.

5. Projects and Other Performance Assessments

To assess learning goals that transcend mere recall, educators are turning to performance assessments such as projects, exhibitions, investigations, and portfolios (see below). Today's teachers don't want to just dispense knowledge; besides teaching *about* history, literature, math, and science, teachers also want to give students opportunities to *be* historians, literary critics, mathematicians, and scientists. Performance assessment tasks call on students to write, debate, create products, conduct experiments, and so on. Using such performance assessments sends a new message to students: that teachers value in-depth understanding, the ability to apply knowledge in new situations, and high-quality work.

For example, Larry Lewin, a middle school teacher in Eugene, Oregon, asked himself: "How should a present-day teacher assess his students' understanding of 1492?" Lewin wanted to assess his students' understanding of the relationships among Columbus, the Spanish, and the Native American Tainos, but he didn't want to give a traditional short-answer test, which would "put a ceiling" on how much learning his students could demonstrate. So Lewin asked his students to write a persuasive letter to the monarchs Ferdinand and Isabella of Spain. In their letters, students were expected to define the encounter between Europeans and Native Americans by a key word of their choice—discovery, visit, invasion—and then argue why that word fit. Students had to call upon their newly acquired knowledge of history to defend their points of view. When finished, the letters were assessed against criteria that the class had helped generate.

The letter-writing task revealed more about the students' learning than a traditional test would have, Lewin says, because it required students to *do* something with their knowledge—not just regurgitate it. For the same reason, the task was "definitely more inherently motivating," he believes. "Kids are more motivated to write to dead monarchs than to take a test" (ASCD).

Examples of other performance assessments are: a teacher teaching/evaluating research methods asked her class to research how their town got its name, she evaluated their choice and appropriate use of multiple research methods to obtain the answer; a math teacher asked students to read and critique the use of statistical methods in news articles on current events such as the Florida net ban and its effects on fish and people; a social studies teacher asked her class to prepare an exhibit on their family histories and roots as a project to accompany a unit on immigration.

6. Portfolios

A portfolio is a purposeful and systematic collection of student work to reflect growth and the achievement of curriculum objectives over time. The portfolio itself may be bound like a book, in a folder or binder, in a box, or on audio- or videotape.

Usually, the teacher is responsible for choosing the *purpose* of the portfolio and the *contents* (categories of work to be included); setting the timetable for the work; and determining who evaluates the portfolio. Usually, the student selects the individual items to be included, explains *why* each item is included (e.g., this is my best essay; this one shows that I learned ...), updates the table of contents, sets personal goals for learning, and assess his personal goals. Teachers and students jointly develop criteria for assessment and determine how the portfolios will be shared with others.

Portfolios need not be restricted to language arts. For example, in a math class, a portfolio might include: a way I used math in real life, an article I read that used statistics, the hardest problem I learned to solve this month, etc.

References:

Association for Supervision and Curriculum Development (ASCD). On the cutting edge of assessment: Testing what students can do with knowledge. *Education Update*. Volume 38, Number 4, June 1996.

Empowering ESOL Teachers: An Overview. Menu of alternative assessment instruments. Section IX.3, Handout 7, 1996 Revised Edition.

Alternative Assessment Worksheet

Directions: Read the handout *Practical Alternative Assessments for the Content Areas.* Choose one of these assessments to use as a complement to or substitute for the material tested by your classroom test that was evaluated earlier. Then, think through the steps to implement this alternative assessment in the classroom and complete the Worksheet items below. Be prepared to share your assessment briefly with your small group.

Content Area Topic: _____

1. What do you want the students to know and be able to do at the end of the unit?

2. Which alternative assessment have you chosen to demonstrate this?

3. What are the criteria for excellent performance? (List at least three.)

4. How will you provide students ongoing support and ongoing feedback during this work? What additional support can you provide to ESOL students?

5. Does the activity require students to learn new knowledge and skills (not just do nifty things)? What new knowledge and skills?

6. How are students made aware of what they have learned and how they have learned it?

7. What are the "pros" of this assessment for ESOL students?

8. What are the "cons" of this assessment for ESOL students?

Enriching Content Classes
for Secondary ESOL Students

Study Guide

**Section 7
Culture, Part B**

Culture, Part B

Goals

To understand how to use a variety of approaches and strategies for multicultural
education in the content areas.

Performance Objectives

• Understand Banks' four approaches to multicultural education.

• Apply the multiple perspectives strategy in the content areas.

• Adapt sample lessons for secondary content areas.

• Reflect on one's feelings about multicultural education in the content areas.

SECTION 7

Approaches to Multicultural Education

<u>Contributions Approach</u>—adds ethnic heroes to the curriculum

<u>Additive Approach</u>—adds content or units to the curriculum without changing its basic structure, purpose, and assumptions

<u>Transformation Approach</u>—changes the basic assumptions of the curriculum and enables students to view concepts, issues, themes, and problems from several perspectives

<u>Social Action Approach</u>—includes all elements of the Transformation Approach and adds components that require students to make decisions and take actions related to the concept, issue, or problem that they have studied

Source: Banks, J.A. (1988). *Multiethnic education: Theory and practice* (2nd ed.). Boston: Allyn & Bacon.

Enriching Content Classes for Secondary ESOL Students (National Edition)
Study Guide Section 7: Culture, Part B

Beautiful Women in Literature

MEXICAN AMERICAN

"Mamacita is the big mama of the man across the street....Mamacita ...arrived in a yellow taxi. The taxi door opened like a waiter's arm. Out stepped a tiny pink shoe, a foot soft as a rabbit's ear, then the thick ankle, a fluttering of hips, fuschia roses and green perfume....All at once she bloomed. Huge, enormous, beautiful to look at, from the salmon-pink feather on the tip of her hat down to the little rosebuds of her toes."

from: Cisneros, Sandra. (1983) "No Speak English": in *The House on Mango Street*. Houston: Arte Publico Press.

AFRICAN AMERICAN

"Celine was thin like a puma, with mahogany-tinted, pure flesh. No eyebrows or hair on her head; just rich skin and line. Celine usually painted her cheeks and eyes with bright geometric shapes. Her lips were always deep purple....Celine smiled a lot and never...slumped carelessly into a seat or neglected to breathe evenly and deeply when anyone was looking."

from: Shange, Ntozake. (1982) *Sassafras, Cypress, and Indigo*. New York: St. Martin's Press.

NATIVE AMERICAN

"Woman-on-the-wall was the most beautiful woman she had ever seen....In and of herself there was nothing about her that was unusually striking. She was dark. Indian or Mexican. Black, black hair. Big, sturdy thighs. There was just something about her....This woman...had nice teeth. She had shiny black hair pulled back, half in a ponytail and half down...."

from: Castilla, Ana. (1993). *So Far From God*. New York: W.W. Norton.

VIETNAMESE AMERICAN

"In her prime she was nearly five feet tall, which is very big for a Vietnamese woman. Her hair was beautiful, long, and black, and whenever she cut it, which was usually once a year, village women would gather round and offer money for the clippings....She had two other signs of beauty. One was her "Buddhist ears," which, with their long lobes, showed she would live a long and fruitful life. The second was her blackened teeth, made dark from the three-day process of *nhom rang*, and strong from chewing betel nuts."

from Hayslip, Le Ly. *(1989). When Heaven and Earth Changed Places.* NY: Doubleday

SECTION 7

ANGLO-AMERICAN

"Flo March was then twenty-four years old, perhaps not the smartest girl in town but one of the nicest and, certainly, one of the prettiest, if red hair, blue eyes, and creamy-colored skin were an appealing combination for the beholder....She was young and very pretty....She exuded sensuality rather than fashionableness....There was a sway to her walk....Whether she meant it to be provocative or not, it was."

from: Dunne, Dominick. (1991). *An Inconvenient Woman.* Boston: G.K.Hall.

CHINESE-AMERICAN

"Your...ears, a big thick lobe, lots of meat at the bottom, full of blessings. Your...nose. The hole is not too big, so your money will not be running out. The nose is straight and smooth, a good sign...chin...not too short, not too long...your forehead is wider, so you will be even more clever. And your hair is thick, the hairline, is low on your forehead."

from: Tan, Amy. (1989) *The Joy Luck Club.* New York: Ballantine.

1492

Perspective 1

In the fifteenth and sixteenth centuries, European nations began to explore and colonize the world, in part in a search for goods from exotic countries. In time these voyages expanded the "known world" and led to the development of the current civilizations in North and South America, though not without some abuses of power along the way.

[Excerpted from an older, middle school text: Frederick M. King, et al. (1979). *Understanding the World*. River Forest, IL: Laidlaw Brothers, Publishers.]

In 1469 the Spanish kingdoms of Castile and Aragon were joined. That came about through the marriage of Ferdinand of Aragon and Isabella of Castile....Ferdinand and Isabella used a special church court called the Inquisition to add to their power. This court was used to find and to try people who did not follow the teachings of the Roman Catholic Church. It was also used to try people who were against the king and the queen....Ferdinand and Isabella wanted everyone in Spain to belong to the Roman Catholic Church. So, many Jews and Muslims were forced to leave Spain. But the Jews and the Muslims were the major craftspeople and business leaders in Spain. How do you think their leaving hurt Spain? Why do you think so?

...In the late 1400s an Italian named Christopher Columbus thought he could reach the East a new way. Columbus and a number of other people believed the earth was round. If this was true, ships sailing west from Europe could reach the East.

King Ferdinand and Queen Isabella of Spain helped Columbus by giving him three ships with crews and supplies. These ships sailed from Spain in August of 1492. On October 12, 1492, they reached islands Columbus believed were close to India. These islands, however, were really part of North America. Columbus made three more trips, but he never reached the East. However, he did explore other lands. Those lands were in what is today called South America.

...During the 1500s the Spanish began to go to the lands that Columbus had reached. People from Spain who came to these lands looking for fame and wealth were called conquistadores. The conquistadores used their power to overcome other peoples.

...One person who helped to build Spanish power was Hernando Cortes. Cortes went to Mexico in 1519 looking for gold and silver. The Aztec Indians in Mexico had an advanced way of life. They lived in beautiful cities, and they had gold and silver mines. Cortes and his soldiers fought the Aztecs and defeated them....Spanish conquistadores also went to other places in the Americas....

The Spanish Empire was closely controlled by the rulers of Spain. They wanted to use their overseas lands to make Spain rich and powerful. The Indians who lived on the lands taken over by Spain were generally not treated very well. Sometimes the Indians were worked as slaves to help add to Spain's wealth. How do you think the Indians felt toward the Spanish?

Perspective 2

The name Columbus and his "discovery of the New World" are common knowledge, but Columbus as a man; the civilization, suffering, and extinction of the Taino Indians; and the objections of Spaniards such as Las Casas; are often omitted.

[Excerpted from "Timeline: Spain, Columbus, and Native Americans." In *Rethinking Columbus*. Washington, D.C.: Network of Educators on Central America (NECA).]

Approximately 13,000 B.C.: First known human beings live in the Caribbean.

Approximately 8 B.C.: The people who call themselves Taino, or "men of good," arrive in the region. With great care for the earth, the Tainos are able to feed millions of people. No one in a community goes hungry. They play sports and recite poetry. They are great inventors and travel from island to island. One Spanish priest reported that he never saw two Tainos fighting. There are frequent skirmishes between Tainos and Caribs on nearby islands, but these threaten neither civilization.

1450: There may be as many as 70 to 100 million people living in what will one day be called the Americas. They are of many nationalities, with perhaps 2,000 different languages.

August 3, 1492: Columbus departs from Palos instead of the port of Cadiz, which is filled with ships taking some 8,000 Jews into exile [as a result of the Inquisition].

October 12, 1492: The ships arrive at the island, Guanahana, where Columbus takes possession of the island for Ferdinand and Isabella. Columbus receives presents from the people he encounters and gives them some red caps, glass beads, and "many other things of little value." The first thing he tries to ask the people is "if they had gold."

October 14: Columbus's thoughts turn to slavery. He writes: "...When Your Highnesses so command, they [the Indians] can be carried off to Castile or held captive in the island itself, since with 50 men they would be all kept in subjection and forced to do whatever may be wished."

December 25: Columbus's ship, the Santa Maria, hits rocks off Espanola. He is forced to abandon it. The Taino cacique (leader), Guacanagari, weeps when he hears of the shipwreck. Tainos help unload the ship "without the loss of a shoe string." "They are," Columbus writes, "a people so full of love and without greed...I believe there is no better race or better land in the world."

January 13: First reported skirmish between the Spaniards and Indians: After landing on an island to trade for bows, Columbus writes that many Indians prepared "to assault the Christians and capture them." The Spaniards "fell upon" them, "they gave an Indian a great slash on the buttocks and they wounded another in the breast with an arrow."

February 15: Columbus returns [to Spain] with relatively little of value. In a letter written aboard ship, Columbus lies, saying that on Espanola, "there are many spices and great mines of gold and of other metals."

September 25, 1493: Columbus's second voyage begins....At least some of the money to finance the voyage comes from wealth taken from Spanish Jews.

Early February, 1494: Columbus sends 12 of the 17 ships back to Spain for supplies. Several dozen Indian slaves are taken aboard—"men and women and boys and girls," he writes. He justifies this by writing that they are cannibals and thus slavery will more readily "secure the welfare of their souls." Spanish priest Bartolome de las Casas later writes that claims of cannibalism are used to "excuse the violence, cruelty, plunder and slaughter committed against the Indians every day."

November 1494: Returning to Spain, mutineers against Columbus complain to the king and queen. They say there is no gold and that the enterprise is a joke.

February 1495: Columbus must be desperate to prove that his "enterprise" can be profitable. He rounds up 1600 Tainos—the same people he had earlier described as "so full of love and without greed." Some 550 of them—"among the best males and females," writes colonist Michele de Cuneo—are chained and taken to ships to be sent to Spain as slaves. "Of the rest who were left," writes Cuneo, "the announcement went around that whoever wanted them could take as many as he pleased; and this was done."

1495: Columbus establishes the tribute system. Every Taino, 14 or older, is required to fill a hawk's bell full of gold every 3 months....Where Columbus decides there is little gold, 25 pounds of spun cotton is required. The Spaniards cut the hands off those who do not comply; they are left to bleed to death. As Las Casas writes, the tribute is "impossible and intolerable." Columbus will soon replace the tribute system with outright slavery....

May 20, 1506: Columbus dies in Valladolid, Spain.

1542: Bartolome de las Casas writes that a mere 200 Tainos still live in Espanola. One scholar recently estimated that perhaps more that 3 million Tainos lived there when Columbus first arrived.

<u>Perspective 3</u>

For Spanish Jews and Muslims the year 1492 meant the Inquisition: religious persecution, death and torture, and being driven out of Spain, their country for hundreds of years.

{ This story is based on a history of the Ben-Isaac family that has been handed down through oral tradition. It was written by a Florida resident, the great-granddaughter of Solomon Ben-Isaac, who immigrated with his family to the United States from Rabat, Morocco, in the early part of this century.}

My name is Mara Ibn-Isak, and I will remember 1492. I am 16 years old. It is the Christian year 1492, and I live in Cordova in Spain, but not for long. Soon I will have to leave here and go to somewhere else. I am looking at every corner of my house so that I can remember it. This house and this land have been part of my family for over 500 years. Life was good for all of us here for a very long time. The Christians and the Jews and the Moors all lived peacefully with each other. Together we produced great art and music and philosophy. My father said business and trade were good too. But the Christians have always thought of us as different. The Rabbis tell me that about 100 years ago, the real troubles started. On the Christian holy day of Ash Wednesday in 1391, a mob broke into the Jewish quarter of our neighbor city Seville and demanded that all Jews convert to Christianity. Four thousand of our people were killed. Our homes and businesses and synagogues were burned. There were almost 10,000 Jewish families in Seville. Many became outwardly Christian, because the alternative was to be burned or butchered. Secretly, they practiced their Jewish faith.

Somehow, most of the Ben-Isaks managed to survive as Jews over these 100 years. That was until 10 years ago, when the priest Tomas de Torquemada was appointed Inquisitor General. He made our lives miserable. He tortured and killed relatives and friends. Ferdinand and Isabella wanted to get rid of all the Muslims and Jews in Spain, and they got the church to help them do it. Five years ago, a special tax was levied on all Jewish families. The 14,000 families in my province became almost bankrupt. Some families were ransomed as slaves and transported to Africa.

In March of this year, 1492, Ferdinand and Isabella decreed that by July 30 (that's next week), not a single Jew was to remain in Spain. If a Jew remained, he had either to submit to baptism or pay with his life. We can take with us only what we can carry, except gold and silver and coins. These, and all of our property, become the property of the crown or the church.

Now we are making our final preparation to leave. We must visit the graves of our ancestors because we will never be able to come to their burial sites and remember them again. My family is honored by our ancestor, Solomon Ibn-Gabirol, who found the works of the Greek philosopher Aristotle and translated them into Arabic; then the Christian Tomas Aquinas took his translation and translated it into Latin and wrote many books. I am told that this man Aquinas was a priest of the Domincan order. So is Torquemada. I find it all confusing. Now Ibn-Gabirol will have only the dead as company.

My father will see that the less fortunate Jewish families have money for passage to Morocco or Tunisia, because we have more left than others. My uncle and many of his friends are trying to sail with Senor Columbus to the orient to find spices and treasures. My uncle speaks many oriental languages and will be an asset to Senor Columbus.

My father says we will go to Fez, in Morocco, and start again. My Arabic is not good. Will anyone in Fez understand my language? {Ladino, sometimes called Judeo-Spanish.} Will I have to learn a new language? My mother says that when she bakes her "pan de casa" {special holiday bread} our house will be the same. My father and all our family will have to work hard to build a new life. Our Jewish community will be dispersed again, this time throughout Africa and Europe, and maybe even the orient, if Senor Columbus gets there. I will remember July of 1492, and tell my children about it, and they will tell their children, so generations will remember that 1492 was a bad year for Mara Ibn-Isak.

Fishing Net Ban

Perspective 1

The use of gill nets by commercial fishermen in Florida should be banned because the nets are not selective, contribute to overfishing, endanger certain species such as sea turtles, and take fish that sport fishermen want to catch.

[Based on articles and letters to the editor published over a period of several weeks in the *Gainesville Sun*.]

Supporters of a ban on net fishing claim that commercial fishing shows a "callous disregard" of natural resources. They state that the nets are not selective in catching the intended prey and that they kill other marine life including young fish, fish that are less valuable as a food source, dolphins, and sea turtles.

James Bohnsack of the National Marine Fisheries Service in Miami told a state coastal-management conference in Jacksonville, "For every pound of fish landed, there are nine pounds thrown overboard." This bycatch, or bykill, is often smaller fish which are critical as food for larger fish or which would grow larger if not killed prematurely. Supporters of the net ban point out that once the fish are gone, they are gone permanently. Now is the time, they say, to ban the nets and let the fish population begin to come back.

Net ban supporters say that the economic impact on the commercial fishing industry that is predicted by commercial fishermen is completely overstated. Ban supporters say that only about a thousand jobs will be affected because many commercial fishermen will use hook and line or fish for other species such as crabs that are not affected by the ban.

Ban supporters also point out that prices of fish to the consumer did not rise in other states that passed a net ban because the majority of food fish are not caught by nets in Florida waters. Most food fish are farm-raised, caught by another method, or caught further offshore.

Ban supporters say that the big money to be made by net fishermen in Florida is fishing for mullet roe to be sent to Taiwan. They say that a few commercial fishermen with lots of political power and financial backing from Taiwan, are spearheading the fight against the ban so that they can make a lot of money before the mullet are fished out.

Ban supporters also say that the commercial fishing industry is trying to portray them as selfish sport fishermen, but that thousands of concerned citizens signed the petition to amend the state constitution to ban the nets and that they are supported by every major environmental organization in the state.

[see next page for Perspective 2]

Perspective 2

The use of gill nets should not be banned. A ban will destroy the commercial fishermen's way of life, bankrupt many families, and reduce the amount and quality of seafood available to Floridians.

[Based on articles and letters to the editor published over a period of several weeks in the *Gainesville Sun..*]

Commercial fishermen oppose a ban on net fishing and claim that it will destroy their way of life and reduce the quality and quantity of seafood available in Florida.

Commercial fishermen state that perhaps 50,000 people will lose their jobs as a result of a ban. Fishers would be put out of business, and many wholesale seafood houses, suppliers, truckers, and markets would close. The commercial fishermen say that there will be less seafood available to Florida consumers and that the prices will be considerably higher. Further, they feel a ban would destroy their way of life.

One commercial fisherman says, "Being a waterman, like being a farmer, is a way of life. Nets and boats, like cattle and land, have been handed down from generation to generation. The art of providing food for millions of Americans has been refined over generations, knowing when, where and how much to harvest."

Opponents of the ban see supporters as a group of self-interested sport fishermen and related businesses. They feel that the sport fishermen want to limit commercial fishing so that they can take more fish themselves. Ban opponents say that non-fishing consumers, the vast majority, will be hurt by the ban. Besides, the extra fish for the sport fishermen will be very little.

Organized Fishermen of Florida claims that the fiercest competition between sport and commercial fishermen is for speckled trout. Sports fishermen catch 78 percent of all trout landed. Jorge Laguna, a state fisheries management analyst testifying before the Marine Fisheries Commission, stated that if nets were banned and their entire catch recovered by sports fishermen, each east coast angler would catch one additional trout once every three years (.28 per year). West coast anglers would catch one additional trout once every eight years (.13 per year).

A commercial fisherman states, "I simply cannot believe I live in a state ...in favor of devastating an entire industry, putting thousands of families in the shadow of bankruptcy and removing more than 90 percent of domestic seafood affordable to poor and low-income families for the frivolous reward of the one additional trout every eight years."

Commercial fishermen state that existing regulations are sufficient to protect the fish and other sealife. They say that net ban supporters overstate the damage done to sealife by nets and that many more sea turtles are killed on the highways than in nets. Further, they say that the bycatch is not a problem because it goes back into the water and provides food for other sealife and birds.

SECTION 7

Organized Fishermen of Florida (OFF) is angered by the charge that they are wasteful of natural resources and point out that three decades ago they contributed to the successful passing of a ban on purse seines for good fish. OFF states that the image of gill nets capable of indiscriminately inhaling fish of every size and shape is a big hoax—a bogeyman constructed of newsprint and malicious intent. OFF points to the Everglades National Park as an example of a park in serious trouble because exclusive fishing rights were granted to sport fishermen.

Multiple Perspectives in the Content Areas

Help students:

- Understand that many issues and topics have more than one "valid" perspective.

- Know how to learn about multiple perspectives.

- Know how to talk with and work with students who have a different perspective.

Multicultural Education: Strategies for Linguistically Diverse Schools and Classrooms

By Deborah Menkart

With lesson plans by
Andrea Vincent
Debbie Wei
Ellen Wolpert

SECTION 7

Introduction

We were reading three books and they all dealt with houses. We were reading Vladimir Nabokov's *Speak Memory*, Isak Dinesen's *Out of Africa*, and Gaston Bachelard's *Poetics of Space*. When we got to the third book I was terribly confused and I couldn't make sense of what they were talking about. So I thought, it must be because I am not smart enough. So I'll just go to class and I won't say anything. Maybe no one will notice that I am not as smart as they are. But then it suddenly occurred to me when they started talking about the attic they weren't talking about my house. We didn't have an attic in our house. You don't usually have an attic when you live in a third floor front. Then I thought about the basement. I thought nobody went there but the landlord, and only if he had to. There were wild things that grew and prowled in the basement. Nobody wanted to go there. And then I realized–Nabokov's house wasn't mine. Isak Dinesen's house wasn't mine. Then I thought about all the books I ever had, all the way back to Dick and Jane and Sally and Spot. We never talked about my house. It was a horrific moment. My temperature changed. I remember going home and getting so frightened that at that moment I think I could have given up my education. I felt I don't belong here.

–Sandra Cisneros (April 17, 1993, excerpt from speech at TESOL Convention, Atlanta , Georgia), author of House on Mango Street, Woman Hollering Creek, and My Wicked, Wicked Ways

Luckily, Sandra Cisneros did not give up her education. Instead, she decided to write a book that had been missing all through her school life: a book about her home and her family. A book that would feel like home to many students who did not live with Dick and Jane. A book about a house on Mango Street.

But for every Sandra Cisneros, thousands of other potential poets and leaders drop out each year–thousands of students who, because they see nothing familiar in the curriculum or school environment, begin to believe that they are not smart. They feel, "I don't belong here." This sense of alienation from school is reflected in the higher dropout rates and lower test scores for language minority students. Schools are failing their students.

Source: Menkart, D. (1993). *Multicultural education: Strategies for linguistically diverse schools and classrooms* (Program Information Guide No. 16). Washington D.C.: National Clearinghouse for Bilingual Education.

Multicultural education seeks to reverse that trend. The aim of multicultural education is to ensure equity in education for all students and to help empower young people to make the world a better place both individually and collectively (Bigelow, 1993). As leading multicultural theorist James Banks explains, "Multicultural education, as its major architects have conceived it during the last decade, is not an ethnic- or gender- specific movement. It is a movement designed to empower all students to become knowledgeable, caring, and active citizens in a deeply troubled and ethnically polarized nation and world" (Banks, 1993).

This program guide will share strategies that teachers in linguistically diverse schools and classrooms can use to create a successful environment for all students.

The Origins of Multicultural Education

Many popular journals cite America's new and growing multicultural population as the impetus for the move toward multicultural education. But, of course, the population of the United States has always been multicultural. Think of all the peoples from Senegal, Ghana, the Congo, China, Japan, England, Ireland, Italy, Poland, Germany, Mexico, and the Caribbean, as well as Iroquois, Apache, Hopi, Cherokee, and more who make up the population of this country.

What is new is the national commitment to seek equity for all people within this pluralistic society. The Civil Rights and women's movements of the 1950s and '60s pushed the country in this new direction. In addition to political and economic equity, the demand was raised for the right to cultural integrity. The image of the melting pot, all cultures blending into the image of the dominant culture, was replaced by the societal salad or mosaic.

Education became a central focus of the Civil Rights movement. If blacks and Latinos were to have an equal opportunity in politics and employment, then they had to be afforded an equal education. But schools were literally failing Latino and African American students. Prior to the Civil Rights movement, the lower test scores and higher dropout rates among certain races, ethnic groups, and women were attributed to "racial" or "cultural" differences. For example, in the early 1900s, persons of eastern and southern European origins and blacks were considered to have lower IQs (Suzuki, 1984; Fairtest, 1991). Women were considered to have lower aptitudes in math. Black and Latino families were said to place a low value on education.

The Civil Rights movement shifted the blame from the students to the system of schooling. If women or blacks had lower test scores, then schools were failing, not students. As a public institution central to our democracy, schools needed to change. First came the admission that separate was not equal and that there was a need for integration. Other aspects of schools came under scrutiny and are still in the process of revision. There was the recognition, for example, that
- The school curriculum needs to reflect our full history, including the contributions and experiences of people of color and women. Thereby, all students can see themselves in history and students of all races can develop a greater respect and appreciation for each other.

- Testing and assessment need to be culturally and linguistically sensitive.
- Sorting or tracking systems should not segregate students within schools based on race or native language.
- School policy and pedagogy should promote cooperation among students of all races to prepare them for life in a pluralistic, multicultural, and global society.
- The native languages of nonnative English speakers and their parents should be treated as an asset, not a weakness.

The combination of these reforms came to be known as multicultural education. Just as there was much debate about the Civil Rights and women's movements, so there is much debate about multicultural education today. And just as there were many interpretations of the Civil Rights movement, so there are many interpretations of multicultural education.

Focus on curriculum

Curriculum and classroom literature are the areas over which teachers have the most direct control. James Banks (Banks and McGee, 1989) outlines four levels of integration of ethnic content into the curriculum. This provides a helpful framework for teachers to use in their classrooms. Examine the four levels below and determine which most closely reflects your current practice. Then you can plan how to move specific lessons up to the next level. This is more fruitful if done with a partner and has proven to be an extremely useful exercise for departmental meetings, inservices, and peer coaching sessions.

Level 1–Contributions: Focus on heroes, holidays, food, and other discrete cultural elements. During special commemorative days (e.g., Cinco de Mayo, Martin Luther King's birthday, the Chinese New Year), teachers involve students in lessons and experiences related to the ethnic group being studied.

Level 2–Additive: Add a unit or course on a particular ethnic group without any change to the basic curriculum. For example, the teacher may add a unit on Native Americans or Haitians to the traditional social studies course.

Level 3–Transformation: Infuse various perspectives, frames of reference, and content material from various groups that extend students' understanding of the nature, development, and complexity of American society. The basic curriculum is changed. For example, the conquest of American territory is viewed from multiple perspectives, including those of Native Americans, African Americans, wealthy European settlers, and indentured servants from Europe.

Level 4–Decision Making and Social Action: This includes all of the elements of the Transformation approach (Level 3) but also encourages students to make decisions and to take action related to the concept, issue, or problem they have studied in the unit. The goal at this level is to help students develop a vision of a better society and to acquire the knowledge and skills necessary to bring about constructive social change. At this level, students do more than identify social problems; they move to the higher-level thinking skill of analysis. As high school social studies teacher and curriculum developer Bill Bigelow explains, "Multicultural education should be based on a problem-solving approach, using inequity in this society as the core problem. The curriculum should pose the big 'why' questions: Why is there racism? Why is there sexism? What are the roots of social conflicts?" (Bigelow, 1993).

In practice there is often overlap between Banks' four levels of integration. The emphasis in this publication is on strategies for facilitating multicultural integration at the transformation and decision-making and social action levels (Levels 3 and 4). For example, when studying the economy in the United States, students might examine the plight of unemployed factory workers or homeless people today. For their final project, they could be asked to take individual or small-group actions to address the problems. Students should be asked to evaluate the relative effectiveness of the proposed actions. Action for the sake of action is not enough. Letter writing is probably one of the most common forms of "student action." There are times when letter writing is very effective but there are also times when the letters will not make a difference. They are simply an assignment. Students should begin with an analysis of the root cause of the problems. How can their actions get to these roots? What can they learn from historical movements for social change?

Questions and Answers about Implementing Multiculturalism

Teachers are always looking for ways to reach their students more effectively, especially when their classes include students with diverse backgrounds. However, they are also wary of techniques that create more work for them without producing clear benefits for their students. This section addresses some of the most common questions teachers have before they implement multicultural strategies in their classrooms.

1. *Why do we have to add something else to the curriculum? I am already trying to do too much!*
Teaching about culture is not the addition of something new. We already teach about culture every day by what we include or exclude from our curriculum. The goal is to make this aspect of the curriculum more complete, more accurate, and more sensitive. Stop and look at any classroom. Lessons about cultures fill the room (Lee, 1993). Here are some examples:

Classroom Example #1: The children's books feature light-skinned children with rosy cheeks. A few books include an African American or Asian child. There is one book on the Mexican holiday, Cinco de Mayo. One wall is filled with portraits of famous people. All the famous people on this wall are white men who have made advances in science, the military, and politics. There is one poster of a woman.

What are the children in this classroom learning about culture? They are learning that European-American culture is the norm, that people from countries outside the United States only celebrate holidays, and that people make scientific or political advances all by themselves.

Classroom Example #2 : A teacher reads *The Three Little Pigs* to the class. Through dramatic story reading, all the children huff and puff as they blow down the straw and the wood houses. Only the brick house stands firm.

SECTION 7

With this lesson, the children learn that brick (urban) houses are best, and straw and wood houses are pretty worthless. Of course, in certain contexts, a brick house is preferable. In other climates, though, a straw or wood house is more appropriate. The story needs to be placed in context rather than giving the impression that brick houses are universally the ideal home (Wolpert, 1993).

Classroom Example #3: A sixth grade textbook describes the high level of adult illiteracy in Latin America. It describes a U.S. -supported literacy program to help Latin American governments address the problem. The text does not mention that before the conquest, the Mayans in Latin America had vast libraries with volumes of advanced historical and scientific documents; nor does it discuss the profound worldwide influence of contemporary Latin American literature. In addition, the book does not mention the current high levels of adult illiteracy in the United States or the fact that certain groups in the United States, such as women and African Americans, have historically been denied the right to literacy.

Here children learn that people in other countries are "behind" the United States in their development. They are not learning about the richness of the region's literary history. They do not learn that illiteracy is the result of social or governmental policies, not the ignorance or "backwardness" of a country's population.

2. How long will it take to implement a multicultural curriculum?
Substantive change will probably take one to five years, but it is worth the effort! (Suzuki, 1984; York, 1991). Investing a little time–giving priority to human relations over activities covered–is important for a successful multicultural education program. As we move toward a fully enriched curriculum (using Banks' Level 4 as a goal), we can make incremental changes in cultural awareness and sensitivity. For example, we can learn to pronounce our students' full names correctly instead of relying on shorter, simpler "American" nicknames, "affirming who students are rather than who we may want them to become" (Nieto, 1992). This also demonstrates our respect for their families, who gave them these names.

3. Won't multicultural education simply divide the school along racial and ethnic lines?
As Banks (1993) points out, "Multicultural education is designed to help unify a deeply divided nation rather than to divide a highly cohesive one." Multicultural education may bring problems to the surface, giving the appearance of creating conflict. But if a school's entire staff and faculty are committed to working through that conflict, then unity based on new, more equitable relationships can be achieved. See *Freedom's Plow* (Perry and Frazer, 1993) for teachers' descriptions of their schools' conflicts in the process of transformation.

In *Roots and Wings* (York, 1993) and *White Teacher* (Paley, 1993), the authors describe the importance of talking openly about differences rather than ignoring them. York points out that "phrases such as 'We are all the same' and 'You are just like me' deny the differences between people...they very subtly use European American values as the norm–the point of reference" (York, 1993).

Conflicting descriptions of history can become a valuable part of the learning process. A junior high history teacher in San Diego begins one lesson by discussing Pancho Villa, who is a hero of her Mexican American students. She tells them that, in her school, Villa was depicted as a "bad guy, a bandit" (Willis, 1993). The history lesson becomes richer as students examine these different perspectives.

4. How can I know about all cultures?
You need not become an expert on all cultures represented in your school, but there are many ways you can learn about them. Talk to the students, their families, and other teachers. Explain that you want to learn more about their culture(s) so that you can have the best possible communication with them. Visit community centers and houses of worship. Read fiction and poetry from these cultures.

When approaching students and their families, keep two points in mind:
1. Culture is not uniform; within a country it varies by region, class, religion, and many other variables. Just imagine if someone asked you to teach them all about the culture of the United States. You could tell them about your own family's traditions, which would shed some light on U.S. culture.
2. Some students, especially adolescents, may not want to be singled out as the in-house experts on their cultures and nationalities.

Multicultural Education in the School Environment
Multicultural education encompasses all aspects of school life. The values of multicultural education must be modeled throughout the school environment. In a school, there may be posters in the hallway that celebrate diverse cultures, but a disproportionate number of language minority children are suspended each week. There may be welcome signs in multiple languages, but school policy does not encourage children to maintain their native language(s). We must look below the surface to see how the whole school environment impacts students.

> We need to consider the role that schools and society in general have in creating low self-esteem in children. That is, students do not simply develop poor self-concepts out of the blue. Rather, they are the result of policies and practices of schools and society that respect and affirm some groups while devaluing and rejecting others (Nieto, 1992).

The following categories can be reviewed as your school focuses on developing its multicultural curriculum. Although all aspects are integral to a successful program, it is often more manageable for a school to concentrate on one or two areas at a time. Each category includes only a few indicators. Rather than provide a fully prescribed list, we encourage you to brainstorm with fellow staff members to decide which additional factors should be considered.

Language

• What is the official policy regarding native language use and development?

• What is the prevailing attitude toward students' native languages? (This includes non-standard English.)

- Are students provided native language instruction in the core subjects so that they learn the same grade-appropriate concepts as their native English speaking peers and develop their native language proficiency while they become proficient in English?

Discipline

- Is a higher percentage of language minority students suspended or kept after school as compared to the overall school population?

Community

- How does the community perceive the school? What kind of outreach programs are there to help determine these perceptions?

- Does the curriculum connect to issues in the local community?

Assessment and Testing

- Are the assessment tools culturally and linguistically sensitive and unbiased?

- Are various methods of assessment used, such as performance-based and portfolio evaluation?

Staffing (Administrative, Instructional, Counseling, and Support)

- Does the school staff reflect the cultural diversity of the student population?

- Are there staff members who can speak the native languages of the students and their families?

Families

- How much does the staff know about the children's lives outside of school? Do they ever visit the families' homes?

- When do families receive a call from school staff? Only when there is a problem? Are there programs to involve families in school activities?

Curriculum

- Does cultural pluralism permeate the curriculum or is it the same old curriculum with a sprinkling of ethnic holidays and heroes?

- Is the curriculum rigorous and challenging to all students? Are there high academic expectations for all students?

- Does the curriculum portray culture not as a static identity but as a dynamic characteristic that is shaped by social, political, and economic conditions?

- Does the curriculum include people of various cultural and class, backgrounds throughout–not just as a side bar, separate bulletin board, or special afternoon activity?

- Does the curriculum help students learn to understand experiences and perspectives other than their own (e.g., through role play, pen pals, interior monologues, dialogue poems, autobiographies, or other activities)?

Instructional Materials and School Library

- Do the textbooks and literature reflect the cultures of the students in the school?

- How are women portrayed in the textbooks?

- How are the students' native countries portrayed in the textbooks and literature?

- Does the library have contemporary music available from various parts of the United States and the world?

- Who selects the textbooks?

Classroom Practice

- Are cooperative learning and whole language methods used?

- Is there equitable participation in classroom discussions?

- Does the question-and -answer practice encourage or discourage participation by female and minority students?

- Does the classroom model a democratic and equitable environment as closely as possible? Is it collective or hierarchical?

Tracking or Sorting

- Are students separated within a grade level based on supposed differences in ability? For example, are students separated into different reading groups at the elementary level? Are students pulled out for talented and gifted classes? Are there different levels of secondary English or history?

- Is a disproportionate number of minority students placed in vocational or technical classes?

- What percentage of young women is in the higher-level math and science classes in relation to the percentage of young men?

Conclusion

In summary, multicultural education strives for equity regardless of race, gender, culture, or national origin. Students' lives are shaped by both school and society. So, in order to be successful, multicultural education encompasses both the effort to create more equitable schools and the involvement of teachers and students in the creation of a more equitable society. As educator Bill Bigelow (1993) states, "[Students] are given the opportunity to flex their utopian imaginations, and further, the opportunity to try to make their dreams real."

Sample Methods and Lessons

What is a multicultural classroom? First and foremost it is a classroom characterized by an ethos of caring and equity. The pedagogy supports active participation through role plays, simulations, and hands-on activities. Students learn, through their own experiences, that people's actions make a difference. (Bigelow, 1993).

A multicultural curriculum should help children discover their connection to a broader humanity–breaking down the invisibility of working people, women, and people of color. It should help students identify with a much more profound sense of "we." The traditional European-American-centered curriculum excludes not only people of color but also the majority of white people. The stories feature white (male) leaders–usually military, political, or economic. Students learn that isolated, independent individuals make history. A multicultural curriculum seeks not only to include other cultures but also to tell the more complete story of our social history. It acknowledges the value of the lives of common people (Bigelow, 1993).

The following are examples of techniques that teachers have used in their classrooms to make their lessons multicultural.

Lesson One
Pictures, Pictures, Pictures
(Grades K-3, can be adapted to any grade,)

[Particularly good for beginning ESOL students]

Ellen Wolpert, director of Washington-Beech Community Preschool in Boston, MA, has developed an extensive picture collection that helps to integrate a multicultural approach across the curriculum.

The pictures show culturally diverse people throughout the United States and the world. Teachers can use these images throughout the week for math, social studies, and language arts. These diverse images of people–a woman carrying groceries on her head in Brooklyn, a man vacuuming the house, a factory worker reading a book during his lunch break, or parent testifying with a translator at a school board hearing–represent a significant shift from the norm as it is defined by the mass media. They are not only more inclusive but also more accurate in their representation of our multicultural country.

The following is a brief description of how to develop and use your own picture collection.

1. Collect pictures that challenge the biases and stereotypes that children are subjected to. Categories may include the following:

• Economic standing	• Physical ability	• Family	• Race
• Gender	• Nationality	• Culture	• Age

SECTION 7

Within each of these categories, consider the stereotypes children are most typically exposed to and look for images that emphasize all cultures' humanity. For example, children are currently exposed to stereotypical images of Arabs which impact their attitudes about the Middle East and toward Arab Americans. To address this, include pictures in your collection of Arabs participating in different aspects of life-with family members, shopping, worshipping, and at work.

The elderly is the fastest-growing population in this country, yet our stereotypes of people in their senior years have not changed. Counter our limited assumptions about old age with images of elderly people of all nationalities actively engaged with life.

Most literature refers to Native Americans in the past tense. Counter this with images of contemporary Native Americans from the United States and Latin America. Within any of these categories, include people engaged in daily routines such as work (inside and outside of the home), at play, and learning. Show their transportation, housing, art, and health care. Include people from various parts of the United States–rural and urban, south and north, small towns and big cities.

Include in every collection images of your own students, their families, and the school staff. This tells children that they and their families are an integral part of the school's instructional base. It also keeps children's attention. Most importantly, it demonstrates that students and teachers are part of the diversity, not outside of it (Wolpert, 1993).

2. Mount the images on mat board and laminate. Use them in games based on familiar formats, including matching games, sorting games, classifying games, counting games, dominoes, puzzles and so on. Here are some ideas for using these pictures in exercises across the curriculum.

Math: Have students create addition, multiplication, division, or subtraction problems using the number of people in the pictures. For example, select two pictures, one with three people and another with six people, for a total of nine people. Students must find cards with the correct number of people to create their own math problems and solutions.

Problem solving: One of the goals of multicultural education is to show that culture is not a collection of quaint customs but actually a system of strategies for living. To teach this, have students look to the images for solutions to challenges in their own lives. For example, when students study transportation, have them look at pictures of how people from many parts of the world carry children, food, firewood, and other things. Then give them a problem to solve, such as how to carry a baby doll and some groceries from the class store to the class house. Ask them to study the pictures of people from other countries and other parts of the United States for ideas. Some children may choose to strap the baby doll around their backs with a scarf. Others may try to balance the groceries on their heads so that their hands will be free to carry the baby, while other may put everything into a basket on wheels. Through this lesson, students learn skills of observation, analysis, and problem solving while also gaining a respect for other cultures as sources for information and strategies for their own lives.

Language and Communication: Select a group of pictures that can be paired by themes (e.g., pictures of painted Ukrainian eggs, Navajo rugs, paintings from the Harlem Renaissance, or Sunday Easter hats). Tape the pictures onto students' backs, so that they cannot see their own pictures. Then have them walk around the room and describe the images they see to each other until each student has found his or her match. Through this exercise, students learn keen observation, descriptive language, and communication skills and have opportunities to dialogue with students in the class with whom they may not normally interact.

The examples provided were of artwork, but this works equally with houses, families, or any other theme your students are studying. This is a successful activity for K-12 or even for staff development ice breakers.

Match: Spread dozens of cards on the table. Leave a replacement pile in the middle and one card in the match pile. Students must place cards from the pile in front of them onto the match pile. They must be able to find a common feature (e.g., both have vehicles, both have people who look worried, both have people cooking), although these may be in very different conditions.

(Lessons provided by Ellen Wolpert, Director, Washington-Beech Community Preschool, Boston, MA.)

SECTION 7

Lesson Two
Hold Fast to Dreams
(Grades 3-12)

Linguistically diverse students often face special difficulties in their daily lives. This can easily lead to frustration. Teachers need to find ways to keep students hopeful. The poem "Dreams" by African American poet Langston Hughes (1960) can be used as a catalyst for a writing exercise that encourages students to explore their hopes and aspirations.

> ### Dreams
> *Hold fast to dreams*
> *For if dreams die*
> *Life is a broken-winged bird*
> *That cannot fly*
>
> *Hold fast to dreams*
> *For when dreams go*
> *Life is a barren field*
> *Frozen with snow*

From *The Dream Keeper and Other Poems* by Langston Hughes. Copyright 1932 by Alfred A. Knopf, Inc. and renewed 1960 by Langston Hughes. Reprinted by permission of the publisher.

Read the poem aloud to students. Ask them to draw or write about their own dreams and how they can hold on to them. Share their work. By sharing their dreams, students who are feeling less optimistic can be inspired by the dreams of others. By talking about "how they hold on to them," students learn strategies to hold on to their own dreams.

Lesson Three
My Life is History
(Grades 6-12)

Traditional textbooks can make students (and teachers) feel pretty small compared to the heroes who "made history." As teachers and as linguistically diverse students, we are pushed to the margins of the textbooks. Multicultural education seeks to present a larger and more social history of this country. Multicultural texts bring out the stories of women, working people, and people of color, who have traditionally been ignored. (The resources listed later in this monograph provide good sources for multicultural histories of the United States.)

The ideal place to start writing these new histories is with ourselves. The goal of this lesson is to assert the connections that we all have to history. It allows us to examine the roles that we play in history and to see how history can help us gain insight into our lives today and ideas for the future.

1. Read aloud an excerpt from *Childtimes: A Three Generation Memoir* by children's authors Eloise Greenfield and L.J. Little.

> People...are affected...by big things and small things. A war, an invention such as radio or television, a birthday party, a kiss. All of these experiences help to shape people, and they in turn, help to shape the present and the future...

Share stories of how events in history have dramatically impacted your own life. A teacher in Washington, DC, shared the following examples with her English as a second language (ESL) class:

   a. During the 1968 racial riots in Detroit, she and her family were among the few non-African Americans she knew who stayed. Her old friends moved to the suburbs while she made new friends and learned among a community from which she had been previously isolated.

   b. The invention of word processors has opened up a world of writing she would never have pursued by hand.

   c. The economic crisis in Latin America forced her husband to leave Colombia. Because of this, she met him in Washington, DC, got married and had a child.

Have students think of ways in which historic events or developments have impacted their lives. After a few have shared their stories, ask the whole class to write (draft without concern for spelling or grammar) on the topic. In the class mentioned above, one student wrote about how her family had to stay in the house for weeks during the U.S. invasion of Panama; a number of students from Ethiopia wrote about how the war affected their lives;

and one student wrote about how her role as a woman has shifted now that she lives in the new cultural environment of the United States.

2. Time lines: By creating personal time lines, students can see how their own lives and the lives of their classmates are tied to history.

Begin by having students phrase in their own words the quote "An unexamined life is not worth living." Explain that the class will study the history of the community and the country we live in–beginning with the lives of the students in the class.

The teacher should prepare in advance a time line of his or her own life to share with the students. Highlight dates that you know will trigger ideas for students (e.g., when you met your best friend, your first day of school, your first day at work, times you have traveled, the gain or loss [birth or death] of a family member, when you learned a second language, and so on).

Have students begin to develop their own time lines. Students can expand the time lines by interviewing family members to collect dates that go back a couple of generations. When did their parents or grandparents get married or come to the United States? What are other highlights in their lives? Again, model first with your own time line so that students can get ideas about the kind of information they might solicit from their relatives.

Combine the student and teacher time lines into a collective class time line. This can be illustrated with drawings or bar graphs. Add key historical events to the personal time lines of the collective time line so that students can see the relationship between their lives and history.

3. Questions for History

Discuss the following statement by noted historian Howard Zinn:

> I started studying history with one view in mind: to look for answers to the issues and problems I saw in the world about me. By the time I went to college I had worked in a shipyard, had been in the Air Force, had been in a war. I came to history asking questions about war and peace, about wealth and poverty, about racial division.

> Sure, there's a certain interest in inspecting the past and it can be fun, sort of like a detective story. I can make an argument for knowledge for its own sake as something that can add to your life. But while that's good, it is small in relation to the very large objective of trying to understand and do something about the issues that face us in the world today (Zinn, 1991).

Teachers can share some of their own questions about history based on their own life experiences. For example, a teacher shared how she and her husband both work, but when they go home in the evening, it is expected that she should take care of their baby. So her

SECTION 7

question is "Why do women have to do more work than men?"

Ask students to look at their own lives—what problems do they have? Ask history—where does this problem come from? Be prepared for some pretty profound questions. Use these to shape your teaching of history. For example, the following are a few of the questions asked in a class with students from Ethiopia, El Salvador, the Philippines, and Vietnam:

- Why is there so much discrimination?
- Why do we have fights between different countries and why do we fight our own people?
- Why do women still get raped? (A boy asked this question.)
- Why are so many people poor? Why do some people have more money than others?
- Why do people make so many bad comments about Africa? So many people tell me. "If you come from Africa...did you live like an animal in the jungle?"
- Why did racism start? When did it start?)We found this to be a burning question and concern for ESL students. Studies of the 1600s and 1700s when racism was institutionalized [Zinn,1981; Bennet,1992] help to address many questions on this topic.

This personal connection should be made not just at the beginning but also throughout your study of history. This helps students understand the themes and concepts in terms of their own experiences. Students also learn about each others' strengths and cultures.

Prior to their study of the Civil Rights movement, a teacher asked students to write about a time they had stood up for what they knew was right. "In school I was punished once. I was made to stand in a corner on one foot," wrote a student from Laos. "After a while I put my other foot down and told the teacher that it was enough." The student will be able to connect her experience to those of the students who participated in Freedom Summer in Mississippi, and the other students have learned about one student's experience of life in Laos. The same student might have been uncomfortable making a class presentation about life in Laos, but within the context of the history curriculum, this student shared a profound experience.

(Lesson provided by Andrea Vincent, ESL teacher, Washington, D.C.)

SECTION 7

Lesson Four
Reading the Media
(Grades 6-12)

An important skill in multicultural education is the ability to read critically for biases in textbooks and the media. The local paper often provides ample material for students to hone their critical reading skills.

For example, an ESL teacher in Philadelphia brought an advertisement from the *Philadelphia Inquirer* for her students to critique. The ad read, "Come to Philadelphia and Celebrate New Year's Every Month of the Year." It portrayed the cultural activities of Philadelphia's many ethnic groups as a tourist attraction, and listed the Chinese New Year, the Cambodian New Year, and so on. The teacher posted the ad on the chalkboard and asked her students for comments.

The Cambodian students noticed that the Cambodian New Year was listed in the wrong month. The teacher asked them to probe deeper–what else did this ad make them think about? One student commented that if the newspaper had Cambodians on its staff, the incorrect date might have been avoided. Others noted that the paper rarely included news about the political situation in their home countries that they, as readers and residents of Philadelphia, would find important. "Why," they asked, "was the paper using our culture as an advertisement when the staff obviously does not even know anything about us?"

As a class project, the students wrote letters to the paper complaining about the trivialization of their cultures. In addition to learning to read the media for bias, students learned about each other's cultures.

(Lesson provided by Debbie Wei, ESL Teacher, Philadelphia Public Schools, PA.)

Acknowledgments

My appreciation to Bill Bigelow, Enid Lee, Denise McKeon, Linda Mauro, Christine Sleeter, Lynda Tredway, Andrea Vincent, Ellen Wolpert, Debbie Wei, and the entire NECA staff and board for their invaluable feedback on this publication.

References

Banks, J. (1993). Multicultural education: Development, dimensions, and challenges. Phi Delta Kappan Vol. 75(1), pp.22-28.

Banks, J. and McGee, C.A. (Eds.). (1989) *Multicultural Education: Issues and Perspectives.*

Bigelow, W. (1993). "Limits of the new multiculturalism: The 'good' children's literature and the quincentenary." Unpublished manuscript. Available from NECA.

Fairtest. (1990). *Standardized Tests and Our Children: A Guide to Testing Reform.* Cambridge, MA: National Center for Fair and Open Testing.

Greenfield, E. and Little, L.J. (1979). Childtimes: *A Three Generation Memoir.* New York: HarperCollins.

Hughes, L. (1960). *The Dreamkeeper and Other Poems.* New York: Alfred Knopf.

Lee, E. (1993, May 8). "Strategies for building a multicultural, anti-racist curriculum." Presented at the Books Project Seminar, Washington, DC.

Sleeter, C.E. and Grant, C.A. (1988). *Making Choices for Multicultural Education.* Columbus, OH: Charles E. Merrill.

Sleeter, C.E. and Grant, C.A. (1987) An analysis of multicultural education in the United States. *Harvard Educational Review* Vol. 57, pp. 421-444.

Sleeter, C.E. (Ed.). (1991). *Empowering through Multicultural Education.* Albany: State University of New York Press.

Suzuki, B.H. (1984, May). Curriculum transformation for multicultural education. *Education and Urban Society* Vol. 16, p.3.

Willis, S. (1993, September). Multicultural teaching: Meeting the challenges that arise in practice. *ASCD Curriculum Update*, p. 2.

Wolpert, E. (1993, August). Presentation at the National Coalition of Education Activists Building Bridges Conference, Washington, DC.

York, S. (1991). *Roots and Wings: Affirming Culture in Early Childhood Programs.* St. Paul, MN: Redleaf Press.

Zinn, H. (1992-93, Winter). Why students should study history: An interview with Howard Zinn. *Rethinking Schools.* Vol. 7, p.2.

SECTION 7

Curriculum Guides

Banks, J., Cortes, C., Gay, G., Garcia, R., and Ochoa, A. (1991) *Curriculum Guidelines for Multicultural Education.* Washington, DC: National Council for the Social Studies.

Curriculum guidelines and a multicultural education program checklist.

* Belli, G. et al. (1992). *Rediscovering America.* Washington, DC: NECA.

Excellent readings and lessons for providing a multicultural history of the Americas. Includes two dialogue poems that can be used to teach about multiple perspectives on many issues.

Caduto, M.J. and Bruchac, J. (1988). *Keepers of the Earth: Native American Stories and Environmental Activites for Children.* Golden, CO: Fulcrum.

Native American stories are linked to classroom lessons on science and the environment.

*Derman-Sparks, L. (1989). *Anti-bias Curriculum: Tools for Empowering Young Children.* Washington, DC: National Association for the Education for Young Children.

Chapters include "Learning about Racial Differences and Similarities," "Learning about Gender Identity," "Activism," "Holiday Activities," "Working with Parents," and "Ten Quick Ways to Analyze Children's Books for Sexism and Racism."

* Peterson, B. et al. (1992). *Rethinking Columbus.* Milwaukee, WI: Rethinking Schools.

Lessons, essays, short stories, interviews, and poetry critique the traditional versions of the encounter and offer teachers creative approaches for engaging young people in an evaluation of the hidden assumptions within the discovery myth.

* Schniedewind, N. and Davidson, E. (1983). *Cooperative Learning/Cooperative Lives.* Dubuque, IA: Brown.

More than 75 excellent interdisciplinary activities that are easily integrated into the upper elementary and middle school curriculum for language arts, math, social studies, art, and science.

* Schniedewind, N. and Davidson, E. (1983). *Open Minds to Equality: A Sourcebook of Learning Activities to Promote Race, Sex, Class, and Age Equality.* Englewood Cliffs, NJ: Prentice-Hall.

Lessons address building trust, communication, and cooperation; stereotypes; the impact of discrimination; and creating change.

York, S. (1991). *Roots and Wings: Affirming Culture in Early Childhood Programs.* St. Paul, MN: Redleaf Press.

A wonderful collection of hands-on activities for children that shape respectful attitudes toward cultural differences. Also includes recommendations for staff training and parent involvement.

* The starred items in the resource section are among the many resources and publications listed in the NECA catalogue. Write or call for a free copy. (See Sources, below).

Literature Reviews

Harris, V. (Ed.). (1992). *Teaching Multicultural Literature in Grades K-8.*

An opening chapter on the politics of children's literature is followed by critical reviews of children's literature featuring Native Americans, Puerto Ricans, African Americans, Mexican Americans, people of the Caribbean, and Asian Pacific Americans.

Reflections of Teaching and School Reform

California State Department of Education. (1986). *Beyond Language: Social and Cultural Factors in Schooling Language Minority Students.* Los Angeles: California State University Evaluation, Dissemination, and Assistance Center.

Cummins, J. (1986). Empowering Minority Students: A Framework for Intervention. *Harvard Educational Review* Vol. 56, pp. 18-36.

Gould, S. et al. (1991). *Strategic Planning for Multicultural Education.* Chicago: The Joyce Foundation.

Guidelines for schools trying to develop their own model for multicultural education. Includes internal assessments for schools with linguistically diverse populations.

Langer, J.A. (Ed.). (1987). *Language, Literacy and Culture: Issues of Society and Schooling.* Norwood, NJ: Ablex.

Murray, D. (Ed.). (1992). *Diversity as a Resource: Redefining Cultural Literacy.* Alexandria, VA: TESOL.

Examines specific literacies and uses of language among specific groups such as Mexican Americans, Khmer, and African Americans. Offers classroom strategies to realize the potential of linguistically and culturally diverse learners.

Nieto, S. (1992). Affirming Diversity: *The Sociopolitical Context of Multicultural Education.* New York: Longman.

Explores the meaning, necessity, and benefits of multicultural education for students from all backgrounds. Nieto explains in clear, accessible language how personal, social, political, cultural, and educational factors interact to affect the success or failure of students in our schools and offers a research-based rationale for multicultural education.

Olsen, L. and Mullen, N.A. (1990). *Embracing Diversity: Teachers' Voices from California's Classrooms*. San Francisco: California Tomorrow. San Francisco: California Tomorrow.

Teachers talk about how they are creating classrooms that allow them and their students to transcend barriers of language, cultural differences, and national background. Focus on curriculum, pedagogy, and teacher education.

Paley, V.G. (1989). *White Teacher*. Cambridge, MA: Harvard University Press.

A review in the Phi Delta Kappan says, " A wonderful useful book–short, warm and to the point. Using entertaining, well-chosen incidents from her own teaching experience, Paley examines a question that concerns teachers at all levels: How do I use my own behavior as a teacher to help my students learn to deal constructively with racial and social differences?"

* Perry, T. and Fraser, J.W. (Eds.). (1993). *Freedom's Plow: Teaching in the Multicultural Classroom*. New York: Routledge.

The voices and experiences of first grade to college level teachers who are actively engaged in multicultural teaching efforts.

* Sleeter, C. (Ed.). (1991). *Empowerment through Multicultural Education*. Albany: State University of New York Press.

The strategies section includes a chapter on the empowerment of language minority students.

Walsh, C. (Ed.). (1991). *Literacy as Praxis: Culture, Language, and Pedagogy*. Norwood, NJ: Ablex.

Examines the relationship between literacy and empowerment for language minority students. Includes an excellent chapter on a fifth grade bilingual classroom and two chapters on family literacy programs.

Background Reading

Amott, T.L. and Matthaei, J. (1991). *Race, Gender and Work: A Multicultural Economic History of Women in the United States*. Boston: South End Press.

Bennet, L. (1992). *The Shaping of Black America: The Struggles and Triumphs of African Americans, 1619 to the 1990s*. New York: Penguin Books.

What forces transformed Africans into African Americans? How did they sustain themselves during centuries of captivity and oppression? In what way did their presence shape the attitudes–and fortunes–of white America? How did black people become a nation within a nation? And what are the prospects for that nation in the 1990s?

Takaki, R. (1993). *A Different Mirror: A History of Multicultural America.* Boston: Little, Brown and Co.

A lively account filled with the stories and voices of people previously left out of the historical canon.

* Zinn, H. (1980). A People's History of the United States. New York: HarperCollins.

The lives and facts that are rarely included in textbooks. An indispensable teacher resource.

Journals

Multicultural Education
Published quarterly by the National Association of Multicultural Education ($40/year). Contact Caddo Gap Press, 3145 Geary Blvd. Suite 275, San Francisco, CA 94118; 415/750-9978.

* Rethinking Schools
1001 E. Keefe Ave., Milwaukee, WI 53212. ($12.50/year individuals, $25 organizations)

The Spring 1993 issue on parent involvement programs also featured a bibliography of children's literature about the elderly–a group often ignored in discussions of multicultural education. The bibliography includes titles in Spanish.

Teaching Tolerance
400 Washington Ave., Montgomery AL 36104. (Free subscription for teachers.)

This is a 64 page, full color magazine published by the Southern Poverty Law Center. Free for educators. The Fall 1992 issue had an excellent article titled "The Peacekeepers: Students Use Mediation Skills to Resolve Conflicts," which described programs nationwide and provided a detailed resource list.

Sources

California Tomorrow
Fort Mason Center
Building B
San Francisco, CA 94123

Research, advocacy, and technical support for California schools on education in a multicultural and multiracial society. Write for a list of their excellent publications, including Embracing Diversity: Teachers' Voices from California Classrooms (see Reflections on Teaching and School Reform section).

Multicultural Publishers Exchange
Highsmith Co.
W5527 Highway 106
P.O. Box 800
Fort Atkinson, WI 53538-0800
800/558-2110
    Catalogue of books by and about people of color.

Teaching for Change Catalogue
Network of Educators on the Americas
P.O. Box 73038
Washington, DC 20056-3038
202/429-0137
NECA Catalogue containing items in this list.

About the Author

Deborah Menkart is the director of the Network of Educators on the Americas (NECA) and the Books Project. NECA, a nonprofit organization, produces and distributes materials on critical teaching and multicultural education. NECA copublished the popular publication *Rethinking Columbus* and sponsored the Rethinking Columbus/Rethinking Our Classrooms workshops. The Books Project is a federally funded teacher training project on the teaching of reading and writing to linguistically diverse students. Menkart is co-editor of the curriculum series *Caribbean Connections,* which includes titles on Haiti, Jamaica, and Puerto Rico. She is currently co-editing a guide for elementary and secondary schools titled *Beyond Multiculturalism: Roots of Racism/Stories of Resistance.*

SECTION 7

Expert Group Tasks for Menkart Reading

Each Expert Group will become "experts" on one of the sample lessons in the Menkart reading, *Multicultural Education: Strategies for Linguistically Diverse Schools and Classrooms.* (You may write notes on the bottom of this page.)

1. Read half-page introduction entitled *Sample Methods and Lessons*, then read the lesson assigned to your group.

2. Be able to briefly summarize the essence of the lesson in your own words.

3. With your group, determine which of Banks' approaches to multicultural education the lesson represents. Be able to justify your decision.

4. With your group, identify the three most important ways that the sample lesson helps linguistically diverse students learn language, academic content, and US school culture.

5. With your group, determine how to expand or adapt the lesson to be more appropriate to secondary students in the content areas. If the lesson idea can be adapted to different content areas, list a few ideas. (This step should result in ideas, not full-blown lesson plans.)

6. As an individual, review the steps above and evaluate your readiness to present them to your home group. Work out any difficulties in your expert group.

SECTION 7

Home Group Tasks for Menkart Reading

A. Each "expert," in any order, will teach the home group about his/her sample lesson using the following outline:

1. Describe the lesson briefly.
2. Tell how the lesson helps linguistically diverse students learn language, academic content, and US school culture.
3. Tell which of Banks' approaches it represents and why.
4. Give ONE example of how your expert group suggested the lesson could be expanded or adapted to be more appropriate to secondary students in the content areas.
5. Elicit additional suggestions from your home group about how they might expand or adapt the lesson for their classes. (Some adaptations will only use a general idea from the original lesson, depending on the content area.)
6. Ask each Home Group member to record the best idea for his/her classroom in the appropriate space below.

B. All Home Group members will listen to each expert presentation, then record a possible adaptation of each lesson for their own classroom below.

Lesson #1: Possible Adaptation for My Classroom

Lesson #2: Possible Adaptation for My Classroom

Lesson #3: Possible Adaptation for My Classroom

Lesson #4: Possible Adaptation for My Classroom

Enriching Content Classes for Secondary ESOL Students

Study Guide

Section 8
Putting It All Together

Putting It All Together

Goal

To integrate the strategies learned in this session in a unit, in case studies, and in a framework for school reform.

Performance Objectives

• Prepare a unit plan that integrates language development, academic development, and multicultural education strategies.

• Apply strategies to case studies of issues that face secondary students.

• Consider characteristics of schools that support ESOL students' academic achievement.

• Share the unit with other participants in order to learn from each other.

SECTION 8

Developing the Unit Plan

Part A: Recommended Approach

1. Identify a <u>topic or organizing concept</u> for the unit.

2. Decide on a <u>culminating activity</u> (project, display, debate, essay, chart) in which students will demonstrate their understanding of and ability to use the unit's most important concepts; decide how to grade this activity.

3. Choose <u>holistic activities</u> to build on students' prior knowledge, contextualize the concepts, and teach students what they need to know to understand the unit's concepts and to do the culminating activity.

4. Identify the <u>high priority language</u> needed to do the activities and explain the concepts, and how this language will be taught.

5. Identify the <u>higher-order thinking skills</u> needed to do the activities and use the concepts, and how these skills will be taught.

6. Identify <u>ESOL students' cultural needs/contributions</u>, for example: Are there cultural assumptions/background knowledge he/she may need? Can the ESOL student make a unique contribution to the unit?

7. Select a method of assessing <u>individual learning</u>, adapt it for beginning ESOL students, and determine how to grade it.

Part B: Other Strategies to Consider

1. The Three Principles
2. Connecting across the content areas
3. Promising Practices from the Anstrom reading
4. Banks' approaches to multicultural education
5. Your personal priorities for teaching diverse students

Part C: Presenting the Unit Plan

1. Each unit plan will be presented to other participants in a Poster Session. You must visually show how your plan <u>has identified</u> and <u>will teach</u> the underlined items listed in Part A. Think of having a large bulletin board that you can use to show these items. You may use pictures, drawings, outlines, graphic organizers, etc. Your display should be self-explanatory.

2. You will receive written feedback on your display from other participants. In addition,

participants will select the display that they feel best exemplifies the criteria listed below.

Part D: Evaluating the Unit Plan

1. Does the display: identify a <u>topic or organizing concept</u> for the unit?

2. Does the <u>culminating activity</u> (project, display, debate, essay, chart) require students to demonstrate their understanding of and ability to use the unit's most important concepts?

3. Do the <u>holistic activities</u> build on students' prior knowledge, contextualize the concepts, and teach students what they need to know to understand the unit's concepts and to do the culminating activity?

4. Is the <u>high priority language</u> needed to do the activities and explain the concepts identified and taught?

5. Are the <u>higher-order thinking skills</u> needed to do the activities and use the concepts identified and taught?

6. Are <u>ESOL students' cultural needs/contributions</u> recognized in the unit?

7. Is there a method of assessing <u>individual learning</u> and an adaptation for beginning ESOL students?

Issues that Secondary Schools Face in Educating
Language Minority Students

Scenario #1 - Low Literacy

Mrs. Brown teaches a tenth grade, mainstream Social Studies class. Each day when she writes the instructional objective on the board or asks students to copy notes from the blackboard, Ahmed, an ESOL student, is always the last to finish. When Ahmed is called on to read instructions out loud or when any reading is done within cooperative groups, he almost always looses his place within the text and has great difficulty with the pronunciation of words. Since there is only one blackboard in her classroom and often a lot of information for students to copy, Mrs. Brown frequently has to erase what she has previously written. Ahmed always protests by saying "wait, I'm not finished yet!" and the class has to wait for several minutes before proceeding. At other times when Mrs. Brown does not write on the board but presents her lesson in a lecture format, she asks students to take notes. She has noticed that Ahmed always sits and never writes anything. When homework is assigned or students are asked to complete a major paper, Ahmed almost never completes any homework or submits any written paper. In addition, when students are given any type of test, Ahmed sits for long periods of time before attempting to begin. If anything is written on the paper, the letters are usually very large and all of the words are written in one continuous line.

Possible approaches/suggestions:

Scenario #2 - Standardized Tests

Within the last ten years, School District "Y" has had a large influx of immigrant students. Open Door High School, located in School District "Y," has the largest percentage of immigrant students. Out of the total school population, 75% of the students are recently arrived immigrants. The school has an English as a Second Language (ESL) program where students receive intensive language development for the first year. Many of these students, however, are between the ages of 15-20 years old when they arrive and have had minimal schooling experiences. While many of them make progress during their first year, their linguistic and cognitive abilities still fall far below grade level compared to their mainstream peers. Because of their chronological ages, after the first year these students often receive instruction from mainstream teachers who have had little experience teaching second language learners and employing instructional strategies to accommodate their needs. In addition, the native English speakers are often unaware of or insensitive to these students' needs in these classes. At the beginning of this school year, the superintendent of

School District "Y" issued a mandate stating that all schools, regardless of their student populations, would be required to administer a standardized exam. Test scores from each school in District "Y" would have to reach a standard determined by the district, or the school would be identified as a targeted assistance school. Teachers were also informed that low test scores could possibly result in the loss of their jobs. In an effort to improve test scores, teachers were forced to "teach to the test." Two months after the administration of the standardized test, the results arrived at Open Door. While there were some gains in student performance, the overall gains were minimal.

Possible approaches/suggestions:

Scenario #3 - Lack of Parent Participation

Mr. Juarez is the principal of a middle school in a fairly large city. Many of the students who attend this school come from families where English is not the dominant language of the home. Recently, the school was cited in the city's major newspaper as having one of the lowest records for student achievement in the district. Enraged by this type of publicity concerning his school, Mr. Juarez called the paper and arranged to have an interview with the reporter to defend his school. Mr. Juarez explained that not only were most students at the school limited English proficient, but their parents spoke little or no English. Secondly, he explained that at parent/teacher meetings, less than half of the parents were in attendance since most worked at night. Thirdly, even when fliers in students' native language were sent home to announce upcoming school events or when important letters or documents were mailed, less than a quarter of the students' parents responded. Finally, when calls were made to the homes of parents to notify them that their child(ren) were in danger of failing or facing disciplinary action, there was almost never any response to messages left for the parent(s) to return the call. Even native language parent groups were poorly attended.

Possible approaches/suggestions:

Scenario #4 - High Turn Over (Transitory Population)

Ms. Jacobs is a young, enthusiastic and innovative ESOL teacher. This is her first year teaching at a large high school located in a rural area outside Philadelphia. At least 45% of the English language learners live in the nearby communities where their families are migrants who work in the mushroom nursery. Since this type of work is the only means of income for these families and the work is seasonal, the children often are forced to work long hours and to miss school to assist their parents. Prior to the beginning of the school year, Ms. Jacobs attended staff development sessions for the purpose of identifying and developing appropriate curricular materials for beginning level ESOL students. To facilitate language acquisition and to make the instruction more relevant for her students, she decided that she would center her instruction around thematic units. When classes started in September, the class enrollment was thirty. By mid-October, the class size had been reduced to fifteen. Half of the students had to drop out because the work had ended for their families, and it was time to relocate to another area. One week later, when she had already completed half of the first unit, a new group of students enrolled in her class. Ms. Jacobs was faced with a dilemma; she did not know whether to continue with the same unit or start a new unit. She made the decision to begin a new unit, and within two weeks the other half of the first group of students had left. Ms. Jacobs is finding it extremely challenging to teach this population of students because she cannot have continuity in her instruction.

Possible approaches/suggestions:

Scenario #5 - Limited Resources

Mr. Pertuzzi has been a principal in the Tecumseh Valley School District for the past ten years. Prior to his appointment as principal, he taught both at the elementary and secondary levels. His experience working in the Tecumseh School District can be sharply contrasted with that of the earlier schools where he was employed with respect to the types of educational resources and instructional materials that were readily available for teachers' use. Freedom High School, where he currently works, is located in an economically depressed area of the city. The student population consists of the following ethnic groups: 45% Caucasian, 30% Hispanic, 15% African American, and 10% Asian. The educational needs of these populations are as diverse and varied as their cultural and linguistic backgrounds. Monies for the purchase of books and other instructional resources come from a fund designated for this purpose. Teachers are requested to place their orders prior to the end of the school year, from a specified book list published by the school system. Often the books listed by the Tecumseh School District are outdated and not relevant to the needs of the student population. In addition, the books that are ordered almost never arrive prior to the beginning of the following school year in time for teachers to make adequate preparations for classes. On the other hand, when teachers are fortunate to get good and relevant books, materials and other instructional equipment, they are often lost or stolen. In frustration, teachers are forced to violate copyright laws to provide printed materials for the students in their classrooms and the copier often stays in need of repair. Without appropriate textbooks and other equipment, students at Freedom High School are unable to achieve the same high level of academic standards as the other schools in the Tecumseh School District.

Possible approaches/suggestions:

Scenario #6 - Mixed Ability Groups

Since 1995 Becky Thompson has seen a steady increase in the population of English language learners in her school. When she first started teaching ESOL in 1988, the primary focus of the ESOL Department was a grammar based approach with the intent of preparing students who already had strong academic skills to quickly exit the ESOL sequence into mainstream classes. In recent years, however, the department has been forced to change its curricular focus to accommodate students who have varying levels of literacy and, in some cases learning disabilities. Realizing that these students require different instructional approaches and additional time to acquire both content and language skills, the department increased the instructional course load of the ESOL teachers, requiring them to teach both language and sheltered content classes. At the same time, the school decided to change the former fifty minute class to a block schedule where students would take fewer classes in ninety-minute blocks. While Ms. Thompson likes the idea of having more time to teach students, she also has concerns. Her class sizes are much larger than a few years ago, and she has to teach students at multiple literacy levels and with a variety of learning problems. With this type of heterogeneity in her classroom, it is extremely difficult to develop one lesson to meet the needs of all students. Although the school has been identified as a Title 1 school and has some money to pay for bilingual aides, the people who apply for these positions are not always the most qualified and the number of aides available is not sufficient to meet the growing needs of the students.

Possible approaches/suggestions:

SECTION 8

Source: Cathy McCargo, Center for Applied Linguistics, Washington, DC, 1998.

Exemplary Schooling for Language Minority Students

Directions: . Read the following attributes carefully and rate your school on each attribute using a five point scale, then total your ratings at the bottom of the page. These ratings will be confidential.

Scale: 5=school does exceptionally well
       4=school does very well
       3=school does pretty well
       2=school could improve
       1=school needs substantial improvement

In 1996, Beverly McLeod published the findings of her intensive study of selected schools in four states (Texas, Illinois, California, and Massachusetts). The schools were chosen for study because they served highly diverse and poor student populations, and demonstrated high levels of academic success. McLeod investigated each school, looking for attributes that related to the functioning of the school, then looking for common attributes across sites. Seven attributes were identified. The schools made decisions and organized services in order to:

_____1. **Foster English acquisition and the development of mature literacy**. Schools utilized native language abilities to develop literacy that promoted English literacy development. Programs in these schools were more interested in this mature development than transitioning students quickly into English language instruction. This approach paid off in English language development at levels that allowed students to be successful in English instruction.

_____2. **Deliver grade-level content**. Challenging work in the academic disciplines was perceived and acted on simultaneously with the goals of English language learning. Teachers organized lessons to deliver grade-level instruction through a variety of native language, sheltered English, and ESL activities.

_____3. **Organize instruction in innovative ways**. examples of innovations included: (a) "schools-within-schools" to more responsively deal with diverse language needs of the students; (b) "families" of students who stayed together for major parts of the school day; (c) "continuum classes" in which teachers remained with their students for two to three years, helping teachers become more familiar with and respond to the diversity in the students; and (d) grouping of students more flexibly on a continuous basis to respond to the developmental differences between their native language and second language.

_____4. **Protect and extend instructional time**. Schools utilized after-school programs, supportive computer based instruction, and voluntary Saturday schools and summer academies. These school activities multiplied the opportunities for students to engage in academic learning. Regular teachers or trained tutors were utilized to extend this learning time. Not surprisingly, a majority of students took advantage of these voluntary extensions. <u>Care was taken not to erode the daily instructional time that was available</u> -- erosion often related to auxiliary responsibilities by teachers that take away from instruction.

_____5. **Expand teachers' roles and responsibilities**. Teachers were given much <u>greater</u> roles in curricular and instructional decision making. This decision making was much more collective in nature to ensure cross-grade articulation and coordination. Teachers in these schools became full co-partners. They devised more <u>authentic assessments</u> that could inform instruction, developing assessment tools and scoring rubrics in reading and mathematics.

_____6. **Address students' social and emotional needs**. Schools were located in low-income neighborhoods serving poor families. Therefore, a <u>proactive stance</u> with regard to issues in these communities was adopted. An after-school activity that was aimed at families, particularly dealing with issues of alcohol and drug abuse, family violence, health care, and related social service needs, brought the school staff together with social service agencies at one school site. Similar examples of actual family counseling and direct medical care were arranged at other sites.

_____7. <u>**Involve parents** in their children's education.</u> Some of the schools were magnet schools. Parents had chosen to send their children there. In such schools, parent involvement was part of the magnet school contract. This included involvement in school committees, school festivals and celebrations, student field trips, and other activities. In non-magnet schools, parent outreach services were an integral part of the school operation. In all cases, communication was accomplished on a regular basis in various home languages. Parent participation in governance of the school was a common attribute, although levels of parent participation were highly variable.

Source: McLeod, B. (1996). *School reform and student diversity: Exemplary schooling for language minority students.* Washington, DC: George Washington University, Institute for the Study of Language and Education.

Enriching Content Classes
for Secondary ESOL Students

Study Guide

Conclusion

Conclusion

Goal

To review and assess the learning that occurred in the inservice training.

Performance Objectives

• Reflect on each participant's personal learning in this session.

• Complete the post-test.

• Review the post-test.

Note to Participants

Presenter will distribute materials for Conclusion. Participant should place these materials in this section to complete the portfolio.

Enriching Content Classes for Secondary ESOL Students

Study Guide

**Resource Lists
and References**

Supplemental Resources for Working with ESOL Middle School and High School Students with Limited Formal Schooling

Note: Many of the following text resources were compiled by Dr. Catherine Walsh, MRC/UMass-Boston

English/ESL

In Print: Beginning Literacy Through Cultural Awareness-Addison Wesley

Language and Culture in Conflict: Problem Solving in the ESL Classroom-Addison Wesley

ESL for Action: Problem Posing at Work - Addison Wesley

Picture Stories and *More Picture Stories* - Addison Wesley/Longman

A New Start. A Functional Course in Basic Spoken English and *Survival Literacy* - Dormac and Heinemann

New Arrival English - Heinle and Heinle

First Words; Starting to Read; Basic Study Skills for Academic Success; Teen Scenes and *Teen Stories* - all from Linmore Publishing

The New Oxford Picture Dictionary Program - Oxford University Press

Access Fundamentals of Literacy and Communication - Regents/Prentice Hall

Teaching literature to language minority students by L. Sasser, in *The Multicultural Classroom: Readings for Content Area Teachers* (Richard-Amato and Snow, eds.) Longman, 1992

Mathematics

Mathematics Book A /Learning Strategies for Problem Solving - Addison Wesley Publishing

Math for the Real World, Books 1 and 2 - New Readers Press

Basic Essentials of Math, Books 1 and 2 - Steck-Vaughn Company

Working with Numbers - Steck-Vaughan Company

FAST MATH: Promoting Success in Math and Language (A curriculum developed by Fairfax County Public School for students with limited English and prior schooling) National Clearinghouse for Bilingual Education

Reforming Mathematics Instruction for ESL Literacy Students by K. Buchanan and M. Helman - National Clearinghouse for Bilingual Education (Program Information Guide Series No. 15, 1993)

Science

Life Science: Content and Learning Strategies; Earth and Physical Science: Content and Learning Strategies - Addison Wesley

Concepts and Challenges in Earth Science - Globe Book Company

The Wonders of Science (5 volumes) - Steck-Vaughn

LIFE SCIENCE UNITS: 7th grade, modified for ESOL students (a curriculum guide and supplemental materials for beginning and intermediate ESOL students) - available from Prince George's County Public Schools, Upper Marlboro, MD 20772 (Document number: 7690-1566)

Social Studies

Language Development Through Content Series: America the Early Years; America after Independence, Our People Their Stories - Addison Wesley

Explore America - Ballard and Tighe Publishers

Unlocking Social Studies Skills; Unlocking Geography Skills and Concepts, Unlocking the Constitution and the Declaration of Independence - Globe Book Company

Content Area ESL: Social Studies - Linmore Publishing

Maps, Globes, Graphs - An Interactive Program for Adults; World Geography and You, Books 1 and 2 - Steck-Vaughan

Spanish

Longman Photo Dictionary - Edicion Bilingue - Longman

Palabras de lucha y alegria; Cuentos de lucha y alegria; Mas cuentos de lucha y alegria - New Readers Press

America, su Historia hasta 1865; desde 1865 - Steck-Vaughn

El Arrepentimiento de Julian/Julian's Regrets (a photonovel written by HS students with limited formal schooling) Available from: Dr. Catherine Walsh, MRC, Wheatley I-77, UMass, Boston, MA 02125

Study Skills

Basic Study Skills for Academic Success by Hana Prashker - Linmore Publishing

Study Skills for Students of English, 2nd edition, by Richard C. Yorkey - McGraw-Hill

Multiple Subjects

Prince George's County Public Schools has developed several curriculums for teaching literacy and basic academic content to secondary students with limited literacy, English, and academic skills. The materials are available from: Prince George's County Public Schools, Upper Marlboro, MD 20772

Guidelines for Teaching Pre/Non-literate Speakers of Other Languages, grades 4-8 (Document No: 7690-1704)

ESOL AIM literacy, grades 7-12 (Document No: 7690-1514)

ESOL AIM 2 literacy grades 7-12 (Document No: 7690-2813)

ESOL CABLE, grades 9-12 (Document No: 7690-2810)

Resources for Mainstream Teachers of ESOL Students

<u>General Resources: Instructional Strategies and Approaches</u>

Chamot, A.U. and O'Malley, J.M. (1994). *The CALLA handbook: Implementing the cognitive academic language learning approach.* Reading, MA: Addison-Wesley

Law, B. and Eckes, M. (2000). *The more-than-just-surviving handbook: ESL for every classroom teacher.* Second ed. Winnipeg, Canada: Portage and Main Press (Peguis Publishers).

Peyton, J. K. and Adger, C. T., guest editors. (1998). Promoting achievement: Special issue on immigrant students in secondary school. *TESOL Journal,* Vol. 7, No. 5.

Reyes-Blanes, M.E. and Daunic, A. (1996). Culturally responsive pedagogy: An imperative approach to instruction. *The Journal of Educational Issues of Language Minority Students.* 17, 49-66.

Richard-Amato, P.A. and Snow, M. A. (1992). *The multicultural classroom: Readings for content-area teachers.* White Plains, NY: Longman.

Short, D.J. (1991). *Integrating language and content instruction: Strategies and techniques.* Washington, DC: The National Clearinghouse for Bilingual Education, Program Guide #7.

Short, D. J. and Echevarria, J. (1999). *The sheltered instruction observation protocol: a tool for teacher-research, collaboration, and professional development* (Educational Practice Report 3). University of California, Santa Cruz: Center for Research on Education, Diversity and Excellence.

Zehler, A. M. (no date). *Working with English language learners: Strategies for elementary and middle school teachers.* Washington, DC: The National Clearinghouse for Bilingual Education, Program Information Guide No. 19.

<u>Specific Resources: Math and Science</u>

Buchanan, K. and Helman, M. (Fall, 1993). *Reforming mathematics instruction for ESL literacy students.* Washington, DC: The National Clearinghouse for Bilingual Education, Program Information Guide No. 15.

Guillaume, A.M., Yopp, R.H., and Yopp, H.K. (1996). Accessible science. *The Journal of Educational Issues of Language Minority Students.* 17, 67-86.

Khisty, L.L. (1996). Making mathematics multicultural through meaning and empowerment. *The Journal of Educational Issues of Language Minority Students.* 17, 49-66.

Fathman, A. K., Quinn, M.E., and Kessler, C. (Summer, 1992). *Teaching science to English learners, grades 4-8.* Washington, DC: The National Clearinghouse for Bilingual Education. Program Information Guide, No.11.

Minicucci, C. (1996). *Learning science and English; How school reform advances scientific learning for limited English proficient middle school students.* Washington, DC: The National Center for Research on Cultural Diversity and Second Language Learning. Educational Practice Report: 17.

RESOURCES

Other topics:

Flores, J.L. (1996). *Children of la frontera: Binational efforts to serve Mexican migrant and immigrant students.* Charleston, WV: ERIC Clearinghouse on Rural Education and Small Schools.

Germer, L. (1996). *47% American: Coping with cultural issues in middle school.* Studio City, CA: JAG.

Gonzalez, J.M. and Darling-Hammond, L. (1997). *New concepts for new challenges: Professional development for teachers of immigrant youths.* Washington D.C. and McHenry, IL: Center for Applied Linguistics and Delta Systems Co., Inc.

Hainer, E.V., Fagan, B., Bratt, T., Baker, L., and Arnold, N. (Summer, 1990). *Integrating learning styles and skills in the ESL classroom: An approach to lesson planning.* Washington, DC: The National Clearinghouse for Bilingual Education, Program Information Guide, No. 2.

Holt, D.D., Chips, B. ,and Wallace, D. (Summer, 1991). *Cooperative learning in the secondary school: Maximizing language acquisition, academic achievement, and social development.* Washington, DC: The National Clearinghouse for Bilingual Education, Program Information Guide, No. 12.

Lucas, T. (Fall, 1993). *Applying elements of effective secondary schooling for language minority students: A tool for reflection and stimulus to change.* Washington D.C. and McHenry, IL: Center for Applied Linguistics and Delta Systems Co., Inc.

Lucas, T. (1997). *Into, through and beyond secondary school: Critical transitions for immigrant youths.* Washington D.C. and McHenry, IL: Center for Applied Linguistics and Delta Systems Co., Inc.

Mace-Matluck, B.J., Alexander-Kasparik, R. and Quenn, R.M. (1998). *Through the golden door: Educational approaches for immigrant adolescents with limited schooling.* Washington D.C. and McHenry, IL: Center for Applied Linguistics and Delta Systems Co., Inc.

Savage, M.K. and Savage, T.V. (1996). Achieving multicultural goals through children's nonfiction. *The Journal of Educational Issues of Language Minority Students.* 17, 25-38.

Violand-Sanchez, E., Sutton, C. P., and Ware, H.W. (Summer, 1991). *Fostering home-school cooperation: Involving language minority families as partners in education.* Washington, DC: The National Clearinghouse for Bilingual Education, Program Guide Series No. 6.

Walqui, A. (1998). *Accent and engagement: Program design and instructional approaches for immigrant students in secondary school.* Washington D.C. and McHenry, IL: Center for Applied Linguistics and Delta Systems Co., Inc.

Note: for additional multicultural resources see the extensive resource listing following the Menkart article in Section 7 of the Study Guide.

RESOURCES

Other Resources: Organizations and Journals

<u>Organizations</u>

1.   TESOL (Teachers of English to Speakers of Other Languages)
     700 South Washington Street, Suite 200
     Alexandria, VA 22314
     703-836-0774   fax: 703-836-7864
     www.tesol.org

2.   Association of Supervision and Curriculum Development (ASCD)
     1703 North Beauregard Street
     Alexandria, VA 22311-1714
     800-933-ASCD(2723)
     703-578-9600
     www.ascd.org

3.   Center for Applied Linguistics (CAL)
     4646 40th Street NW
     Washington, D.C. 20016-1859
     202-362-0700
     www.cal.org

4.   National Clearinghouse for Bilingual Education (NCBE)
     The George Washington University
     2121 K Street, NW, Suite 260
     Washington, DC 20037
     202-467-0867
     www.ncbe.gwu.edu (includes on-line library)

5.   National Association for Bilingual Education (NABE)
     1030 15th Street , NW, Suite 470
     Washington, DC 20005-1503
     202-898-1829
     www.nabe.org

Journals

ERIC/CLL News Bulletin (free)
ERIC Clearinghouse on Languages and Linguistics
Center for Applied Linguistics
4646 40th Street, NW
Washington, DC 20016-0700
202-362-0700

Language Arts Journal
National Association of Bilingual Education
1111 W. Kenyon Rd.
Urbana, IL 61801-1096

NABE Journal, NABE NEWS
National Association for Bilingual Education
1030 15th Street, Suite 470
Washington, DC 20005-1503
202-898-1829

NCBE Program Information Guides
NCBE Occasional Papers
NCBE Forum
National Clearinghouse for Bilingual Education
The George Washington University
2121 K Street, NW, Suite 260
Washington, D.C. 20037
202-467-0867

Phi Delta Kappan
408 N. Union
P.O. Box 789
Bloomington, IN 47402

The Reading Teacher
International Reading Association
800 Barksdale Road
 P.O. Box 8139
Newark, DE 19714-8139

TESOL Journal, TESOL Matters, TESOL Quarterly
TESOL
700 South Washington Street, Suite 200
Alexandria, VA 22314
703-836-0774; fax: 703-836-7864

References

Introduction

ECS (Education Commission of the States) Clearinghouse. (1997). *When students get behind.* Denver :ECS.

Flores, J.L., Ed. (1996). *Children of la frontera: Binational efforts to serve Mexican migrant amd immigrant students.* Charleston, WV: ERIC Clearinghouse on Rural Education and Small Schools.

Navarette, C. and Gustke, C. (1996) *A guide to performance assessment for linguistically diverse students.* Evaluation and Assistance Center West, New Mexico Highlands University.

Section 1: Academic Competence, Part A

Fogarty, R. (1991). *The mindful school: How to integrate the curricula.* Palatine, IL: IRI/Skylight Publishing, Inc.

Hamayan, E.(1993). Current trends in ESL curriculum. In S. Hudelson et al (Eds.). *English as a second language curriculum resource handbook.* Millwood, N.J.: Kraus International Publications.

Long, M.H. and Porter, P.A. (1985). Group work, interlanguage talk, and second language acquisition. *TESOL Quarterly*, 19(2), 207-228.

Perkins, D. (1993). The connected curriculum. *Educational Leadership*, 51(2), 90-91.

Secretary's Commission on Achieving Necessary Skills (1991). *What work requires of schools: A SCANS report for America 2000.* Washington, DC: Department of Labor.

Section 2: Language Learning in School

ASCD Update. (1994). Teaching language minority students: Role of native-language instruction is debated. Vol. 36, No. 5. Alexandria, VA: Association for Supervision and Curriculum.

August, D. and Pease-Alvarez, L. (1996). *Attributes of effective programs and classrooms serving English language learners.* University of California, Santa Cruz: National Center for Research on Cultural Diversity and Second Language Learning.

Bennett, C. I. (1990). *Comprehensive multicultural education: Theory and practice.* Second ed. Boston: Allyn and Bacon.

Collier, V.P. (1995, Fall). *Acquiring a second language for school.* (Directions in language and education Vol. 4). Washington, DC: The National Clearinghouse for Bilingual Education.

RESOURCES

Cummins, J. (1984). *Bilingualism and special education: Issues in assessment and pedagogy.* San Diego, CA: College-Hill Press.

Cummins, J. (1987). *Empowering minority students. Teacher Training Monograph #5.* Gainesville, FL: The University of Florida.

Empowering ESOL teachers: an overview. (no date). Volume I, Section V. Tallahassee, FL: Florida Department of Education.

Krashen, S.D. (June 1996). A gradual exit, variable threshold model for limited English proficient children. *NABE News.* 19(7):1-18

Krashen, S.D. (1981). Bilingual education and second language acquisition theory. In *Schooling and language minority students: A theoretical framework.* Los Angeles: Evaluation, Dissemination, and Assessment Center, California State University.

Levine, D.R., and Adelman, M.B. (1993). *Beyond language: Cross-cultural communication.* Second ed. Englewood Cliffs, NJ: Prentice-Hall Regents.

National Center for Research on Cultural Diversity and Second Language Learning. (Dec. 1992). Myths and misconceptions about second language learning. *ERIC Digest.* (EDO-FL-92-10).

Navarette, C. and Gustke, C. (1996), *A guide to performance assessment for linguistically diverse students.* Evaluation and Assistance Center West, New Mexico Highlands University.

Pinker, S. (1994). *The language instinct.* NY: HarperCollins

Short, D.J. (1991). *Integrating language and content instruction: Strategies and techniques.* Washington, DC: The National Clearinghouse for Bilingual Education, Program Guide #7.

TESOL (1997). *ESL standards for preK-12 students.* Alexandria, VA: Teachers of English to Speakers of Other Languages, Inc.

Thomas, W.P., and Collier, V. (May, 1996). Language minority student achievement and program effectiveness. *NABE News.*

Thomas, W.P., and Collier, V. (1995). *Research summary of study in progress: Language minority student achievement and program effectiveness.* Fairfax, VA: George Mason University.

Thomas, W.P., and Collier, V. (1997). *School effectiveness for language minority students.* Washington, D.C.: National Clearinghouse for Bilingual Education.

Section 3: Culture, Part A

Damen, L. (1987). *Culture learning: The fifth dimension in the language classroom.* Reading, MA: Addison-Wesley.

Fersh, S. (Ed.). (1974). *Learning about peoples and cultures*. Evanston, IL: McDougal, Littel, and Co.

Fradd, S.H. and Lee, O. (1998). *Creating Florida's multilingual global workforce: Educational policies and practices for students learning English as a new language.* Tallahassee, FL: Florida Department of Education.

Section 4: Academic Competence, Part B.

Anstrom, K. (1997). *Academic acheivement for secondary language minority students: Standards, measures and promising practices.* Washington, D.C.: National Clearinghouse for Bilingual Education.

Guillaume, A.M., Yopp, R.H., and Yopp, H.K. (1996). Accessible science. *The Journal of Educational Issues of Language Minority Students.* 17, 67-86.

Guskey, T.R. (1985). Staff development and teacher change. *Educational Leadership,* 42 (7), 57-60.

Jones, B.F., Pierce, J., and Hunter, B. (Dec. 1988/Jan. 1989). Teaching students to construct graphic representations. *Educational Leadership.* pp. 20-25

Khisty, L.L. (1996). Making mathematics multicultural through meaning and empowerment. *The Journal of Educational Issues of Language Minority Students.* 17, 49-66.

Reyes-Blanes, M.E. and Daunic. A. (1996). Culturally responsive pedagogy: An imperative approach to instruction. *The Journal of Educational Issues of Language Minority Students.* 17, 103-120.

Savage, M.K. and Savage, T.V. (1996). Achieving multicultural goals through children's nonfiction. *The Journal of Educational Issues of Language Minority Students.* 17, 25-38.

Saville-Troike, M. (1984). What really matters in second language learning for academic development? *TESOL Quarterly*, 18(2).

Short, D.J. (1991). *Integrating language and content instruction: Strategies and techniques.* Washington, DC: The National Clearinghouse for Bilingual Education, Program Guide #7.

Tang, G.M. (Winter 1992/1993). Teaching content knowledge and ESOL in multicultural classrooms. *TESOL Journal*, 2(2), 8-12.

Section 5: Literacy Development and Study Skills

Chamot, A.U. and O' Malley, J.M. (1994). CALLA handouts from a University of Florida workshop.

Chamot, A.U. and O' Malley, J.M. (1994). *The CALLA handbook: Implementing the cognitive academic language learning approach.* Reading, MA. Addison-Wesley.

Law, B. and Eckes, M. (2000). *The more-than-just-surviving handbook: ESL for every classroom teacher.* Second ed. Winnipeg, Canada: Portage and Main Press (Peguis Publishers).

Lopez-Valdez, J. and Reed, T. (June, 1989). *Building competencies to serve LEP vocational students: An inservice manual.* Des Plaines, IL: Northwest Educational Cooperative.

Section 6: Assessment

Anstrom, K. (1997). *Academic achievement for secondary language minority students: Standards, measures and promising practices.* Washington, D.C.: National Clearinghouse for Bilingual Education.

Education Update. (June, 1997*).* Assessment that serves instruction. Vol. 39, No. 4 Alexandria, VA: Association for Supervision and Curriculum Development.

Education Update. (June 1996). On the cutting edge of assessment: Testing what students can do with knowledge. Vol. 38, No. 4. Alexandria, VA: Association for Supervision and Curriculum Development.

Education Update. (June 1998). Matching assessment with curriculum. Vol 40, No.4. Alexandria, VA: Association for Supervision and curriculum Development.

Empowering ESOL teachers: An overview. (Revised 1996 edition). Volume II, Section IX. Tallahassee, FL: Florida Department of Education.

Herman, J.L. (1992). What research tells us about good assessment. *Educational Leadership*, May, 1992.

Lopez-Valadez, J. and Reed, T. (June, 1989). *Building competencies to serve LEP vocational students: An inservice manual.* Des Plaines, IL: Northwest Educational Cooperative.

Navarette, C. and Gustke, C. (1996) *A guide to performance assessment for linguistically diverse students.* Evaluation and Assistance Center West, New Mexico Highlands University.

Solis, A. (1995). Grading LEP students: Developing sound practice. *NABE News.* pp. 21-44.

Section 7: Culture, Part B

Banks, J.A. (1988). *Multiethnic education: Theory and practice.* (2nd ed.). Boston: Allyn and Bacon.

Banks, J.A. (1994). Transforming the mainstream curriculum. *Educational Leadership.* Vol. 51, No. 8.

Menkart, D. (1993). *Multicultural education: Strategies for linguistically diverse schools and classrooms.* (Program Information Guide No. 16) Washington, DC: The National Clearinghouse for Bilingual Education.

Section 8: Putting It All Together

Fullan, M. (1998). Breaking the bonds of dependency. *Educational Leadership* 55(7).

Goldenberg, C. and Sullivan, J. (1994). *Making change happen in a language minority school: A search for coherence.* Educational Practice Report 13. Santa Cruz, CA. National Center for Research on Cultural Diversity and Second Language Learning.

McLeod, B. (1996). *School reform and student diversity: Exemplary schooling for language minority students.* Washington, D.C.: George Washington University, Institute for the Study of Language and Education.

RESOURCES

Achieving Multicultural Goals Through Children's Nonfiction

Marsha K. Savage
Tom V. Savage

Introduction

The advantages of using children's literature to achieve important educational goals have long been recognized. Well-written children's books can capture student interest and motivation much better than textbooks (Norton, 1994). In addition, children's books are often written in a narrative format appealing to students who come from cultural backgrounds where narration and storytelling are common,

Typically, the type of literature recommended for this purpose is fiction. While a number of excellent fiction books can be used in the classroom, nonfiction is often overlooked because of the perception that it tends to be less interesting and motivating than fiction. In fact, since the inception in 1922 of the Newbery Award for the most distinguished contribution to children's literature, only four awards have been presented to authors of nonfiction. The same pattern seems to hold true for other awards such as the Boston-Globe Horn Book Award or the National Book Award (Meltzer, 1994b). Why? Fisher (1972) contends that part of the problem is that writers of nonfiction for children are not viewed in the same light as authors of junior novels, and their works are considered as more "information books" than creative works. A children's book editor of the *New York Times* dismissed nonfiction works as "non-books" (Meltzer, 1994b). It appears that many judges of book awards for children do not believe that nonfiction books can have any literary merit (Meltzer, 1994b, p. 28). Meltzer (1994a) reacts to the charge that a nonfiction book is simply an information book by asking the question, "Information about what?" He points out that young readers need to be informed not only about how trucks run and how weather is formed, but on how character is shaped, how handicaps are overcome, and how the whole world works (p. 19). He also points out that "imagination, invention, selection, language, form...are just as important to the making of a good book of biography, history, or science as to the making of a piece of fiction" (Meltzer, 1994b, p. 25). Well written nonfiction books can be as captivating and engaging as fiction books and have some important advantages.

Nonfiction has the capacity to "raise questions in the minds of young readers. Teach them not so much facts and dates or formulas but the art and necessity of asking questions" (Meltzer, 1994a p. 22). Whether it is a story of the Civil War or a moving biography of someone who met with critical acclaim, quality nonfiction encourages young people to think–and to inquire. Consequently, students begin to relate to the accounts and the people in a personal way. These are not contrived stories, they really happened. This focus on reality helps establish a record of the experiences of a particular group (Pugh & Garcia, 1990). Reading stories of real people helps students develop an understanding of the values, the perspectives, and the frames of references of individuals from a variety of cultures. Reading about real people and events can help students develop a sense of pride and provide them with some parameters for thinking about their values and sense of purpose.

Another advantage is that nonfiction books provide a sense of identity or rootedness for readers by recounting the ethnic histories and accomplishments of African Americans,

Hispanic Americans, Native Americans, and Asian Americans as well as other cultural groups.

Several categories of nonfiction books should be considered for classroom use. One category is biographies and autobiographies which celebrate the lives of people who have overcome barriers and made important contributions. While some of these might be about famous individuals who are generally well known, such as Cesar Chavez or Martin Luther King, Jr., at least as valuable are the stories of those common or less known individuals who have not been considered important enough to be mentioned in mainstream textbooks. Many of these stories provide examples that are closer to the lives of the students in our classrooms and provide valuable insight into the culture of which they are a part.

For example, Elsie Kreischers' *Maria Montoya Martinez: Master Potter* (1995), published by Pelican Publishing Company, is an engaging account of the struggles of a sick little girl, born on an Indian reservation, who grew to become an award winning potter. Similarly, William Loren Datz's *Black Women of the Old West* (1995), published by Atheneum Books for Young Readers, tells the often ignored stories of African American women who challenged bigotry and prejudice and helped transform the West as school teachers, poets, nurses, cowgirls and business owners.

Another category of nonfiction literature is those books that provide glimpses and insight into other cultures. Examples include George Ancona's *Fiesta U.S.A.* (1995) published by Lodestar Books and Peggy Thompson's *Katie Henio: Navajo Sheepherder* (1995) published by Cobblehill Books. Ancona's book contains beautiful photographs and stories of the celebrations of Spanish-speaking people in the United States. Thompson's engaging book includes photographs and accounts of people and their lives on the Navajo Reservation.

A third type of nonfiction book that can be especially valuable in the classroom is one that portrays children living in different cultural settings. These books help children relate their lives to the main character in the book. They can also help students develop a sense of identity and self-esteem, achieve academic success, and develop proficiency in English (Savage, 1990). Examples of these books include the beautifully illustrated *Konnichiwa: I am a Japanese-American Girl* (1995) by Tricia Brown, published by Henry Holt; Monty Roessel's *Songs From the Loom: A Navajo Girl Learns to Weave* (1995), published by Lerner Publications; and Kathleen Krull's *The Other Side: How Kids Live in a California Latino Neighborhood* (1994), published by Lodestar Books. These books illustrate the great potential of nonfiction books as powerful tools in accomplishing important multicultural education goals.

As noted earlier, the lack of recognition accorded to nonfiction children's books can make the identification of quality nonfiction books problematic. There is, however, one award given annually to multicultural nonfiction children's literature: The Carter G. Woodson Award, sponsored by the National Council for the Social Studies, honors Carter G. Woodson, a prominent African American educator and historian. In addition to his own writing and publishing, Woodson originated Negro History Week in 1926. Each year the committee solicits participation from over 150 publishing houses for nonfiction books that deal with minority, ethnic, and multicultural themes. These books are systematically reviewed, and those books that treat minority and ethnic groups accurately and sensitively are recognized. A secondary and an elementary book are selected to receive the annual award. Other especially worthwhile books receive merit awards (Savage, 1995).

RESOURCES

Selecting Nonfiction Books

Just selecting nonfiction books that discuss a variety of multicultural topics is not enough. Teachers must plan carefully to make sure that powerful ideas are developed and misconceptions avoided. Simply reading a book is not enough, either. For example, students who read about people different from themselves may develop the perception that the people about whom they are reading are "strange" or "funny." Careful guidance from a knowledgeable teacher can assist them in understanding the concepts and the people (Savage & Savage, 1994).

Initially, the teacher must consider how the book relates to important multicultural goals. Some literature might focus on what Banks (1994) calls the contributions approach, where the focus is heroes, heroines, holidays, and discrete cultural elements, or the additive approach which does not change the curriculum in depth. The additive approach might extend a unit or add concepts without changing structure. Ultimately, however, teachers should include books that deal with what Banks calls the transformation approach. This approach is much more time-consuming and requires significant reflection because it changes the structure of the curriculum to "enable students the opportunity to view concepts, issues, events, and themes from the perspectives of diverse ethnic and cultural groups" (p.25).

Another important step when using literature is to identify the important concepts that might be useful for studying the experiences of people from different cultures. Identifying these concepts provides a foundation for selecting books that will then allow the students to develop more than a superficial understanding of a cultural group (Banks. 1994). Some concepts that can be used include: shared culture, values, and symbols; ethnic identity and a sense of peoplehood; perspectives, world views, and frames of reference ethnic institutions and self-determination; assimilation and acculturation.

One way that these concepts can be used in the classroom is by providing questions as advance organizers for students when they read a book. These questions might include:
- What is most important to the people in the book?
- How do people in this book relate to each other?
- How do the people help each other?
- What makes the people in the book proud?
- How do the people in the book view the world around them?
- How do they relate to other people who are from different groups?
- What can you find in the book to indicate that the people have changed to be more like other cultures who live near them?
- What can you find that indicates that the people in the book are trying to keep some parts of their traditional way of living?

When students have addressed some of these questions, they can then compare what they found with classmates' observations and compare the characters in the books with themselves. As they read additional books dealing with a particular cultural group, they can continue to refine and expand their understandings of the concepts. In addition, they can compare cultural groups. They can compare the values and the symbols of different cultures, consider how they are trying to preserve a sense of ethnic identity, and how they are adapting to the world around them (Savage & Savage, 1993).

RESOURCES

Examples of Nonfiction Books

The following are reviews of some of the past winners and merit books that have received the Carter G. Woodson Award. Each review includes suggestions for including some of the concepts suggested by Banks. Many of the award-winning books are now translated into several languages providing the bilingual teacher with a variety of options for using them with all students.

Levine, Ellen. (1995). *A Fence Away From Freedom. New* York: G. Putnam's Sons.
Level: Secondary.
This book which won the 1995 Woodson Award in the secondary category, tells the story of the internment of Japanese Americans during World War II. It helps the reader view an event from a variety of perspectives as it tells the stories of the internment through the voices of young children. Each chapter of the book is composed of a series of short stories told by young people who were sent to the internment camps. The chapters include: The Years before Pearl Harbor, Life in the Camps, Homeless Children, Japanese Peruvians in the U.S. Camps, and Life Outside the Camp. The voices speak with humor as well as with pain and tell of hateful discrimination as well as courage. Because these are the voices of young people, the book is accessible to the young people in our classrooms. Comparing the different accounts of these participants can help readers learn that there are multiple perspectives to any event. Viewing an event from those perspectives is important in arriving at a more complete understanding.

Lyons, Mary. (1993). *Starting Home: The Story of Horace Pippin, Painter*. New York: Charles Scribner's Sons.
Level: Upper Elementary
This award-winning book in the elementary category is one of a series of books written by Mary Lyons dealing with the topic of African American artists and artisans. It fits into the category of a biography about a generally unknown person who has not been mentioned in textbooks.

This book presents the fascinating story of Horace Pippin, a self-taught painter. Pippin was born in 1888 and exhibited a talent for drawing relatively early in his life. A fascinating aspect of the book tells of Pippin's experiences as a soldier in World War I. He was shot in his right shoulder and lost the ability to use his right arm. For 11 years Pippin was unable to draw or paint. How he overcame this handicap and was finally recognized as a painter is a captivating story that holds readers' interest. The book includes a number of color photographs of his paintings. In addition to learning about Pippin and his life, readers gain insight into issues of prejudice, African American culture, and American history. The element of Pippin's injury adds an additional opportunity to examine how courage and persistence can assist individuals in overcoming a disability.

Several of the concepts identified by Banks can be explored using the story of Horace Pippin. Ethnic identity is easily explored through the themes of many of the pictures that Horace painted. They include paintings of African American families in their homes, men harmonizing on the street corner, and other scenes depicting aspects of African American life.

RESOURCES

The concepts of prejudice and racism are prominent in the story. Horace was placed in an all-Black regiment for his service in World War I. The training of the regiment was cut short because of tension created in South Carolina where the regiment trained. One of the paintings displayed in the book, entitled "Mr. Prejudice," provides an excellent opportunity for discussion of issues of racism and prejudice.

Haskins, James. (1993). *The March on Washington*. New York: Harper Collins.
Level: Secondary.

James Haskins has painted a vivid picture of the most significant events in the history of our nation – the March on Washington of August 28, 1963. Although the March on Washington is mentioned in most history books, Haskins provides a glimpse of this event through a perspective different from that normally found in textbooks. He presents it with passion and a dramatic flair that makes readers feel as if they are there.

His story begins in the early days of the civil rights movement with people like Asa Philip Randolph, who had the dream for this march many years before it actually commenced. As the dream unfolds, Haskins introduces each of the major characters who contributed to the success of the event. As August 28 approaches, Haskins takes us inside the minds of those traveling to Washington, and we learn why the trip was so important to them. The climax of this drama is the final speech by Dr. Martin Luther King, Jr. Surprising to many readers is that much of his speech was extemporaneous.

Haskin's book offers a chance to experience vicariously a signal event in the history of the civil rights movement. In this book which reads more like fiction than nonfiction, readers can trace not only the events but the lives of individuals who were instrumental in shaping American history.

This book is an excellent source for exploring a number of the concepts identified by Banks. Racism, prejudice, ethnic identity, and ethnic institutions play a prominent role. The topic of intraethnic diversity can also be explored by identifying the differences between key groups and leaders in the March on Washington. This book offers a good opportunity to deal with the concepts of knowledge construction and revolution since The March on Washington was a major revolutionary event in the history of civil rights in America. Students can look at the March on Washington from different perspectives and can be challenged to construct their own interpretation of this momentous event.

Echo-Hawk, Roger and Walter Echo-Hawk (1994). *Battlefield and Burial Grounds: The Indian Struggle to Protect Ancestral Graves in the United States*. Minneapolis: Lerner Publications Company.
Level: Secondary

This book, a Woodson Merit book in 1995, helps students learn to view events from multiple perspectives. One perspective is that of the Native Americans and their rights, and the other is the research perspective of anthropologists and museums. This book deals with the efforts of the Pawnee Tribe to reclaim the remains of their ancestors.

This book is especially useful for dealing with the relationships between different groups and how there is often a double standard applied to minority groups. The book also provides insight into another culture as it discusses the culture of the Pawnee and their burial practices.

Concepts of racism and prejudice are apparent in this book as it includes the work of earlier anthropologists who used skull measurements to provide evidence of the inferiority of Native Americans and Blacks. These earlier "scientific findings" can be compared to more contemporary efforts aimed at providing the superiority of one group over others.

Klausner, Janet. (1993). *Sequoyah's Gift*. New York: Harper Collins.
Level: Secondary.

    This 1994 merit award winner of the Woodson award is a well-written biography of the great Cherokee leader. Although Sequoyah is a name frequently mentioned in American history textbooks, this account provides great insight into his life.

    Several dimensions of his life provide a basis for classroom discussion. One deals with his devotion to reading and writing. Sequoyah exhorted everyone to learn to read and to teach another in return. Another theme that can be discussed is how Sequoyah overcame hardship, deprivation, and physical handicap to make an important contribution. The issues of racism and injustice are easily discussed in the context of the removal of the Cherokees from their eastern lands on the infamous "Trail of Tears."

Codye, Corinn. (1990). *Vilma Martinez*. Milwaukee: Raintree Publishers.
Level: Elementary.

    This merit-award winner is the inspirational story of an Hispanic woman who was schooled in Texas in an environment that typically trained Hispanics for low-paying jobs. She overcame the prejudice, completed college in two and one-half years, and earned a law degree from Columbia Law School. This degree allowed her the opportunity to fight those who have discriminated against minorities. This book, written in both English and Spanish, chronicles the life of a woman who eventually became the lawyer for the Mexican American Legal Defense and Educational Fund. It is more than just her story, however. *Vilma Martinez* is inspirational for anyone who has faced prejudice and adversity.

    In addition to being a powerful resource for discussing the concepts of prejudice and racism, this book is useful for exploring the concepts of political and economic status. Readers can see how the economic status of a group is often reinforced by the majority culture. This story provides readers with insight into how political power can be used to change the economic and educational status of groups.

Hoyt-Goldsmith, Diane. (1992). *Hoang Anh: A Vietnamese-American Boy*. Holiday House.
Level: Elementary.

    This merit book uses excellent photography by Lawrence Migdale and well-written text to tell the story of Hoang Anh who immigrated to the United States about twelve years ago. This story of a young Vietnamese refugee is an excellent tool to help children and adults understand the experiences encountered by young children as they leave their home country to start fresh in a new country.

    Concepts that can be discussed after reading this book include those of acculturation and assimilation. Readers can see how individuals from other cultures face pressures to adopt the language and the values of the dominant culture. This leads to cultural conflicts as the children grow up torn between two sets of cultural expectations. This book is also useful in helping individuals understand the frames of references and the perspectives of different cultural groups.

RESOURCES

Jenness, Aylette and Alice Rivers. (1989). *In Two Worlds: A Yup'ik Eskimo Family.* Boston: Houghton Mifflin Company.
Level: Elementary.

As technology forces itself into Scammon Bay, Alaska, Alice Rivers is torn between the family structure to which she is accustomed and the lure of an easier life. Jenness, an ethnographer, has provided a poignant glimpse inside a culture often overlooked–the American Eskimo. As teachers and students research and study the various cultural groups within the United States, they should not omit this excellent resource.

This is an especially powerful book for dealing with the issues of acculturation and assimilation. Too often, groups of individuals lose their culture and sense of identity as they interact with the dominant culture. Readers are challenged to consider how the ethnic identity of a culture can be preserved.

Summary

Nonfiction is often overlooked when using children's literature to explore important multicultural concepts. However, it is a powerful tool because real people and real events often stimulate students to question and to think in a way fictitious characters cannot. Fortunately, quality nonfiction literature is increasingly more available for students at both the elementary and secondary levels. Teachers are encouraged to search for books that will be appropriate for their classrooms.

Source: Savage, M. K. and Savage, T. V. (1996). Achieving multicultural goals through children's nonfiction. *Journal of Educational Issues of Language Minority Students*, Vol. 17, 25-37. Used with permission.

RESOURCES

Enriching Content Classes for Secondary ESOL Students

Study Guide

Appendix

Study Guide Appendix

Table of Contents

Teaching Content Knowledge and ESOL in Multicultural Classrooms

Gloria M. Tang

ESOL students in the United States and Canada who study in multicultural settings take approximately 2 to 3 years to reach proficiency in basic communication skills in English (Cummins, 1984). However, they take more than 5 years to reach native-speaker levels in academic content language (Collier, 1987; Cummins, 1984). By implication, unless ESOL students learn language and content simultaneously, they will be denied the full benefits of education. However, school-age students, particularly those at the upper intermediate and secondary levels (ages 12-18), have difficulty understanding content knowledge written and presented orally in English, and they have difficulty expressing concepts in English, even when they have learned them in their first language.

How can we help students learn new content knowledge written or spoken in English? How can we enable them to demonstrate their content knowledge in English? How can we assist them in using and expressing their background knowledge in English and linking it to new knowledge?

Methods which endeavour to answer these questions can be divided into two categories: those which bring the students' English proficiency to a level at which they can read expository text in content textbooks, or those which bring the language in content textbooks to the level of the students.

Traditionally, the former has involved removing students from the regular stream and giving them intensive courses to develop their written and oral English skills until they have acquired adequate proficiency for enrollment in content-area classes. However, marginalized or segregated programs mean denying students the full benefits of education, that is, full access to content-area subject matter and, possibly, development of thinking skills. The alternative approach involves modifying the text, and, perhaps, using adjunct materials to bring the language in classroom texts to students. This process commonly results in watering down the course content and exposing students to language that is not usually found in real textbooks.

A more effective solution is to employ a model which combines the two, a model which systematically integrates language and content. The proposed classroom model enables ESL students to access the language of textbooks and, at the same time, helps them reach a level at which they can read the language of content classroom texts independently as well as write academic

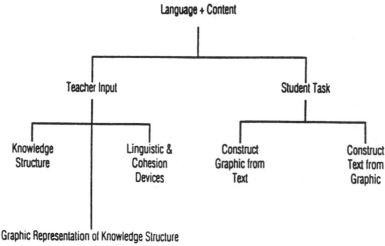

**Figure 1
A Classroom Model**

Language + Content

Teacher Input

Student Task

Knowledge Structure

Linguistic & Cohesion Devices

Construct Graphic from Text

Construct Text from Graphic

Graphic Representation of Knowledge Structure

APPENDIX

Figure 2
Knowledge Structures of Chapter 1: *Other Places, Other Times*

CLASSIFICATION/CONCEPTS	PRINCIPLES	EVALUATION
Homo Habilis—early tool-using ancestors of modern man **Homo Erectus**—first human to walk upright **Neanderthal**—more sophisticated tools and social structure **Cro-Magnon**—most technically advanced of early people	**Homo Erectus** • use of fire allowed migration to colder climates • development of stronger tools and weapons allowed Homo Erectus to kill larger animals **Cro-Magnon Man** • sophistication allowed them to survive the ice age • development of farming provided food for long periods of time	
	Homo Habilis • 1.75 million to 800,000 years ago **Homo Erectus** • 1.25 million to 250,000 years ago **Neanderthal Man** • 130,000 to 30,000 years ago **Cro-Magnon Man** • 30,000 to 10,000 years ago	
DESCRIPTION	SEQUENCE	CHOICE

discourse in English. It takes into consideration systematic development of students' thinking skills. It consists of five components (see Figure 1. p. 8) which can be sequenced in a variety of ways:

1. Explicit teaching of text/knowledge structures of text organization
2. Explicit teaching of graphic representation of text/knowledge structures
3. Explicit teaching of linguistic and cohesion devices of text/knowledge structures
4. Setting student tasks which involve constructing graphics from expository prose, and

5. Setting tasks which provide opportunities for students to practice constructing expository prose from a graphic.

The rest of this paper shows how the model can be successfully implemented in seventh-grade social studies classes by describing the work of one teacher.

Implementation

A teacher from the Burnaby School District (in British Columbia, Canada) introduced some of the components of this model into her seventh-grade social studies class

and found the strategies successful. The textbook she used was *Other Places, Other Times* (Neering & Grant, 1986), a social studies textbook widely used in public schools in the Vancouver and Burnaby school districts.

The teacher planned her lesson according to Mohan's (1986) knowledge framework. She read each chapter to determine the top-level structure of the text, to organize the content according to the knowledge structures in the knowledge framework (see Figure 2, above), and to prepare a structured overview, or graphic organizer, which best

Figure 3
Time Line of Early People to accompany Chapter 1: *Other Places, Other Times*

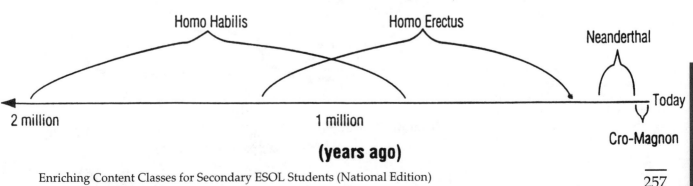

Early People

(years ago)

Figure 4
Graphic Representation of Homo Habilis to accompany
Other Places, Other Times

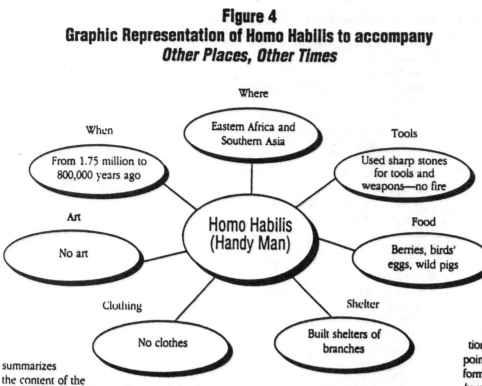

same linguistic devices repeatedly to reinforce learning. She decided on a web because this graphic was familiar to her students.

The teacher presented the first of these completed graphic organizers, Figure 4, on the overhead projector (OHP). She used the language of description consistently to answer the questions *when?, where?,* and *what?* After the graphic presentation, she referred students to the text, explicitly drawing their attention to the knowledge structure, description, and the linguistic devices specific to that knowledge structure. In presenting the next two major groups of early people, she varied her strategies. She built up one of the graphics on the OHP while presenting the section, and she built up the other cooperatively with the students by assigning the paragraphs to be read and by again asking the questions *when?, where?,* and *what?* The linguistic points she focused on were verbs in the past form, for example, *were, was, lived, ate, hunted;* adjectives and adverbial phrases of comparison, for example, *longer than, short, erect, sharp, pointed, different from, the same as, similar to,* and *as large as.* By building the graphic together with students, she was helping them to make the link between the graphic and the text and to see that the two are giving the same information but in different forms. She was also exposing students to the real language of description found in textbooks, a step towards

summarizes the content of the chapter. Chapter 1, entitled "Early People," (Neering & Grant 1986, pp. 1-27) looks at the Earth from 1.75 million years ago until the time of the first civilizations. It concentrates on the development of the four major classifications of early humankind: Homo Habilis, Homo Erectus, Neanderthal Man, and Cro-Magnon Man. The top-level structure of the chapter is a temporal sequence of descriptions, so she decided that the structured overview that would best represent it was a time line (see Figure 3, p. 9). The graphic helped her plan the content she was going to present, that is, early people, as well as linguistic devices associated with the time line, for example, *lived from ... to ... , began in ... and ended in ... , inhabited the earth for ... years, during that period.* In presenting the chapter overview, she explicitly introduced the knowledge structure "sequence" and the language used in chronologically ordered texts.

Having identified the knowledge structure of each section, she decided that the chapter could be divided into four sections according to the four major groups of early people. Each section describes one group of early people, their way of life, the change and development they experienced, and the impact the environment had on them. She put the information in each section

in a graphic and because similar information can be extracted from each of the sections, she organized the information in the same web-like graphic form for all the sections (see Figure 4, above). The purpose of recycling the same graphic form was to provide a schema students could access again and again. It also allowed her to use the

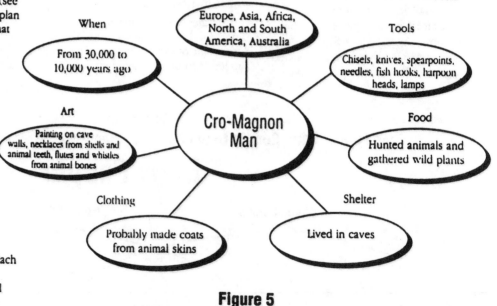

Figure 5
Graphic Representation of Cro-Magnon Man to accompany
Other Places, Other Times

Enriching Content Classes for Secondary ESOL Students (National Edition)
Study Guide: Appendix

Figure 6
Chapter Review: *Other Times, Other Places*

	When	Where	Tools	Food	Shelter	Clothes	Art
Homo Habilis	From 1.75 million to 800,000 years ago	Eastern Africa and Southern Asia	Used sharp stones for tools and weapons—no fire	Berries, bird's eggs, wild pigs	Built shelters of branches	No clothes	No art
Homo Erectus	From 1.25 million to 250,000 years ago	Africa, Asia, and Europe	Fire, flint blades, pointed wooden spears	Wild animals • elephant • cooked meat	Probably built shelters of branches	No clothes	No art
Neanderthal Man	From 130,000 years ago to 30,000 years ago	Europe, Middle East	Knives, borers, spear sharpeners made from stone	Wild animals • bear • cooked meat	Lived in caves	Animal hides for clothes	No art
Cro-Magnon Man	From 30,000 to 10,000 years ago	Europe, Asia, Africa, North and South America, Australia	Chisels, knives, spearpoints, needles, fish hooks, harpoon heads, lamps	Hunted animals and gathered wild plants	Lived in caves	Probably made coats from animal skins	Painting on cave walls, necklaces from shells and animal teeth, flutes and whistles from animal bones

managing school knowledge independently. After sufficient exposure to the structure and the language in two similar graphics on Homo Erectus and Neanderthal Man, the students were able to complete the section on Cro-Magnon Man (see Figure 5, p. 10) on their own.

To bring the whole chapter together, she prepared a table (see Figure 6, above) and required students to complete it using the information in the webs. Using such a graphic serves several purposes: It summarizes the chapter; it reinforces the content knowledge students have learned; and it enables the students to see the relations of the knowledge in the slots, that is, the development of the early peoples. The teacher was moving them from managing information in isolation to managing the relations of information, which is a step forward in their cognitive development. The table also provides further opportunities for students to use language to compare and classify.

Note that while the vocabulary inside the cells are

terms which show the content schemata of the information, the shape of the web, and the lines which join them, the headings such as *Where*, *When*, and *Tools* represent the formal schemata or the linguistic devices specific to that knowledge structure or genre. These are terms which can be used again and again across topics and curricula.

The students were gradually trained to build similar graphics on their own after working cooperatively with the teacher a number of times. The teacher pointed out

Figure 7
Student-Generated Time Line

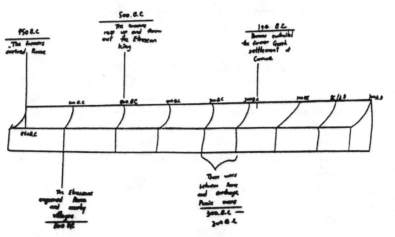

linguistic devices and provided opportunities for them to practice constructing graphics from similarly structured text. The teacher introduced the time line in chapter 1, and she was delighted when all her ESL students could build up a time line on their own when they came to chapter 5 (see Figure 7).

To give students practice in writing a coherent passage from a graphic, the teacher provided familiar graphic representations of familiar knowledge structures and asked students to write an essay based on the graphic. She found that she had to provide linguistic devices and ensure that students knew "how to link sentences together ... and how to present and focus information" (Mohan, 1986, p. 94).

Only by requiring students to interact with the graphic after explicit teaching can they truly learn to read and write graphics and to recognize text structure. Constructing a prose passage from a graphic is also a step towards writing expository text. The graphic and the text are semantically comparable (see Mohan, 1989): They convey the same information and they have the same knowledge structure. But in order to convert the graphic into expository prose, students have to translate the lines, arrows, and spatial arrangement, which are graphic representations of linguistic and cohesion devices, into linguistic and cohesion devices in text form. Figure 8 is a cause-effect graphic. The title and the headings give the signal that it is a table showing a series of causes and effects, and spatial arrangement, the lines or arrows connecting the slots, signify *caused, brought about, resulted in, leading to, so, because, the effect of ... was ...* or *as a result of ..., ...* .

The teacher had taught the knowledge structure of cause-effect and exposed the students to cause-effect tables. She had also pointed out the linguistic devices many times and given the students practice in constructing text passages from graphics. Figure 9 shows that students could write a coherent passage on the events leading to the end of the Roman Republic and that they could produce expository prose using devices of cause-effect (e.g., *cause, the reason was, so,* and *because*).

I should, perhaps, reiterate that the process is slow. Students cannot be expected to be able to understand a social studies text or to write expository prose using linguistic devices of description, classification, or cause-effect after simply having gone through the five components once. They need explicit teaching and practice to acquire the skill of understanding and expressing content knowledge and academic language.

Conclusion

Results of research (Early, Mohan, & Hooper, 1989) carried out in schools in Vancouver point to the fact that adopting the proposed

model in classroom teaching, that is, explicit teaching of text/knowledge structure and graphic representation of knowledge structures; and providing practice in constructing graphics from text and text from graphics in intermediate and secondary ESL social studies classes can help to increase students' ability to read and write academic discourse. In other words, this classroom model appears to have the potential for bringing classroom texts to a level students can comprehend, and at the same time, bringing students to the English proficiency level where they can read and write classroom texts.

Figure 8
A Cause-Effect Table for *Other Places, Other Times*
Events Leading to the End of the Roman Republic

Cause	Effect
The Roman Empire expanded rapidly.	Romans had to spend a lot of time and energy defending their empire from invaders.
Angry Italians wanted the advantages of Roman citizenship. They threatened to rebel and attack Rome.	The Romans granted citizenship to the Italians.
Many internal problems existed • Poor people were starving • Government officials became corrupt • Consuls were assassinated • Slaves rebelled against rough treatment from masters.	The republican system was weakened.

Figure 9
Student-Generated Text

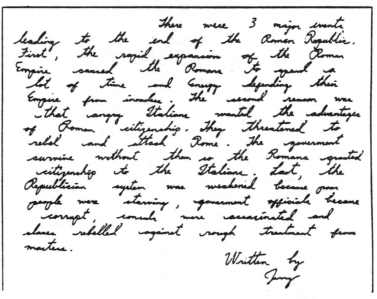

References

Collier, V. P. (1987). Age and rate of acquisition of second language for academic purposes. *TESOL Quarterly, 21.* 617-641.

Cummins, J. (1984). *Bilingualism and special education: Issues in assessment and pedagogy.* Clevedon, England: Multilingual Matters.

Early, M., Mohan, B. A., & Hooper, H. R. (1989). The Vancouver School Board language and content project. In J. H. Esling (Ed.), *Multicultural education and policy: ESL in the 1990s* (pp. 107-122), Toronto: The Ontario Institute for Studies in Education.

Mohan, B. A. (1986). *Language and content.* Reading, MA: Addison-Wesley.

Mohan, B. A. (1989). Language socialization. *Word, 4,* 100-114.

Neering, R., & Grant, P. (1986). *Other places, other times.* Toronto: Gage Educational.

Acknowledgment

I wish to thank Cathy Humphries of the Burnaby School District, Burnaby, British Columbia for permission to use her graphic supplements to *Other People, Other Times* (Neering & Grant, 1986).

Author

Gloria M. Tang is Assistant Professor of ESL in the Department of Language Education at the University of British Columbia, Vancouver, Canada. Previously, she was head of the Educational Technology Department at Northcote and Grantham Colleges of Education in Hong Kong. Her research interests include studying the relationship between academic discourse and graphic literacy across languages and cultures and devising tasks and graphics for enhancing ESL student learning in multicultural classrooms.

Assessment
Participation and Portfolio Checklist

Enriching Content Classes for Secondary ESOL Students

Name: _____

School: _____

Identification #: _____

A. Participation
In order to receive credit for a section, the participant must attend and actively participate in all discussions unless alternate arrangements are approved in advance.

	Yes	No
Introduction		
Section 1: Academic Competence, Part A		
Section 2: Language Learning in School		
Section 3: Culture, Part A		
Section 4: Academic Competence, Part B		
Section 5: Literacy Development and Study Skills		
Section 6: Assessment		
Section 7: Culture, Part B		
Section 8: Putting It All Together		
Conclusion		

B. Products
Complete all products as assigned in the Study Guide. Place outside assignments and your journal in a folder to be evaluated by the facilitator. Only completed products are acceptable.

	Yes	No
Introduction		
Demographics Anticipation Guide		
Evaluating Techniques for ESOL Students		
Section 1: Academic Competence, Part A		
Easy as Pie Lesson Modification		
Easy as Pie Lesson Modification Partner Checklist		
Sequenced Topics or Shared Topics		
Webbed Topics		
Section 2: Language Learning		
Inferences About Language Acquisition		
Implications for the Clasroom		
Civics Classroom Activity		
Case Studies		
Program Models for Second Language Learners: Pros and Cons		
Section 3: Culture, Part A		
Cultural Diversity Profile		
Cultural Vignettes Activity		
Section 4: Academic Competence, Part B		
Content Area Tasks and Lesson Outline		
Selecting and Adapting a Content Area Text		
Practice Activity Using "From Text to Graphics and Back Again"		
Draft Criteria to Evaluate Outside Assignment #2		
Strategies and Techniques: Content Area Priorities		
Section 5: Literacy Development and Study Skills		
Passages Worksheet		
DRTA Worksheet		
Student Study Guide		
Section 6: Assessment		
Teacher-made Test Checklist		
Top Ten Test-taking Strategies		
Specific Test-taking Strategy		
Alternative Assessment Worksheet		
Section 7: Culture, Part B		
Home Group Tasks for Menkart Reading		
Section 8: Putting It All Together		
Unit Plan		
Conclusion		
Post-test		
Other:		
Outside Assignment #1		
OA #1 Feedback Form (Criteria)		
Outside Assignment #2		
Journal		